CRIMINAL SHADOWS

David Canter, Professor of Psychology at Liverpool University, is the pioneer and leading expert in psychological profiling and has been the subject of nationally broadcast TV documentaries, including 'Murder in Mind' and 'Helping the Police'.

Also by David Canter

Architectural Psychology (*ed.*) (*1970*)

Psychology for Architects (*1974*)

Psychology and the Built Environment (*ed. with T. Lee*) (*1974*)

Environmental Interaction: Psychological Approaches to our Physical Surroundings (*ed. with P. Stringer*) (*1975*)

The Psychology of Place (*1977*)

Designing for Therapeutic Environments: A Review of Research (*ed. with S. Canter*) (*1979*)

Psychology in Practice: Perspectives on Professional Psychology (*ed. with S. Canter*) (*1982*)

Facet Theory: Approaches to Social Research 1985 (*ed.*)

The Research Interview: Uses and Approaches (*ed. with M. Brenner and J. Brown*) (*1985*)

Environmental Social Psychology (*ed. with J. C. Jesuino, L. Soczka and G. M. Stephenson*) (*1988*)

Environmental Perspectives (*ed. with M. Krampen and D. Stea*) (*1988*)

Environmental Policy, Assessment and Communication (*ed. with M. Krampen and D. Stea*) (*1988*)

New Directions in Environmental Participation (*ed. with M. Krampen and D. Stea*) (*1988*)

Football in its Place: An Environmental Psychology of Football Grounds (*with M. Comber and D. L. Uzzell*)

Fires and Human Behaviour (*ed.*) (*1990*)

Empirical Approaches to Social Representations (*ed. with G. M. Breakwell*) (*1993*)

CRIMINAL SHADOWS

Inside the Mind of the Serial Killer

DAVID CANTER

HarperCollins*Publishers*

HarperCollins*Publishers*
77–85 Fulham Palace Road
Hammersmith, London W6 8JB

This paperback edition 1995
1 3 5 7 9 8 6 4 2

First published in Great Britain by
HarperCollins*Publishers* 1994

Copyright © David Canter 1994

The Author asserts the moral right to
be identified as the author of this work

ISBN 0 00 638394 7

Typeset in Sabon at
The Spartan Press Ltd, Lymington, Hants

Printed in Great Britain by
HarperCollinsManufacturing Glasgow

for Sandra

In interiore homine habitat veritas
ST AUGUSTINE, *The Confessions*

Beware the stories you tell yourself for
you will surely be lived by them.
PROFESSOR G. HOWARD, *Culture Tales*

CONTENTS

LIST OF MAPS, TABLES AND FIGURES

A number of people referred to in this book are composite creations based upon more than one person. Descriptions of these people, that have no significance for the point being made, have also been changed to ensure that there is no intentional likeness to any person living or dead. These invented people are either not named or indicated by a fictitious first name only.

FOREWORD

When I first started to write about my experiences of producing 'psychological profiles' to help catch rapists and murderers, using such 'profiles' was a novel idea. Only senior police officers and a few psychologists had heard of the possibilities for deriving clues about an assailant's personality and lifestyle from a careful, behavioural examination of the crime and its scene. During the time it has taken me to write this book, such 'profiles' – often apparently precise predictions about an unknown criminal's domestic circumstances, employment and character – have become the stock-in-trade of the tabloid newspapers, novelists and film producers. Senior investigating officers are under standing instructions to obtain a 'profile' for any major inquiry that proves intractable. Even the continuing supply of authors who are convinced that they have discovered who 'Jack the Ripper' really was require a personality profile to defend their point of view.

Furthermore, such profiles are no longer produced by one or two lone individuals, risking their reputations on a mixture of hunch and experience. A number of psychiatrists and psychologists now offer a service as a sort of clinical Columbo to any major police investigation that makes the national press, basing their contributions on a growing number of systematic studies.

These developments have been much more rapid than I ever expected. They have caused me to add another layer to this book which began simply as a direct description of my work with the police. It is now also important to show why detectives require an understanding of criminal behaviour that goes beyond experience and intuition; an understanding that also has to go beyond the personal insights of clinicians and others who have had direct dealings with violent offenders.

The new level of understanding required is really a demand for a special type of theory of violent crime. Not a theory that assigns the cause of these crimes to a specific factor such as genetic make-up, birth trauma, lack of self-control or social pressures, but a theory about what drives a person beyond the bounds of socially acceptable aggression into the realms of criminal violence. In the chapters that follow I have taken some preliminary steps towards developing such a theory.

In order to be both valid and useful this theory of violent crime must have its roots in the actual events that constitute rape, murder and other forms of vicious assault. Precisely those actions and locations which are the focus of police attention must be the building blocks of any fruitful theory of interpersonal violence.

I have, therefore, described how I became involved as a university psychologist in helping police inquiries, and how my practical successes led me to search for the themes central to all interpersonal violence. The variations on those themes provide the basis for a preliminary, evolving framework for distinguishing between different acts of violence. Those variations in the violent actions themselves can be used as clues to a criminal's personality and identity.

The practical mission of my work, helping to solve rapes and murders, has thus combined with the more academic quest of understanding the various roots and routes to rape and murder. The quest to understand violence has led me to view a criminal's actions as the shadows cast by his own inner narratives. The task, for investigative psychologists and detectives to tackle together, is how to interpret those criminal shadows.

Part One

PROBLEM

What the police need is a net with smaller holes in it, so that the villains can't swim through.

CHIEF SUPERINTENDENT
VINCE MCFADDEN, MBE

Chapter One

A BETTER NET

In July 1980 the body of an eight-year-old girl was found in a layby in Staffordshire, 264 miles from where she had been abducted. For eleven years the coordinated searches of six police forces were unable to find the man who had killed her. During that time at least two other young girls were murdered by the same man and two more are known to have been abducted by him, escaping alive. He undoubtedly molested many other young children before he was caught.

Despite the use of a specially-dedicated, vast computer system containing the details of thousands of suspects, a solitary, middle-aged man, Robert Black, who had first been convicted of assaults on children a quarter of a century earlier at the age of sixteen, completely eluded the attention of police investigators. Until his fortuitous capture in September 1991, country-wide searches had failed even to include his name as one of the 185,000 people whose details had been amassed.

Senior police officers leading the investigation privately admitted that they were likely to catch him only if he 'showed his hand' again. This deceptively benign euphemism proved to be an accurate prediction. A village shopkeeper, working in his garden on a hot summer's day, saw a six-year-old girl being forced into a van. He called the police who stopped the van when it returned through the

References for each chapter and a select bibliography can be found at the end of the book.

village. The girl's father was the police officer who opened the van doors to find his terror-stricken daughter inside, bound in a sleeping bag, almost suffocated.

Subsequent inquiries led to Black's arrest and conviction for the murder of three young girls as well as the abduction of a fourth.

The search for Robert Black highlights the problems of finding a criminal when there is no known connection between him and his victim. For although a modern police force can fill rooms with details of possible suspects, they still have the enormous problem of finding the vicious needle in their haystack of paper. Is there an alternative to waiting for a criminal to make a mistake? Can huge resources and fast computers not avoid the need for the killer to 'reveal his hand', as in Black's case, doubling back unaware that he had been noticed? Must investigators hope for 'good luck', for an alert neighbour who happens to be in his garden at the right time? Must detectives rely on glimpses caught by witnesses, known *modus operandi* of convicted villains and house-to-house trawls of possible suspects?

Is it not possible to focus all this intensive activity and high technology by deriving some knowledge of the criminal from the way he embraces the crime, or how he chooses to commit it? Does a criminal not indicate something about himself from the way he carries out a crime? Something that will help sift the possible suspects or even point to places where a likely suspect may be found?

To find ways of focusing police investigations the answer to a fundamental question must be found: what does a criminal reveal about himself by the way he commits a crime?

A criminal may reveal what shoes he was wearing from his footprints. His blood-type can be determined from any body-fluids left at the scene. But as well as these *material* traces, he also leaves *psychological* traces, tell-tale patterns of behaviour that indicate the sort of person he is. Gleaned from the crime scene and reports from witnesses, these traces are more ambiguous and subtle than those examined by the biologist or physicist. They cannot be taken into a laboratory and dissected under a microscope. They are more like shadows which undoubtedly are connected to the criminal who cast them, but they flicker and change, and it may not always be obvious where they come from. Yet, if they can be fixed and interpreted, criminals' shadows can indicate where investigators should look and what sort of person they should be looking for.

Changes in the demands made on police forces around the world mean that they are increasingly in need of such help. The lone detective, so popular in fiction, has given way to organized teams which require systematic guidance. These days, such teams have limited resources, yet changes in the law and changes in crime are putting increased demands on their capabilities. The application of scientific psychology is being seized on by senior police officers as a way out of this impasse.

Although enormous strides have been made in analysing the material clues, by contrast the interpretation of psychological shadows has made only a few faltering first steps. This book is an account of my involvement, as a psychologist, in a number of police investigations in which I took some of those steps.

In trying to interpret criminals' shadows, I was following many other footsteps. Many people have expressed views about how to identify a criminal in a crowd. Shakespeare, after all, has Julius Caesar making what later proves to be an accurate prediction:

> Let me have men about me that are fat;
> Sleek-headed men and such as sleep o' nights.
> Yond Cassius has a lean and hungry look;
> He thinks too much: such men are dangerous.

Shakespeare's view that thoughtful, lean and hungry-looking men were potential criminals accords with many other attempts from the earliest times to say what characteristics of physiognomy or physique are typical of murderers or thieves. Such views were steeped in generalized, untested notions about the behaviour typical of many different types of people. Similar stereotypes still exist today in the form of racial prejudice that assumes certain actions are typical of people with a particular skin colour. The blossoming in the last century of biology, medicine and psychology slowly began to challenge such superficial views of the relationship between a person's appearance and how he or she might be expected to behave. In particular, medicine had proven so successful that madness and evil were regarded as illnesses instead of being attributed to witchcraft and possession by the devil.

After Daniel M'Naghten was acquitted of murder 'by reason of insanity' in 1843, physicians became more involved in the legal process, especially in determining whether the accused suffered from a form of disease, thought to be produced by brain dysfunction, 'mental illness'. The growth of medicine also led to their increasing involvement in criminal investigations as pathologists. Their work further encompassed the treating of the perpetrators of crimes who were regarded as mad rather than bad. It is therefore not surprising that, by the 1880s, medical officers thought it appropriate to offer opinions about the characteristics of an offender, based on their clinical and forensic experience.

The earliest of such opinions for which a copy still exists is that offered by Dr Thomas Bond, in November 1888, in a letter to Robert Anderson, head of the London CID, concerning the likely characteristics of 'Jack the Ripper':

> The murderer must have been a man of physical strength and great coolness and daring. There is no evidence that he had an accomplice. He must in my opinion be a man subject to periodic attacks of homicidal and erotic mania. The character of the mutilations indicate that the man may be in a condition sexually, that may be called Satyriasis. It is of course possible that the Homicidal impulse may have developed from a revengeful or brooding condition of mind, or that religious mania may have been the original disease but I do not think that either hypothesis is likely. The murderer in external appearance is quite likely to be a quiet inoffensive looking man probably middle-aged and neatly and respectably dressed. I think he might be in the habit of wearing a cloak or overcoat or he could hardly have escaped notice in the streets if the blood on his hands or clothes were visible.
>
> Assuming the murderer to be such a person as I have just described, he would be solitary and eccentric in his habits, also he is likely to be a man without regular occupation, but with some small income or pension. He is possibly living among respectable persons who have some knowledge of his character and habits and who may have grounds for suspicion that he is not quite right in his mind at times. Such persons would probably be unwilling to communicate suspicions to the Police for fear of trouble or notoriety, whereas if there were prospect of reward it might overcome their scruples.
>
> Donald Rumbelow, *The Complete Jack the Ripper*,
> 1987, pp. 140–41

There is no information to suggest that Dr Bond was drawing on anything except his professional experience, yet the possibilities he proposes would probably be accepted as thoughtful and intelligent by police forces today. Indeed, when FBI agents acknowledged the 'Jack the Ripper' centenary by drawing up their own account of the offender they produced a description virtually indistinguishable from Bond's.

An experienced Victorian detective might have proposed something very similar. Bond adds a psychiatric flourish with his reference to 'diseases' such as satyriasis or religious mania, but essentially he is pulling together a number of reasonable speculations to form an hypothetical 'pen picture' of the criminal. No one was convicted for the Whitechapel murders so the accuracy of Bond's 'profile' cannot be established. Neither can we be sure if the senior investigators of the day gave it any credence. It is unlikely that they ignored it completely, for although it is rare for detectives to write such speculations down it is not uncommon for them to form a view of the person they are seeking. This is one way in which they make their complex task more manageable. Drawing together the various strands known about the perpetrator, and using this summary as a template against which to measure suspects, is a natural way of giving shape to the potentially confusing range of possibilities that emerge in a large investigation.

The idea that idiosyncratic habits would give away clues to hidden aspects of a person's identity was recorded as long ago as the Old Testament. For example, Gideon chose his army from those men who did not kneel to drink at the stream, preferring those who lay down. The former were secret idolators and therefore less likely to fight the infidel with total commitment. Morelli, the outstanding Victorian art historian, maintained that he was able to distinguish fake Old Master paintings by minor details such as how an ear or nose was portrayed. Predating psychoanalysis, he insisted that the large matters of composition and subject were open to conscious control and therefore readily forged, but that details regarded as trivial by the painter would reveal his true identity.

Perhaps one of the major appeals of twentieth-century psychology has been its promise that even the most trifling aspects of human behaviour, for example when a person crosses their legs or forgets a name, can be shown to have profound significance. Although many attempts to fulfil this promise have failed, most notably in the analysis of handwriting, there have been some small successes. Of particular relevance was the careful consideration of detailed aspects of Germans suspected of war crimes at the end of the Second World War.

Lionel Haward, then a young psychologist working as an RAF officer, was a member of a team attempting to identify war criminals. He drew up a list of factors, such as mode of dress and likely possessions, to help screen people suspected of being high-ranking Nazi officials. The checklist made it much easier to decide whom it was worth investigating closely. This was a direct precursor of my own later activities. At the time I first became involved with police investigations, I was in the same department of psychology as Haward, then Britain's leading forensic psychologist. He retired from the department not long afterwards, but not before he had supported my early attempts to follow in his footsteps.

Haward's simple approach of producing a checklist easily gives way to the less scientific, but seemingly more dramatic, approach of drawing up an account of the wanted person. For instance, it might be known that the criminal is probably white, certainly male and possibly of average height and may have a regional accent. Once all of these factors are used as if to describe a specific individual, the target of investigation becomes apparently easier to understand and to identify.

The general description of the psychology of a target individual had been used at a strategic level for many years before a similar approach was adopted in police inquiries. Not long before Lionel Haward began searching for Nazi officers, the psychiatrist William Langer was commissioned by the US Office of Strategic Services to produce a profile of Adolf Hitler, focusing on how he would react to defeat. A few years later, in the mid 1950s, the New York psychiatrist Dr James A. Brussel gave a very detailed account of the man whom the press had dubbed the 'Mad Bomber of New York' because of his sporadic use of home-made explosives to terrorize the city. Brussel even went so far as to say that the 'bomber' would be wearing a neat double-breasted suit, with the jacket buttoned. Despite his help, the bombing continued for over ten years. However, once the culprit, George Metesky, was apprehended he was indeed found to be attired just as Brussel had described.

By the late 1960s, psychiatrists' involvement with criminals in treatment programmes had become so widespread that from time to time they were asked by police investigators for their views on the character of a perpetrator they were trying to find. For example, in September 1974 Dr Patrick Tooley offered an opinion on the characteristics of the murderer of Susan Stevenson, who was attacked on Great Lines Common in Kent, dying from her wounds soon after she staggered to the local police station. Dr Tooley made the following proposal:

> The man is aged between twenty and thirty-five years, possibly a psychopath with previous convictions. Generally one could expect too from his record that he had made a number of court appearances, was

convicted at an early age and had possibly been in a special home; likely to be a manual worker and either unemployed or frequently changing jobs. Previous convictions could include unlawful sexual intercourse, drunkenness, robbery and assaults generally.

Father absent – mother restrictive, sexually prudish and devoted to son and spoils him. He, in turn, resents this and has a hate complex towards women. Despite that, he wants an affair with a woman but cannot make a normal approach. He does not mix socially and walks alone, in open spaces. He could be a 'peeper' but seldom resorts to indecent exposure.

Tom Tullet, *Clues to Murder*, 1987, p. 155

When the culprit, Peter Stout, was arrested, Dr Tooley's comments were found to be generally accurate.

The background of Peter Stout was revealing. He was aged nineteen, single and had one elder sister, two elder brothers and a younger brother. Both his parents were dead. His father had been a drunkard and a bully and was disliked by all the children, but they had all loved their mother. When Stout was fourteen he was convicted of indecently assaulting a woman and he himself had been the victim of attempted buggery when he was ten years old. This fitted exactly into the pattern of the man described by Dr Tooley and there were other things which also fitted. He was a loner who went for long walks and he did not mix well with others.

The interrogation of Peter Stout was a long drawn-out process of admissions, half-admissions, then a complete retraction and references to the Devil and 'queer turns'.

Tullet, op. cit., p. 157

Around the same time that Dr Tooley gave the description that so fitted Peter Stout, instructors at the FBI's national training academy in Quantico, West Virginia, consciously set about developing the art of providing similar accounts, which they called 'profiles', of wanted killers. Drawing upon their detailed experience of violent criminals, the provision of 'profiles' was incorporated into their training courses for FBI agents. As I was later to discover when I visited this famous academy, what had started out as class discussions between experienced law enforcement agents eventually became a service offered to police forces throughout the world.

The instructors at the FBI academy deliberately went beyond the focus on such issues as the significance of the murder to the murderer, the killer's personality, his internal conflicts and fantasy life; these are all aspects of direct relevance to pleas of insanity and to deciding on the provision of treatment for offenders. But such characteristics are concerned with the inner, psychological nature of the culprit and are therefore not readily open to conventional detection. The FBI agents wanted to get closer to the hunt for the criminal, to point directly to where he could be found.

When FBI agents first began this work they invented a new term to grace their actions: *offender profiling*. By so doing they created the impression of a package, a system that was sitting waiting to be employed, rather than the mixture of craft, experience and intellectual energy that they themselves admit is at the core of their activities.

The term 'offender profiling' has stuck; yet another example of the admirably creative but infuriatingly confusing American reinvention of English words and phrases. Often the key to these word inventions is to take a noun in common use, preferably a noun that is reasonably abstract and is therefore used to describe a relatively complex phenomenon, such as 'police' or 'priority' or 'interface', and to turn these into verbs where none existed before. A rather unclear notion emerges, rich in resonance: 'to police', 'to prioritize', 'to interface'. Now with skilled prestidigitation the verb can creep back in as a noun, but now it is describing a process: 'policing', 'prioritizing', 'interfacing'. Because of its roots in a reasonably specific well-known noun the impression is created that a distinct process exists that can be cut and dried and sold by the pound. This is what has happened to the idea of a 'profile' of a criminal. What is a vague idea as a simple noun, referring to the description a policeman might give of the criminal he is looking for, becomes an esoteric process: 'offender profiling' – a procedure that facilitates interfacing between law enforcement agencies and the FBI, enhancing strategic policing and suspect prioritization.

As it transpired, the FBI found that 'profiling' became far too successful a concept, taking on a life and assumed set of limitations all its own. It hid the fact of direct guidance to investigators and of a range of related involvement in the whole process of detection and examination of crime. So 'Criminal Investigative Analysis' was born, a CIA for the FBI. But the power of gerundic nouns prevails long after their demise and most people still think that CIA is just a piece of jargon to describe old-fashioned profiling.

The first documented use of the 'profiling' services of FBI agents at Quantico came in 1974 when the Montana police asked for help in solving a murder that had not been detected for over a year. In June 1973 a seven-year-old girl, Susan Jaeger, on a camping holiday with her parents, had been taken from her tent as her family slept nearby. No sign of her body had been found nor any ransom demand received. In January 1974 the charred body of an eighteen-year-old girl was found in woodlands near the camp site. Convinced that the same killer was responsible for both crimes and that he would be known to them, but unable to identify anyone definitely, local police approached the FBI.

FBI agents proposed that the murderer was a young white male who kept very much to himself. They suggested that he did not live far from the camp site and was therefore already likely to have come to the attention of local police officers. The possibility that he may have kept mementoes of his victims was also noted.

This description closely fitted David Meirhofer, a suspect named by an informant. There was no strong evidence to connect him with the crimes and he had taken both a 'lie-detector' test and a 'truth serum' interview without implicating himself in the killings. At the insistence of the FBI, Susan's mother kept a tape-recorder by her telephone. When, as predicted, an anonymous caller telephoned and said that he had abducted Susan, her mother was able to record his voice. It was identified as that of Meirhofer. A search of his home revealed the gruesome body parts, kept as 'souvenirs'. He later admitted to both murders as well as two others of local boys, before hanging himself in his cell.

The continuing successes of the FBI profilers captured the imagination of journalists and novelists long before most detectives in Britain or America had any idea what was happening at Quantico. Fiction writers readily moved into the richer, psychological pastures opened up by these developments in criminal detection. In Ruth Rendell's thrillers of rural murder, as in Thomas Harris's American massacres, the character and lifestyle of the offenders is often more significant than the detective. Fiction, as ever, was in advance of real life, but it did capture a move in police work towards a desire to understand the nature of the criminal and how his personality may be revealed through his crimes.

The change in emphasis from looking for clues to looking for a person has created a different approach to detection from that of the past. The specific clue that has a direct link to a specific characteristic gives way to looking for patterns in behaviour that add up to a certain style of life. Conan Doyle's fictional detective, like Agatha Christie's, often bases his judgements on some very specialist, typically technical knowledge, such as access to rare poisons, impossibilities in the event sequences described by the suspects, rare skills available only to the culprit, or other one-to-one relationships between known aspects of the offence and identifiable quirks of the villain. The examination of the character of the criminal, as revealed by the behavioural traces he leaves at the crime scene, is an attempt to get beyond a mere list of clues in order to recognize a pattern, an identifiable silhouette, a distinct shadow cast by the offender.

In the interests of a good plot, fictional police officers are often more amenable to new ideas and approaches to detection than are their real-life counterparts. The change in style of detection required by psychological input has not been adopted unreservedly by any police force. Perhaps the recent challenges to detectives have made them more open, but in my early discussions with police officers about the potential contribution of psychology to detection one detective sergeant, who had been in the force for many years, summarized the views of many of his colleagues when he said, 'Why do we need all this new-fangled stuff, Professor? After all, we've got 150 years of police experience to draw upon.'

The significance of this comment has stayed with me ever since. The process of criminal investigation has changed little over the past 150 years but, as my experiences reveal, many pressures from inside and outside the police forces are now producing rapid changes in what it means to be a detective and how detection is carried out. A systematic, scientific understanding of criminal behaviour is increasingly central to those changes.

It is possible to form a view of how the police carried out investigations in Victorian times because detailed information still exists for the most notorious of all serial murderers, 'Jack the Ripper'. A step-by-step procedure was observed with great determination and vigour by a large team of policemen. House-to-house inquiries were conducted, lists of suspects were drawn up and many were interviewed, forensic material was collected and examined.

A close reading of that investigation shows a basic process of identifying suspects, tracing them and deciding whether to examine them more closely or to cross them off the list. This is still the pattern of a major inquiry today. There are, of course, important differences: evidence is much more carefully collected and examined; physics, chemistry, biology and pathology now contribute to a larger degree to the interpretation of stains and fibres, cause of death, and all the other information that provides evidence. The law has also changed, especially in relation to what is acceptable evidence and the forms of expert testimony that can be drawn upon. However, the stages through which police officers go to apprehend the culprit are still much the same. The paper-and-ink record-keeping is done by computer, but otherwise the inquiry leading to the conviction of most killers is very similar to the inquiry that 'Jack the Ripper' evaded. The computer often adds little to the success of an inquiry when compared, for instance, with the lucky break that led to the arrest of Robert Black.

The computer had been installed because it was believed that it would help to overcome the problems that had beset an earlier major investigation, the 'Yorkshire Ripper' inquiry. Completed a few years before the search for Robert Black, it had been widely regarded as remarkably ineffective. The consequences of its failures still echo around government departments and police headquarters throughout Britain. It was an enormous inquiry in the tradition of leaving no stone unturned and eventually led to the conviction of Peter Sutcliffe for the murder of thirteen women.

By the end of the Yorkshire inquiry in 1980, over 150,000 people had been interviewed in order to eliminate them from the lists of suspects. The equivalent of a small town had been involved in house-to-house searches: 27,000 houses. Unlike the Staffordshire case some years later, Peter Sutcliffe had come into the interrogation net on at least five occasions, but had been released each time without raising any suspicions.

The search for the 'Yorkshire Ripper' involved three different police forces and rooms filled with card files. Each police force kept its own separate system. It is reported that when these were eventually housed in one place there was fear that the building would not withstand the weight of all the paper. Peter Sutcliffe's name is reputed to have been in all three sets of files but this was not known until the end of the investigation. In its aftermath, much investment was made in computer systems, the idea being that a computer would have spotted the recurring name.

This search for a mechanical solution to the problem of disentangling all the leads and information that a major inquiry generates has meant that all British police forces now have computers which bury investigating officers under data. Exactly what to do with the data or how to use them is still hotly debated. Centralized indexes for 'Crime Pattern Analysis' and for listing the *modus operandi* of known offenders are maintained, but they still rely enormously on the expertise of the human operators and the sense that they can make of the records that they hold. Confidential studies of these systems also show that they make a real contribution to far less than one in ten investigations that use them. It is also salutary to note that many of the existing police computing systems cannot communicate directly with each other, data being sent by motorbike when combinations of records are needed.

The existence of this vast data set leaves open to question, for example, the direct implications of recurring names and their relevance. What direction could an investigation take when it is known that a name has recurred? To have significance, a name must hold some meaning for the investigating officers, and computers are very poor at giving data meaning; they are much better at numbers, frequencies, percentages or straight description.

For a person running the inquiry, key aspects of any suspect are crucial. These include their having the opportunity to commit the offence and how that fits in with what is known about their *modus operandi* (the distinctive actions of an offender which link his crimes together and link him to his crimes). To locate the suspect, anything that might be publicly available about him can help; where he lives and how are the most obviously important characteristics. Therefore any information that may help with locating a suspect will be seized on. But this can cause its own problems if that information is unreliable. In the 'Yorkshire Ripper' investigation a taped message, thought to have been sent by the killer, misled the police.

Taken as genuine, the tape was submitted to phonetic analysis of the accent by experts at Leeds University. This enabled them to pinpoint the village from Wearside where that particular Geordie accent came from. Sutcliffe was excluded from the inquiry because he had a very different Yorkshire accent. It was later realized that the tape was a hoax; rumour has it that it was sent by disgruntled police officers who did not realize how seriously it would be treated (not unlike the letters supposedly sent by 'Jack the Ripper' a century earlier). By the time alternative possibilities were being considered, a great deal of time and further victims had been lost.

The phonetic experts in Leeds were not, initially, aware of the fact that none of the victims who survived attacks by the 'Yorkshire Ripper' had said he had a Geordie accent. Once it became apparent that every possible suspect who had a Wearside accent had been eliminated from the inquiries, then these broader discussions took place. This led to the conclusion that the tapes were a hoax. Eventually, after the largest investigation ever mounted into crimes that affected people's daily lives throughout Yorkshire, it was old-fashioned police routine and the alert actions of a police sergeant, Bob Ring, that led to the arrest of Peter Sutcliffe.

Sergeant Ring had made a routine check of the number plate of a car parked while the driver was 'doing business' with a prostitute. This revealed that the number plate belonged to a Skoda rather than the Rover to which it was fixed. Subsequent questioning in a police station and a follow-up of the driver of the car showed that he had been a suspect on previous occasions but each time had been dropped from the investigation. He may well have been crossed off the list again if Bob Ring had not remembered that Sutcliffe had gone for a private 'pee' before being taken in for questioning. When he searched the spot used he found a hammer and knife that were eventually linked to the murders. Presented with this evidence Sutcliffe confessed.

Two years after Sutcliffe was caught, two teenage girls were murdered near the village of Narborough just south of the city of Leicester. The detectives given the task of finding the killer were determined not to make the same mistakes as had been made in Yorkshire. They had computers and the possibilities of DNA 'fingerprinting' were just emerging. These new tools, however, were used indiscriminately. The investigating officers decided that they would take blood samples from every man who could possibly have been near the crime scene at the time of the murders. This included men of all ages and backgrounds residing in villages in a very wide area. For months well over 3,000 blood samples filled the laboratory, waiting to be tested. Investigations today can still produce the same overload, generating long queues of samples taken from even the most unlikely suspect.

In Narborough, this massive forensic onslaught nearly failed. If the culprit, Colin Pitchfork, had not had a workmate whose friend was a relative of a policeman, the fact that Pitchfork had got someone else to take the blood-test in his place might never have become known to the police. With the large number of samples being taken, like a routine survey, it was not possible for the officers involved to make detailed checks on the identities of all those who came to give blood.

Many senior officers now recognize that a behavioural analysis can help to identify the most likely suspects. An order of priority can then be assigned to the testing of each suspect. With a more focused approach it would also be possible to check the identity of everyone giving a blood sample.

All these manhunts, which took such enormous effort and very nearly failed, were not searches for arch-villains, brilliant minds that outmanoeuvred the plodding police and covered their traces with fiendish cunning. Robert Black returned through a village where he might have been seen abducting a young girl; Sutcliffe carried incriminating weapons with him when he visited potential targets whom the police were known to be watching; Pitchfork left semen that, even before DNA, could be used for blood-typing.

To check an offender's view of police effectiveness, I spent some hours talking to 'Andrew', a man convicted of a series of violent crimes. I asked him how he managed to evade capture when there were so many police looking for him. He answered that he constantly expected to be caught, he made no very careful plans to avoid detection and was surprised that they took so long to capture him. As in so many other cases they had waited for him to show his hand, spotting him running away from a victim he had left in an alley.

To go beyond the approach of blanket coverage, pouring resources into the investigation in the hope that something will turn up somewhere, requires a very different style of investigation in which various possibilities are weighed and the most fruitful courses of action are given the emphasis they deserve. This more scientific approach requires that investigators have a rich understanding of criminal behaviour and have the information and analytic tools to act on that understanding. This requires changes throughout police training and management; changes which have implications far beyond the drawing up of 'profiles' to help identify suspects.

Recognizing these demands, Surrey's Chief Superintendent Vince McFadden (who was to prove so significant in bringing me into police investigations) summarized the challenge to present-day police forces by saying: 'Sometimes we cast our net so wide that the fish swim through the holes.' His plea was for a more studied approach to fishing for criminals, working out carefully who was being looked for and where they were most likely to be found, using a smaller, finer net to increase the probability of the fish being caught.

There is another pressing reason to develop a smaller, better net. In the past the police could put virtually as much time and effort into a murder investigation as they considered necessary. The scale of this effort strikes police in the United States as beyond belief. In some large US cities a murder investigation has to be dropped if it is not solved by the couple of detectives assigned to it within twenty-four hours. In Britain, ten officers active on one murder investigation for six months is still not unusual. Now, though, police forces have budgets assigned to special inquiries at the start of the financial year and must make that cover all except the most unusual contingencies throughout the year. Inquiries have to be self-consciously managed as effectively as possible. One experienced officer, in charge of a murder inquiry into a gangland slaying, put it this way: 'I've got . . . two hands tied behind my back. That's the way the law's gone down. I'm investigating two dead and five injured and I have to look at my overtime.'

Beyond the financial constraints there are also other legal constraints that require a change in how detectives work. The Police and Criminal Evidence Act, widely known as PACE, grew out of the great disquiet felt by the public during the 1970s and early 1980s with the ambiguities and confusions in the law that appeared to give the police rights that were too easily abused.

PACE made the ground rules for contact between police and public much clearer and in so doing reduced the areas in which police officers could use their discretion. Previously a suspect could be kept for questioning as long as seemed appropriate, provided various routines were observed. The right to remain silent under questioning also had little legal force. With PACE, not only is there a finite limit to the amount of time a suspect can be kept under arrest, but the length of an interrogation session, the time for breaking for meals and a non-coercive style of contact are specifically stated. In the past a police officer could hint that he would keep a person in the cell until he or she confessed, or lay out objects found at the crime scene and indicate that the suspect's fingerprints were on them. Although the officer had to be very careful not to transgress the bounds of legal propriety in these approaches, there was considerable freedom of action. Now the slightest suggestion that such subterfuge or pressure has been used would invalidate any criminal charge in court.

Other pressures on detective work also strengthen the need to follow up opportunities for increased effectiveness. These include a community that is sometimes less sympathetic to the police and less prepared to help an inquiry than in the past; and a more mobile population, making the search for suspects more difficult. Increasing public awareness of the prevalence of violent crime, especially where the offender is unknown to the victim, also makes the detectives' task more demanding.

Whether they like or not, then, senior police officers are aware that there is a need to go beyond their current methods. They know they must challenge the cherished view that '150 years of experience' are all that is necessary to solve crimes. In the past, detectives could treat speculation about a villain's personality and background as something to chat about in the bar. Now they need to pull that discussion out of the realms of instinct and gut feeling and put it on a much firmer footing. One direction for them is to learn to read more clearly the shadows that criminals cast.

Chapter Two

FIRST PRINCIPLES

In 1985 I was invited for lunch at Scotland Yard. Two Metropolitan Police officers, Detective Chief Superintendent Thelma Wagstaff and Detective Chief Inspector John Grieve, wanted to discuss the feasibility of detectives using the behavioural science of psychology to cope with the challenges and difficulties they faced.

My contact with Thelma and John had been established, like many of my significant professional contacts over the years, because an enthusiastic student-turned-colleague, in this case Lorraine Nanke, believed that my academic discourses could have some practical value. Lorraine had met John Grieve in her capacity as a clinical psychologist working with drug addicts and other patients who had run foul of the law. She had studied research methodology with me. So, when she happened to talk to John about 'criminal profiling', she told him that she thought my approach to research might prove appropriate for that type of task. Lunch at the Yard was the first meeting to explore the possibilities.

John Grieve and Thelma Wagstaff (both of whom have subsequently reached the status of Commander) are practical detectives highly experienced in criminal investigation. John Grieve also has higher degrees in psychology and is well-versed in some of the more arcane aspects of personality theory. His informal, throwaway style masked his thoughtful explorations of how police officers could be better equipped to understand criminals and investigations.

Thelma had done a considerable amount to heighten the awareness of the Metropolitan police of the need to change the way rapes were investigated. She had been successful in establishing programmes of training for women police officers involved in rape investigations and setting up clean and comfortable interview suites for use with rape victims. The idea of using behavioural science to help find a rapist appealed to her as a way of increasing the success of investigations, especially of sexual assaults against strangers. Her unassuming, amiable dealings with me did not immediately reveal the ability and determination that had enabled her to reach the highest ranks ever for a woman in the Metropolitan police. I was to learn of her force of personality when she silenced a room full of top-ranking policemen by saying: 'The problem with rape investigation is that half the population don't think it's a crime. That's the men!'

The three of us met for lunch in early November when the tables in the dining-room were adorned with declarations that Beaujolais Nouveau had arrived that very morning. In this relaxed atmosphere we talked over my earlier research identifying patterns of behaviour of people caught in a building on fire. We discussed how the approach I had taken then to studying such traumatic events could be relevant to police investigations. We explored the possibility that psychological research could contribute directly to detection, complementing experience, intuition and foot-slogging with scientifically established facts and principles.

Some years later I was told that, from the police point of view, I had said all the right things at that lunch. I had expressed curiosity without over-confidence, having honestly admitted that I knew little of police procedures. It was only subsequently that I realized how suspicious the police are of people outside the force who offer help. When

I later examined published FBI material and commented positively on some aspects of it, this was also well received. Thelma and John were impressed that although it weakened the case for using my services, as opposed to the services of the FBI, I had none the less spoken positively about the FBI approach. University researchers pick and choose all the time from the published literature, consciously building on what they find valuable in other people's ideas. This can be seen by police officers as welcome naivety, unexpected in the tougher, overtly competitive world in which they live.

At the time of that first lunch I had never heard of 'profiling', but the whole idea of reading a criminal's life from the details of how he carries out his crime was enormously appealing. It presented a challenge to the very heart of professional psychology. Was our adolescent science robust enough to give an account of a person when he was not sitting in front of us, when all we knew about him were the shadowy traces he had left at the scene of the crime? Sigmund Freud had been impressed by the way Sherlock Holmes studied the minutiae of a criminal's actions to make inferences about the mind behind the crime. Freud believed that there were parallels in the clues given to the workings of the unconscious from a close examination of slips of the tongue and lapses in thought. Were we now ready for a less fanciful combination of scientific psychology and criminal detection? One that could save lives?

A couple of months after that lunch I sent a note to Thelma Wagstaff commenting on a series of rapes I had read about in the London *Standard*. Travelling home by train from London to Guildford in January 1986 I happened to see that the *Standard* had devoted its front page to a description of a series of twenty-four sexual assaults committed in London over the previous four years. It was believed all involved the same assailant. Sometimes the attacker was alone, sometimes he had an accomplice. The list gave only brief, incomplete details, but there were some dates and times. The train was not too crowded, so I settled down for the forty-minute journey to see if there was any obvious pattern in the list.

Two general psychological principles seemed relevant to the newspaper list. One was that people influence each other's actions. My thoughts were that the difference between the attacks involving two men and those involving one might tell us something about both individuals. According to the London *Standard*, all the assaults had been linked by the police, so why was there a variation in who had committed the crimes? What might that variation indicate?

The second principle derived from the very extended time-scale. Most human behaviour develops and changes over time, often in relation to direct experience of the consequence of the actions taken. What was changing here? Did time and partnership indicate anything about the character or lifestyle of these offenders?

The starting point, then, was to look at the relationship between partnership and time. The highlighting of graphic details in the chronological list on the tabloid page made it rather difficult to see if there was any change over time and how that might be linked to the assault being by one or two people. It was also difficult to disentangle the times of day and days of the week from the dates dotted around the page, in order to see if these very overt aspects of daily life revealed a pattern. After all, most of us live through a daily and weekly cycle that shapes what we do and when. At that stage I had no basis for thinking that violent criminals were any different.

I drew up a simple calendar of events, listing the offences committed by two people together in one column and those by a man alone in another. Although my work as a research psychologist makes commonplace the examination of rows and columns of numbers that describe human actions, this list was different from any I had used in the past. I was harnessing the rows and columns so that they might tell me their violent story. By reducing the complex, organic texture of actual events to the simplest form I could, I was hoping that they would reveal their central themes. I was asking of this rudimentary table if there was any hidden shape within it, trying to find an angle from which a light could be shone that would show something of the skeleton within the amorphous, complex form of the original vicious actions.

The resulting chronological table, with days and times put in a column for either a two-man or a single assault, turned the tabloid descriptions into a manageable summary with some intriguing qualities. Although some of the days of the week and times were missing (it also later became clear that some were inaccurate), I had only wanted to get a feel for the overall trends. Any research based on data taken from records, or other naturally occurring material, has to assume that there is some distortion in the information so that only broad patterns are likely to be reliable; precise inferences that rely on particular details may well prove unfounded. Any pattern at all is a bonus and can be used cautiously to explore the material further. I felt the overall pattern was clear enough to be worth thinking about and therefore sent the calendar of assaults with my thoughts about it in a letter to Thelma Wagstaff. I was curious to see if it made any sense to her and whether my conclusions added anything to what detectives were already considering:

I had a look through the details of the recent series of rapes that were given in the London *Standard* on 9th

January 1986. This is the series where there were two
or one man involved.

Of course, the details I have are very sketchy, but I
wondered if anybody had prepared a summary table
like the one enclosed. Although this is very rough and
ready it does show that the individual acting on his
own is very much a recent event and it tends to come
in runs after both have been involved.

I have no evidence that the one individual is the
same person, but if it were then one could see something about the relationship between the two men as a
possible clue to the whole series. For example, a
scenario that had one of them working near the
railways mentioned in the Press and only meeting up
with the other under certain circumstances, possibly
related to work, could lead to exploring the evidence
to see whether there might be some recurring event
that brought them together and that led to one 'going
it alone' on other occasions.

This is a speculation that we could possibly check
out more thoroughly in order to see whether hypothesized patterns would emerge.

Looking back on that letter now, having had so much
more contact with police investigations, I realize how
much unsupported speculation it contained. However,
given the remarkable lack of systematic research on the
detailed behaviour of criminals, outside the confines of
treatment programmes and prisons, I felt a start had to be
made somewhere to see whether even elementary psychological principles could be used to help a major police
investigation.

The direct result of this letter was a request, several
months later, for me to visit Hendon Police College in
North London where an incident centre had been set up in

DATE	TWO ATTACKERS	ONE ATTACKER
1982 June 10	Thurs 00.30	
July		
August		
September 15	Wed 00.05	
September 21	Tues 00.30	
September 24	Fri 04.15	
October		
November		
December		
1983 March	Sat 00.30	
1984 January	21.00	
February		
March		
April		
May		
June	00.10	
June 6		Wed 16.30
June 8	Fri 14.10	
July 15	Sun 01.00	
August		

September		
October		
November 22		Thur 22.00
December 7		Fri 19.25
December 11		Tues
1985 January 26	Sat 00.30	
January 30	Wed 19.45	
February 2 (2)	Sat	
February 24		Sun 20.45
March 1	Fri 02.00	
March 3	Sun	
April		
May 22		Wed
June 28		Tues
July 14	Sun	
August		21.25
September 22		Sun 21.00

Table 1. Chronological list of sexual assaults in London adapted from the article in the *Standard*.

a barely furnished room. The walls were covered with hand-written charts, listing the victims who had been assaulted and the descriptions they had given of their assailant and of the attack. Some features, such as the use of a knife, or the binding of the victim, had been underlined in different colours. Other charts had brought these critical features together to show which cases were similar. The overall impression was of a great confusion that was being courageously suppressed by listing every detail that seemed to matter.

Thelma Wagstaff came in, smoking a cigarette as usual. She was accompanied by three high-ranking police officers. Although they towered over her they clearly deferred to her authority. It began to dawn on me that the mood was different from my earlier, informal conversations with Thelma over that bottle of Beaujolais Nouveau. Now they wanted the academic chat to be replaced with action.

Each of the senior officers present was responsible for his own major investigation. Beside the investigation into the rapes (called the Hart inquiry) there were two separate murders being investigated. That morning they had agreed that all the different teams of detectives should be co-ordinated. Examination of the forensic evidence and some of the unusual actions in the offences had led them to conclude that the rapes and murders had been committed by the same man.

I had turned up at the creation of one of the largest detective inquiries that Britain had ever seen, certainly the largest co-ordinated effort since the 'Yorkshire Ripper' inquiry almost ten years earlier.

The officer who had just been put in overall command of the combined investigation, Detective Chief Superintendent Vince McFadden, head of Surrey CID, listened with interest to Thelma's summary of my letter. Before I fully understood the direction in which the conversation was going McFadden asked me if I could help to catch this man before he killed again. With no experience of police investigations and little knowledge of criminal behaviour, I was being asked to use whatever skills I might have as a psychologist to contribute directly to a major inquiry into rape and murder.

Hesitantly I answered that I could try, but that the analysis I had in mind was very time-consuming and, after all, I had a full-time job at the university. I therefore asked if there was anyone who could help me. To my amazement Vince McFadden, hardly pausing for breath, said that two police officers would be with me at the start of the following week.

This set in motion my personal journey to see if a criminal's actions in a crime really could reveal systematically his key identifying characteristics.

The linking of the two murders, and their subsequent connection with the rapes, had started as something of a coincidence. Detective Superintendent Charlie Farquahar was leading an investigation into the murder on 29 December 1985 at Hackney Wick in East London of Alison Day, a nineteen-year-old secretary. He learned from a 'Crimewatch' TV programme of the murder of a fifteen-year-old girl, Maartje Tamboezer, near a village outside Guildford 40 miles south of London. Maartje Tamboezer's body had been found in a wood in the spring of 1986, a few weeks before my visit to Hendon. The wood was covered in bluebells. With a poignancy rare for police officers, they had called their investigation the Bluebell inquiry.

There was something about the account given on television of the Guildford investigation that made Charlie Farquahar wonder if it was linked to his inquiry, even though it was such a distance from Hackney Wick. When he talked to the Surrey police, closer examination was made of the forensic evidence and some gruesome links in the way the murders had been carried out were established. The vicious ligature used to strangle the victims, the cutting of clothing and using it as a gag, the way the hands had been tied, were all unique to these two murders, and the attempt to set fire to one body, especially the pubic region, had never been seen in any other British murder inquiry.

Subsequent comparisons of the murders and of the series of rapes in London also pointed to similarities, especially in the way the victims' hands had been tied and the offender set fire to tissues with which he had wiped the victim after the sexual assault. There was also a link through a relatively rare blood grouping found both in semen left at the rapes and on the body of Maartje Tamboezer. The Hart inquiry had been on the point of being closed for lack of progress when the links to the murders were established. Setting up the combined operation was a last-ditch attempt to find the perpetrator.

Before I got to Hendon I had no idea that the rapes had any connection with the murders, which were also receiving widespread media coverage. My previous discussions with Thelma Wagstaff and John Grieve had been about sexual assaults. Although the focus of our conversations was chilling, meeting these two very unusual police officers had been a real education for me. They had told me that the whole mood of detective work was changing. At the senior levels of the police force, at least, there was an attempt to move beyond a craft, based solely on experience and knowledge of the law, to something more professional, using scientific procedures, methods and theories as central to their investigations rather than as an optional extra.

For my part, if a systematic psychological procedure was to be created that used the actions of criminals to reveal details that might not otherwise be known to detectives, then I wanted to start the research with loaded dice, with crimes where there was a lot of behaviour to work with, especially distinctly personal behaviour. Sexual assaults therefore seemed the best place to begin.

I left Hendon unsure about exactly where the personal journey on which I had embarked would lead. Two police officers were going to turn up at the university in a few days and together we would study the vast amount of material collected by three police investigations. We had to see whether any of the psychological theories and methods I had used to help solve much more benign problems would work with witness statements and crime scene reports; whether this rich and complex material, collected more with an eye to court procedures than to scientific research, could be analysed to reveal characteristics of this violent, devious man before he killed again.

We knew we were following in the footsteps of the Behavioral Science Unit of the FBI, since made internationally famous by the book and film *The Silence of the Lambs*. However, neither *The Silence of the Lambs* nor the publications and lectures of FBI behavioural science agents indicated how to produce an 'offender profile'. The published accounts do reveal a lot about the experiences on which FBI agents draw and the theories they have found helpful, but there is no system from which to produce guidance for investigating officers.

The only way open to me to discover what profiling could be, and how it might relate to the psychological theories and methods that I knew, was by working alongside an ongoing investigation, trying out ideas as they occurred to me. This is not the best way to become involved in any area of research, coming up with possible results without the time or resources to test them thoroughly, but it was the only way forward.

The police officers turned up at the University of Surrey, on the dot of nine on the Monday morning. All they knew was that they were to help with 'the profiling', and they could not have been more different from each other. Even their names could not have been bettered by a thriller writer who wanted to capture their distinct styles. Jim Blann was a square-faced, quietly-spoken detective inspector from the Metropolitan police, closely involved with the Hart inquiry. From the Surrey constabulary came Rupert Heritage, a dapper detective constable with neat moustache and a ready wit, who had been closely involved with the Bluebell inquiry.

Neither Rupert nor Jim had any idea what to expect. They were both detectives with many years of direct, hands-on experience in solving serious crimes. They had been sent to the university out of the blue, in more than one sense. Rupert had just returned from holiday and been told he was getting a computer and a psychology professor to help his work on the murder inquiry. He had never worked directly with either before and did not know which would present the greater challenge.

We had to teach each other a lot about our respective worlds. I was surprised by how much they were prepared to listen as well as to explain their activities to me. I began to realize that they shared the surprise. Not only could they understand what I was saying but they could contribute to the explorations that made sense to me. Jim, though, was on foreign territory, being seconded from London, and his presence in the project waxed and waned as other Metropolitan duties demanded his attention. Rupert was joined by Detective Constable Lesley Cross, an intense, steely woman. She clearly saw her job as part of the helping professions, improving people's lives by reducing crime. Where Jim and Rupert were prepared to follow the research trail I mapped out and give it a try, Lesley also wanted more fundamental answers. She more than the others wanted to know *why*.

Our initial discussions made clear that the newspaper reports, which were all I knew of the cases, implied a clarity and reliability in the police material that was far from the view of it held by police officers. The first task, therefore, was to try and work out which crimes had actually been committed by the same man. I decided that we should work with the rapes to begin with because they provided much more overt behavioural information.

A small research room had already been set up in the Guildford police headquarters by Detective Superintendent John Hurst, who was in command of the Bluebell inquiry. The analysis of the behaviour in the crimes became a focal part of the activity in this unexpected setting. I made frequent visits to this strange laboratory, as much out of curiosity as to supervise the research, watching the painstaking process of analysing the actions that took place in every offence.

Guildford police station seems to have been built deliberately in such a way that the denizens of the town will know without doubt exactly where the police are housed but have no real idea of how to get into it. This anonymous slab office-block can be easily seen on the way into the town centre but its main entrance is tucked away off a side road at the end of a cul-de-sac. My frequent visits there came to represent for me an access to a new world, near my daily existence but strangely isolated from it.

During my visits there, the sense I had of a different reality was magnified by the internal layout and decor. Inside, the building seems to house nothing more interesting than floors of untidy offices. There is no hint of the cells below with their subterranean passage to the next-door courts or the human dramas that pass across the crowded desks. The building did, however, have the distinct advantage to me that it was a five-minute drive from both my home and the university. As I became a regular visitor, parking confidently in a visitor's parking space, my growing familiarity with a part of Guildford and with a particular building came to symbolize my developing relationships with the Surrey police. Eventually I became familiar enough with the building to distinguish the unlabelled floors from each other, so that on the odd occasion when I managed to talk my way past the officer on the front desk, rather than wait to be collected, I was able to find my way to the long narrow room in which Rupert and Lesley and sometimes Jim were ensconced. Typically, though, the officer at the reception desk treated me like any other unknown civilian and I had to wait to be collected by Rupert.

Perhaps surprisingly, this became a pleasant, regular interlude during the early summer of 1986. I enjoyed the change of mood from the hectic, tense and determined atmosphere of the university to the relaxed, coffee-always-ready, cigarette-rolling chats with Rupert, Lesley and any other police officers who happened to pass through.

Rupert and Jim began by listing all the actions that had happened in every rape and then compared the actions across the rapes. This was a development of the charts that had been on the walls at Hendon, with two main differences. First we went into much more detail in considering the actions: did the assailant say anything to the victim before he attacked her? Were the victim's clothes pulled off, cut off or torn off? What sort of threats were made to control the victim? Exactly what sort of sexual activity took place? How did he deal with her after the assault? We soon had over a hundred such categories describing the thirty or so assaults that may have been committed by the same offender. This is where the second important difference from the wall charts came into play: the computer.

For many years I had used computers to help find patterns in data. With data like those available to Rupert and Jim the computer's task is to compare every crime with every other, across all the actions, and to indicate the degree of similarity and difference between crimes. At the university we had powerful computers for doing this, but considerable training was necessary to use them and there was also concern that the confidentiality of the material would be weakened if it were on a large central computer. Fortunately, though, desk-top computers were becoming readily available and the amount of information that we needed to handle at the police headquarters was well within their capability. The problem was that the software to run on these computers was not so readily available, especially software that could be used by computer novices like Rupert and Jim.

When I was originally challenged to help by Vince McFadden at Hendon, it had occurred to me that the inquiry would give me an opportunity to see if some new software that had been developed for me for a personal computer could be used successfully by inexperienced users. Somewhat ironically, the software had been paid for out of profits I had made on market research projects studying people's preferences for biscuits. I had wanted programmes that could be used by respondents in group discussions at the back of pubs, so it had to be very easy to use and very portable. This was what I let Jim and Rupert loose on.

There seems to me to be something remarkably British about the way this whole project began by improvising at every step. Police officers were seconded to help so that no specific budget was assigned to the work. They borrowed a computer and used software that had been paid for by an advertising manager. I fitted in, for free, whatever time I could sneak from the university. Since then, despite our obvious successes, not much has changed.

Rupert and Jim made good progress with the computer analyses of the behaviour. In essence, we got the computer to compare every crime with every other by taking into account all the actions that we had recorded for each crime. It would certainly have been possible to carry out the same sort of analysis by hand but it would have taken much, much longer and have been open to many more mistakes and distortions. The computer analysis was able to assign each pair of crimes a measure of their similarity based on how closely related the patterns of actions in those crimes were. This enabled us to identify a subset of crimes that were very similar indeed. The analysis also drew attention to changes that were occurring in the criminal's behaviour from one crime to the next.

The lone offender showed increasing assurance as the crimes continued. He spent more time with his victims, especially after the sexual assault. On some occasions, even after he had bound a victim to rape her, he sat and talked to her. Within these developments some consistencies could be identified: the tying of the victim's thumbs behind her back, which investigating officers had already used as a link between the rapes and the murders; the questioning of the victim about herself and where she lived; the apparent self-disclosure by the assailant about his ignorance of the locality. These all helped us to identify a subset of the crimes exhibiting enough similar behaviour probably to be the actions of one man.

We were moving into a new approach to police investigation. We were using behaviour to indicate that it was a similar offender rather than the detailed descriptions of what the offender looked like. The descriptions given by the victims varied considerably. Sometimes he was described as having short black hair, sometimes it was longer ginger hair. Estimates of his height and build also differed from a short five and a half feet to over six feet. We discovered, though, that strong similarities did emerge when we considered how the attacker always approached his victims first before returning to rape them and a number of pointers in what he actually did and said before, during and after the sexual assault.

He typically passed his victims, often speaking to them briefly as he passed, then grabbed them from behind threatening them with a knife. In many cases he restrained the women so that he could carry out the rape, fastening their hands behind their backs, using a binding made from their own tights. He also spent time with many of the women after the rape, finding out their name or giving them instructions on how to find the way home. The problem we faced was that his actions were not always the same; there were trends within them that needed careful sifting with the help of the computer. We would exclude some behaviours from our analysis and see if that revealed a more distinct set of offences, then add others to see what the consequence was for the groupings that the computer suggested.

A search for the essence of the offender, his character or what some psychologists would call his 'personality', or 'identity', was behind the computer trawls. We all are aware that there is something about ourselves that makes us distinct. We see that uniqueness reflected in how we think, feel and act. Perhaps with less certainty we also recognize the distinctiveness of other people. It is commonplace to meet a person after an interval of months or years but still to see that they are their 'old self', still talking and acting in ways that we know are typical of them. Psychologists are devoted to questioning what seems obvious and commonplace. This is not, as it sometimes seems, a perverse delight in confusing the layman, but essential to moving our understanding on.

What is consistent about a person from one situation to another? What remains constant from one time and place to another time and place? There are so many ways in which people can differ from each other, what are the major obvious differences that help us to identify each person? It dawned on me that these general questions have a sharp edge to them when applied to criminal investigations. There is a restricted amount of information available about the criminal, what he does and says in the crime. The restrictions are not imposed by the needs of scientific rigour but by the nature of the crime and what can be recorded. There is not, therefore, the luxury of the questionnaire and laboratory experiment, in which the researcher can get people to answer specific questions about themselves or perform particular tasks, that he determines based on theories he has about what distinguishes one person from another. In a criminal investigation we need theories and explanations that will accommodate the type of material we have available. We do not have the opportunity to go looking for particular information shaped solely by our ideas of what might be important.

This is not to say that years of scientific psychology are irrelevant and I had to start from scratch. Instead, I was forced to decide which were the dominant, robust themes of psychology that could be applied even in such a constrained and limited field of human action as violent crime. The conclusion I drew was that violent crime is always a transaction between at least two people; therefore it must reveal something about the way in which the offender deals with people. We had to consider not just the fact that he was prepared to commit a violent crime, although that would never be forgotten, but also all the other implications of his actions, the way he related to other people, especially women. Acts of violence can take many different forms and be preceded and followed by a great range of behaviours. It was my belief that, taken together, these variations could tell us a lot about what was characteristic about the offender's ways of interacting with other people.

Among the plethora of differences in the way people relate to each other that psychologists have explored, two seemed especially relevant to the varieties of violent crime. One was how prepared the criminal was to try and relate to the victim. This mirrors years of debate around terms like 'outgoing', 'extrovert', 'sociable', or even 'warm' and 'considerate'. Within the context of violent crime the key issue may be the attempt to strike up or imply a relationship or not. Given the very distorted nature of the relationship in a violent assault on a stranger this has to be seen through the eyes of the offender. Does he demand of the victim any sense of him as a person? Requests that she kiss him, or asking her name or whether she has a boyfriend (as this offender did) may all indicate a man who is trying to convince himself that there is some personal, even intimate, contact involved in the assault. Perhaps this would indicate that he has attempted such relationships in the past with varying degrees of success?

The second distinct theme that social psychologists have recognized is the desire for dominance. Of course all violent men want to control their victims so that they will allow their urges to be satisfied, but some want to explore and relish the experience of control itself. Deliberately frightening, demeaning and insulting their victims might be expected to be characteristic of such people. Would that indicate a desire to dominate in other aspects of their life? This offender only exerted enough control to rape his victims, so it raised the possibility that he would not be known as a very powerful, secure individual.

There was a feeling of steady progress in our work, but the offender was not waiting for us to develop our scientific theories. He killed again. Another murder took place that bore many of the hallmarks of the previous two. On 18 May, not long after my visit to Hendon, Anne Locke a thirty-year-old secretary working for London Weekend Television disappeared after catching the late evening train to Brookmans Park in North London. This was close to the Hertfordshire border and therefore another police force became involved in the investigation. Her badly decomposed body was not found until 21 July, but the indications from the binding of the fingers and the way it had been set on fire were that she had been killed by the same man who killed Alison Day and Maartje Tamboezer.

To keep some track of all the crimes over the four years from 1982 to 1986 Rupert had carefully marked their locations on a map of London. When I saw this I suggested to Rupert that he produce a separate map for each year. He did a beautiful job. Using a transparent acetate sheet for each year, he carefully coloured in the locations of each attack, using red for the attacks committed by two people together and green for the lone rapist. There were only three years, there being no linked crimes for 1984. Small squares marked the location of each of the three murders.

Sitting on a high stool, nursing my cup of coffee, I watched as Rupert showed me first the locations of all the crimes. Then he peeled off the acetate layers, going back in time, lifting off those including the murders of 1986, followed by the removal of the sexual assaults for 1985, leaving the handful of assaults carried out by two people together, or one alone, in 1982.

What the layers told me seemed obvious enough; so

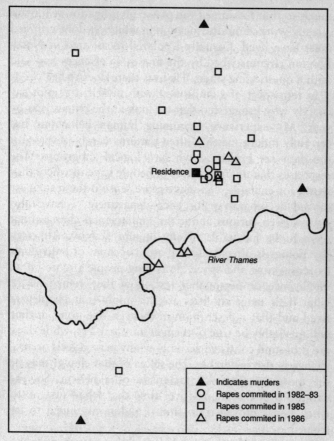

Residence

River Thames

▲ Indicates murders
○ Rapes commited in 1982–83
□ Rapes commited in 1985
△ Rapes commited in 1986

Map i: London, indicating the location of Duffy's rapes and murders and the area in which he lived at the time of his first offences.

much so that I assumed the police investigation team had already worked out the location in which the lone criminal must have lived. Casually I pointed to an area of North London circumscribed by the first three offences and said with a questioning smile, 'He lives there doesn't he?'

In retrospect, if I am honest with myself, I cannot say exactly why I suggested that we look at the crimes year by year. My experience examining human behaviour has certainly taught me that often patterns can be revealed if the data are broken down into logical subgroups. The responses that a large sample of people have to where they work, for example, can make more sense if the results are looked at separately for each department. I have also always been curious about the fundamental changes that seem to be inevitable in any human activity. Although psychology is often presented as an account of individuals frozen in time and space, describing people's score on an intelligence or personality test, how they remember or what their inner conflicts are, all imply that people are fixed and that a description of them at one point in time will inevitably be true of them at another. Yet, while there are profound consistencies in how any person feels or acts, change is also inevitable. The shape of that change may be the most consistent characteristic of a person. So, the variations in the attacks over time that I had first noted when I was on the train from London continued to intrigue me.

The police officers I had discussed this pattern with had never indicated that they had been aware of it. I am sure some had noticed it, but their lack of experience of looking at what people do as a systematic phenomenon had probably led them to undervalue the significance of the patterns or what they could do with them. Like most people who spend their lives dealing with other people, they become aware of the huge variety of human actions and the complex mixture of possible explanations that can account for even the simple fact of a person choosing a weekday to commit a crime. It takes the scientific frame of mind to stand back and say that, confused as it is, the shadow cast by a criminal's actions does have a recognizable shape to it. The shape I saw in the changes in the rapes was just that. They were changing. Something was happening to the criminal as he committed more and more crimes. The fact that the police were convinced that he had gone on to murder, after rapes that were not especially violent, was the clearest possible proof that he was changing.

Here another theme of modern psychology occurred to me as being of central relevance. Everyone changes through life as a result of the experiences they have. However, many different psychologists throughout this century have shown that such changes are not haphazard or arbitrary. In essence, within any particular sphere of experience the changes that take place are those of increasing differentiation and refinement. Furthermore, changes in one aspect of a person are almost invariably reflected in other aspects. A person who tastes many wines, just like a person who uses many computers, or a doctor who treats many patients, not only becomes more able to see (and smell) subtle differences between the subjects of his experience, differences that others are unaware of, he is also more able than others without his experience to distinguish the wines, or computers or patients, or locations for violent crime or ways of controlling victims into more refined categories. With this increasing refinement comes an awareness of the consequences of particular features, an evolving sensitivity to the nuances of the object or situation.

One of the spin-offs of this developing sophistication is that as a person becomes more expert he becomes more able to think of his experience in the abstract, to get outside of the experience itself and look down upon it and its implications. The most dramatic examples of this personal evolution have been shown from studies of children's thoughts and feelings as they grow up. Psychologists have charted the growth from concrete, self-centred childhood in which a child's own place in the world is totally dominant, through to self-conscious adolescence in which more general principles and alternative perspectives can be perceived and acted upon. There is growing evidence that such development processes occur whenever we are faced with new realms of experience. It therefore seemed feasible that this prolific rapist had learned directly from his own experience of the crimes and that this learning process had made him more subtle and sophisticated. But it was certainly not clear how that process had led him on to kill.

The constant question that Lesley Cross had for me was, why had the criminal gone on to murder? He had been successful as a rapist without being caught. He appears, on occasion, to have been almost considerate to his victims after the sexual assault: telling them which train to get home, offering them money for the journey, or a cigarette. Then he murdered three women, one after the other. Why?

Now we have various possible explanations, but in the summer of 1986 the only thing I could say to Lesley in response to her question was that the existence of that very question was the most important thing we knew about him. He had changed his actions. That had to be a clue to who he was and where we could find him. But at that moment I did not know how it could help us.

Like many people, and certainly like all scientists I have ever met, whenever there is such a challenging hint I do not sit back and think about it, or talk about it endlessly to others; I put a big flag on my mental map of the problem battlefield and then fiercely shake every bit of related information I can find to force it to reveal anything that might be relevant. We had the geographical details of many offences. We knew there was a change over time. Did the geography show any change over time that might be relevant?

Rupert's maps showed an explosion of crimes. The area covered was growing each year. This was not a moving on to a new set of locations like some predatory animal that has eaten the game in one region and therefore moves on to new pastures; it was more like a marauding brigand whose confidence grows as he continues to evade capture, spreading his dark influence over an increasing area of the map, the region of each succeeding year encompassing the preceding year. Was the offender exploring ever further outwards from some base? If he was then the most likely location of his base would be in the region of his first known crimes. According to this line of thought, his initial attacks would have been when he was exploring the possibilities close to home; when he was with his accomplice who might have some steady job, for whom rape was an exciting pastime, not a mission; when he was not yet committed to being a 'rapist'.

Together with these conjectures about where the offender might live we were collecting others in the office in Guildford police station. Our ideas about the culprit were growing. We were probably slipping into a relaxed academic exploration that many research teams enjoy, but Vince McFadden wanted to know whether his seconded police officers and borrowed computer really were going to get anywhere with the psychologist from the local university before there was another murder. I was urged to hold a meeting to brief all the senior officers involved.

At the university I was housed in a temporary, one-storey, flat-roofed hut of the sort that still survive in many universities as testament to their rapid expansion in the 1970s. This had the advantage of a central space, with some formica-topped tables, surrounded by open shelves with files on them, in which we held small informal meetings. The hut was set on the edge of the grassed playing fields next to the main university buildings so that the views from it looked out on a somewhat rural Surrey scene. This pleasantly unimposing setting turned out to be ideal neutral territory in which the Metropolitan police, the Surrey police and the Hertfordshire police could meet to hear my deliberations.

With the benefit of the hundreds of cases we have considered since then and the more than sixty reports that we have given to police forces, the presentation in Hut 2 on 28 July 1986 to a handful of senior police officers was possibly a foolhardy act. At that stage I did not appreciate that I was regarded as an insurance policy, to be blamed if the investigation failed. With my ignorance of police investigative procedures I did not appreciate how my thoughts would be dealt with or indeed how seriously they would be taken. From the little we could gather of the FBI work and some simple first principles, together with a gamble that the statistical data-reduction techniques we were using could be relied on for this sort of data, I pulled together some thoughts about the perpetrator.

The notes I produced for this meeting were a rudimentary set of headings.

PRELIMINARY PROFILE

Residence
Has lived in the area circumscribed by the first 3 cases since 1983.

Possibly arrested some time after 24 October 1983.

Probably lived in that area at the time of arrest.

Probably lives with wife/girl friend, quite possibly without children.

Age etc.
Mid to late 20s.
Light hair.
About 5′9″.
Right handed.
'A' secretor.

Occupation
Probably semi-skilled or skilled job, involving weekend work or casual labour from about June 1984 onwards.

Job does not bring him into a lot of contact with public, in all probability.

Character
Keeps to himself but has one or two very close men friends.

Probably very little contact with women, especially in work situation.

Has knowledge of the railway system along which attacks happened.

Sexual Activity
The variety and mixture of his sexual actions suggest considerable sexual experience.

Criminal Record
Was probably under arrest at some time between 24 October 1982 and January 1984.

His arrest may not have been a sex-related crime at all but an aggressive attack, possibly under the influence of alcohol (or drugs?).

I presented the 'preliminary profile' using an overhead projector as I would with any lecture, talking through the points and trying to explain the thinking that had led to them. Copies of the list were handed out, but like most seminars with new students there was little reaction. I was thanked for my efforts and the policemen and women wandered off across the grass to their cars. I continued to have meetings with Rupert and Lesley but these became rarer and little was added to our ideas. Another teenage girl was attacked by a railway line, possibly by the same man. Her mother's timely search for her had frightened the man away. Was he going to kill again before the police got to him? I was given no indication of the directions in which the police inquiry was going and began to think the seminar in the hut had been a waste of time.

In late November 1986 I saw in the local paper that a man had been arrested for the murder of three girls and a number of rapes. I immediately telephoned Rupert and asked him what was happening. He indicated that a lot was going on but he could not speak to me about it then.

A few days later I got a telephone call from Vince McFadden. I still remember the sensation at the back of my neck when he said: 'I don't know how you did it, or if it was all flannel, but that profile you gave us was very accurate and was very useful to the investigation.'

The remarkable accuracy of the profile surprised everyone, especially me.

The huge trawl of possible suspects had led the police to identify nearly 2,000 people who might have committed the rapes and murders, many because they had a blood-group similar to that left at the crime scene which was present in less than 10 per cent of the population. One of these, John Duffy, came into the list of police suspects because he had raped his wife at knife-point after she had left him. Before they were legally separated they had fights in which he bound her to have sex with him against her will.

In the initial stages of the police inquiry Duffy had not been a prominent suspect. He is reported to have been 1,505th on the list. His assault on his wife had been regarded as what police officers often call 'a domestic', merely a contretemps between a married couple. Some officers had assumed that a person involved in such domestic violence was not the sort of man who would go on to kill a stranger in a deliberate, planned way. The prospect that such violence within a marriage could be a reflection of and contribution towards later violence against strangers is still not widely understood.

After Duffy had initially been interviewed by the police about the assaults on his wife, there was another bizarre twist to the story. He staggered into a police station badly injured, saying he had been attacked and had lost his memory. He was admitted to a psychiatric hospital to be treated for this 'amnesia'. He was not under very strict supervision at the hospital, as detectives later discovered, being free to come and go during the day without his absence being noted. It was also curious that the only patient he befriended in the hospital was a man who had strong delusions of having murdered someone. (One day a novelist will explore the relationship between a murderer claiming amnesia, denying any knowledge of a violent criminal past, and a mental patient tormented by his own mistaken belief that he has taken somebody's life.)

Duffy, buried deep in the list of suspects, closely fitted the profile. He was the only one who lived in the Kilburn area predicted and one of very few who fitted the majority of other characteristics. A large-scale surveillance was therefore mounted to watch him. His activities convinced McFadden that Duffy was the man they were looking for. He was arrested.

An acquaintance of Duffy, who practised martial arts with him, came forward to admit to wounding Duffy at his own request. Duffy had told him he wanted to have an excuse to fake amnesia, believing that the wounding would be accepted by the police as so traumatic that it could have produced a loss of memory. Forensic evidence of fibres on his clothing were linked to those found on the bodies of his victims and very unusual string, made out of paper, was found at his family home. This string was the same as that used to bind his murder victims. Identification parades linked him to the rapes as did the original blood-typing.

The case put together in court drew heavily on the ideas behind the profile, giving a story-line to all the disparate facts that had been amassed. John Francis Duffy sat throughout showing little emotion. A small, slim, fair-haired man, bordering on the ginger, with a pock-marked, weasel-like face, he passed notes from time to time to his counsel, but otherwise might have been a casual spectator who would have gone unnoticed in the street. The jury had no difficulty in finding him guilty of two murders and five rapes. He was sentenced to life imprisonment with the recommendation that he serve at least twenty years.

Now that it is known who the 'Railway Rapist' (as the press called him) is, we can see that only his height was overestimated, from victim statements, and the exact timing and pattern of his previous arrests were wrong. The seemingly uncanny accuracy of everything else encouraged us to believe that it may be possible to develop general psychological principles and procedures that can be effective in helping to detect violent crimes against strangers.

Since that first 'profile' we have been trying to pin down the processes that gave rise to it so that a generally available system can be created. I had never thought that this first attempt would become of such interest. In academic terms it was the equivalent of a pilot project that would not normally be published, an exploration that would probably teach us most by how it failed rather than by its success. There were too many scholarly matters demanding my attention to keep extensive notes and looking in my notebook of the time I see that I kept far more detailed accounts of other unrelated, ongoing projects such as the psychology of the nuclear threat and a presentation on the 'Facets of Social Life' to be given in Portugal.

The remarkably positive outcome from the back-room discussions and computer analyses in Guildford police station did lay the basis for future developments. Some of the main arguments are memorable, as well as some of the discoveries we made along the way about what could and could not be relied on in a police investigation.

One of the first problems to face us when we looked at the information that detectives had collected was the variety of descriptions of the assailant given by the victims. These ran from black to ginger-haired and from over six foot tall to under five and a half feet. It seemed very likely that these were not all the same assailant, but how were we to tell which crimes were the actions of the same man? I took the view that the victims' descriptions of an assailant can often be far less accurate than their account of the actions that occurred. Considerable subtlety is required from a visual description of a person for it to be of any real investigative value. Available light or the victim's attention being focused on a weapon rather than the face of the attacker can also, quite understandably, cause the victim not to see the man very clearly. Even if she does see him there is the problem of putting into words what she saw. Slight differences in reports of hair colour or shape of the face can make enormous differences in whether a culprit is recognizable from those descriptions.

By contrast, an account of the actions, engrained into the bodily memory of a victim, will usually capture many distinguishing characteristics of how the assault was carried out. She will have no doubt that he suddenly jumped on her, putting his arm round her neck; she will probably still be able to feel his grip as she speaks. The emotional intensity may actually heighten her memory for what happened to her, just as it may distort what her assailant looked like. There is a sense, then, in which the behaviour is more characteristic of the criminal than descriptions given of him.

We thought it unlikely, however, that descriptions of a criminal's appearance would be systematically biased. Thus for each victim who overestimates his age there can be one who underestimates it. So, if we can identify a group of offences that we can be reasonably sure were committed by the same man, then the common elements of the descriptions given by the victims could possibly be taken as a reasonably accurate description of the offender. Following this line of thought we used the computer-based analysis of the behaviours in the rapes to identify a group of crimes that revealed similar patterns of behaviour. Checking the descriptions of the rapist given by the victims showed some consensus for those crimes and it was this that provided the basis of the physical feature in the profile, of age, hair colour and height.

Duffy was twenty-nine when he was arrested, so victims' estimates of him, ranging from early to late twenties, were reasonably accurate. The inaccuracy in height estimate, though, was an important mistake. It serves to show that some general bias, among even a number of independent victims, is possible. It suggests that victims can be so traumatized by a man who has violently assaulted them that they consistently remember him as taller than he was.

The most dramatic discovery was the way in which the geographical distribution of Duffy's crimes revealed where he was living at the time of his first known rapes. It is easy to forget that his rapes covered the whole of greater London and the three murders were at three distant points on the very edge of London. Looking at a general map of these crimes it is possible to believe that he could have lived anywhere in a fifty-mile radius of central London – an area that houses about a third of the population of Great Britain. He might even have been travelling in from further afield. Yet he was the only one on the list of police suspects who lived in the area we had indicated. His marauding out from the early, less apparently planned sexual assaults to the carefully-conducted murders at the furthest distance, strongly suggested an increasing determination and forward planning in his crimes. This appeared to be based on his identifying suitable locations for these crimes, where solitary, vulnerable females could be found, rather than his searching and targeting of specific women.

The significance of familiarity and convenience in shaping the locations that a criminal will choose for his assaults, at least initially, was one of the clearest suggestions to emerge from looking at Duffy's actions. But when he was convicted we had no idea how generally such a principle might apply. In his particular case we found that even the later rapes happened in areas he already knew. After the trial Rupert discovered that virtually all of the locations in which Duffy carried out his sexual assaults were close to places that he knew from visiting relatives or close friends, or from his recreational activities. This throws an even more chilling light on his killings. It is difficult to believe that the murders were casually opportunist or accidental. There must have been a plan that took Duffy so far from the central London that he knew.

Here was a man, then, increasingly dedicated to crime, developing into a cold-blooded killer. That was the development process that I had glimpsed in the patchy picture of rapes in the London *Standard*. He had become a lone attacker, increasingly devoted to assaults, raping women whenever he could. Perhaps the early attacks when he had a partner were seen by both men as chance opportunities, but as the partner became more aware of how obsessed Duffy was becoming with assaulting women is it possible that he pulled out, wanting no part of activities he could see would lead to arrest?

Throughout his trial, and since, Duffy has claimed amnesia for his actions around the time of the rapes and murders. Consequently, no examination of his own account of what went on has been possible. He did have a known accomplice, arrested with him for earlier physical assaults and burglary but there was not enough evidence to bring that man to court for the joint rapes.

Duffy's prior criminal history for stealing was another suggestion in the 'preliminary profile' that could have been peculiar to this particular man. Perhaps some special circumstances trigger sexual crimes in a man who has previously been a law-abiding citizen, so no record of him would exist in police files. A different possibility, the received wisdom among many police officers, is that there is a natural career for people who are sexually deviant, from voyeurism and indecent exposure through sexual assaults and on to rape. Searches through previous criminal records are most likely, therefore, to be for sexually- linked crimes. Studies by clinicians of people with sexual deviations do not give very strong support to this career path. Some examples of it can be found but many convicted rapists have no obvious antecedents of voyeurism, indecent exposure or less serious sexual assaults. They do, though, quite often have convictions for theft and violence. There are, as a result, many different possibilities to be considered when delving into the files of previous convictions. Every possibility exists from 'no previous' on to prior sex-related crimes and the full gamut of criminal activity. These possibilities are complicated by the very real prospect that although other offences might have been committed by the rapist he may never have been caught or convicted for them, or if the offence was considered rather trivial, like 'peeping', no record would be available to the investigative team.

Our proposal that the 'Railway Rapist' had previously come to the attention of police officers for non-sexual crimes was therefore only one of a large range of possibilities. The fact that we were correct in this one case, our first, opened up the prospect that there may be some discernible principles linking what a criminal does in his crimes and what sort of crimes he may have been arrested for in the past.

One assumption that we very much needed to test in future cases might be called the 'police thoroughness' principle. The thinking behind this was that a man who had committed as many criminal assaults as the 'Railway Rapist' was unlikely to have come to crime all of a sudden. This line of argument proposes that even if there had been some trigger that set him on a particular spree, the fact that his response to that trigger was a series of violent criminal activities suggests that there was some prior criminal involvement in his life. If it were not a response to some perceived provocation then the number of crimes the investigators have associated with the person indicates a style of life that is beyond the law. It is the *number* of crimes that is central to this argument. The same might not be expected to apply to one sudden outburst, although even there precursors in the person's lifestyle may also be likely. The argument may be summarized in the simple notion that we knew the 'Railway Rapist' had committed a lot of crimes during a known time period. We therefore had every reason to think that he had also committed other crimes not linked to the identified series.

The principle behind 'police thoroughness' is that very many men are brought to police attention for a great variety of crimes. Some estimates say a third of the adult male population has some sort of criminal record in Britain. Furthermore, when a major inquiry is launched the net is usually cast very wide indeed in the search for possible suspects. It consequently seems likely that someone who commits a series of grievous crimes has his name logged somewhere in police records. The problem lies in finding him. This principle may be considered optimistic or pessimistic, depending on which side of the civil liberties argument you are, but it does assume a high degree of effort and diligence on the part of the police. Such an assumption may be relevant to major crimes in Britain, but may not apply to other police forces in other countries. However it is viewed, it is a proposal open to testing in other cases. It turned out to be painfully true of John Duffy. If he had been dealt with as soon as he came to police attention for the assault on his ex-wife, he may not have gone on to rape and murder.

We assumed that the 'Railway Rapist' had been caught up in some police investigation during his long period of crime. The problem for Vince McFadden was choosing among the 1,999 suspects those on whom police resources should be expended. Who should be looked at closely? Our suggestion, presented in the profile, of looking for a non-sexual criminal history was based on the idea that there is some central theme, core or objective to a series of crimes, that in some way represents the criminal's way of dealing with other people. A man who rapes many women then starts deliberately to kill his victims shows a central violent nature. In planning some of his sexual crimes he may have had that violence under control to the extent of avoiding immediate detection, but it was a possibility that in other situations his aggression would be less under control, more overt: a brawl in a pub, a fight with his girlfriend.

I think of this as the electrician and the ladder principle. In studies of industrial safety I have found that, typically, electricians who have accidents do not do so by electrocuting themselves; dealing with electricity is such an ingrained habit that they automatically take care. If an electrician has an accident it is more likely to be produced by some part of his job that does not require special skill: he falls off a ladder through stretching too far, or bumps into something because his attention wanders. I speculated that a committed criminal, as Duffy became, is skilled at avoiding arrest when he is consciously going out to commit crimes, but drops his guard and reveals his true criminal nature when involved in activities that he does not think of as criminal, like forcing his ex-wife to have sex at knife-point.

Another hypothesis to emerge from the consideration of Duffy's crimes was that criminals may sometimes betray by their actions that they have already been caught up in a police investigation, attempting to avoid being forensically linked to their crimes. In one case, after he had raped a woman Duffy combed through her pubic hair, presumably so that no traces of his own hair would be found. He also wiped a number of his victims with tissues then set fire to the tissues to get rid of evidence of semen. He was found to have a box of matches with tissues in it, called by the prosecution 'a rape kit'. Setting fire to the pubic region of his murdered victims was one of the factors that convinced the police that it was the same man who had committed rapes in which he wiped the victims. All these actions revealed a detailed knowledge of forensic investigation. He was most likely to have come by this knowledge through being examined himself after his assault on his ex-wife.

A further stage in the logical process that we found useful was the possibility of adding together different conclusions to derive other possible characteristics of the offender. In this case we had formed the view that these violent crimes had been planned and the offender had taken care to avoid detection. Would this not be more typical of an older man who is not likely to be overtaken by the impetuosity of youth? The majority of crimes are committed by young men in their mid- to late teens. Violent, serious crimes such as rape, murder and armed robbery come later in a person's developing criminal career. The studied murders of Duffy were very different from sudden violent outbursts, revealing Duffy's criminal maturity that I assumed, rightly as it turned out, was a reflection in part of his age. He might have been a lot older, in his late thirties or even early forties as many serial murderers are, but that would have been unusual for a rapist who is usually in his early to mid-twenties. The combination of possibilities therefore led to an estimate of this rapist and murderer being in his mid- to late twenties. This estimate was not challenged by the bulk of descriptions by witnesses who gauged their assailant's age. Analyses we have carried out since then do show that victims typically get the age of their attacker broadly correct, within the right decade at least. He was twenty-nine when he was arrested, having started on his crimes in his mid-twenties.

An older man with a history of sexual assault, but probably without any other sort of criminal history, who rapes and eventually murders is most probably unmarried. More of the men who are convicted for rape are unmarried than are married. But in Duffy's contacts with his rape victims he typically approached them first to ask directions, or by a similar subterfuge made contact to give them a false sense of security before assaulting them. After some of his assaults he seemed confident enough with his victims to stay and talk to them, even on some occasions giving them advice on how to get home. Here then was a man who was comfortable being in control of women, who could approach strange women without fear of rebuff. Yet we knew that he raped and violently murdered some victims as well. Women were an obvious vehicle for his control and sexuality. It seemed very likely that he would have wished to have a woman available to him, a wife. The profile therefore proposed that he had been married. Here, then, was the birth of another possible principle that we could develop and test on future cases: a consistency principle. The ways in which he deals with his victims tell us something about the way the offender deals with other people who are significant to him.

It would be strange indeed that a man could have a deep, caring relationship with his wife and still go out frequently with a friend or on his own to rape and then murder. Every case that is published about such men reveals an exploitative relationship between the offender and his partner. On the surface they may seem to be happily married but, more so than in many marriages, it does not take much to find the disruptive chasm between the couple: either an accepting gullibility on the part of the woman that is cynically abused by the man, or a woman kept in a subservient role by vicious manipulation. By the time that the man is involved in violent crime the relationship may have broken up completely.

The breakdown of this relationship may, indeed, be a component in the escalation of the criminal's activities. Crimes of violence are rarely totally removed from the aggressor's feelings of anger and frustration, although these feelings may be confused with thoughts of protection from investigation or the offender believing that he is meting out crude justice. Such feelings are often aggravated by personal traumas. A violent relationship with a woman was therefore a reasonable assumption, derived from the details of the crimes.

This was an interesting example of how confusing common sense can be. Once the original profile became public knowledge there were comments that it was all very obvious that a man who raped and murdered women was antagonistic towards them. But this anger with women could have been a result of lack of contact with them. It would certainly have been a reasonable assumption, at a superficial level, that the offender had never established any long-term relationship with a woman. How could he rape and kill and still have lived with a woman? But such an assumption fails on two counts in this case. First, it does not allow for the development in criminal activity. For a younger assailant, lack of close contact with women of his own age would have been a reasonable assumption, but for an attacker that it seemed was older, some prior association with a woman, out of which his crimes had evolved, seemed more likely. Second, he did indicate in the time he spent with his victims and his conversations with them that in some curious way he wanted a relationship. This is likely to have been reflected in earlier actions and an attempt to establish a relationship with a woman.

The third pointer to a relatively long relationship with a woman was the variety of sexual activity revealed in the sexual assaults. The scientific study of sexual activity does reveal that it is shaped by learning processes. The more opportunity and experience a person has for sex the more varied his or her actions are likely to become. This variety can certainly be enhanced by access to sex manuals and pornography, but first-hand experience has the most potent effect in all aspects of human behaviour. The number of offences that had been linked by detectives allowed me to see a man who carried out every form of sexual behaviour he could with his victims, indicating that he had probably had a relationship in which he had first attempted these actions.

But what of this relationship? I assumed it had been fraught. Would they have had children? The viciousness of Duffy's assault on the fifteen-year-old Maartje Tamboezer seemed to me very difficult to associate with the actions of a man who had been involved in bringing up children himself. There was a carefully planned aggression against this schoolgirl and an inability to empathize at all with her situation in his hands. I thought, perhaps naively at that stage, this could not be the actions of a man who had been a father. (At that stage I did not know of Colin Pitchfork, for example, who killed two adolescent girls while he was married with young children.)

What kind of job, if any, would a man have who was potentially very violent, antagonistic towards women, but who planned his assaults with confidence, going ever further afield to carry out his most vicious attacks? He was clearly a man who exploited and used people but also one who would be intolerant of those who made demands on him, so any job he had would be unlikely to be a 'service' that brought him into direct contact with those he served. His preparation and planning indicated an ability beyond labouring work; the intellectual skills he brought to his murders could have seen the light of day earlier on in the learning of a trade.

If he did have some semi-skilled job, how could he commit crimes so often during the working week, clearly without any fear of being missed? The simplest assumption was that it was weekend work that he did or that it was very casual. I should have realized that the exploitative, confident style of his contact with his victims could easily have been reflected in a poor work record, a man who was often absent from work for no apparent reason. Or that it would fit in with a man who had to travel around to carry out his work on his own, so that absences could go unnoticed for some time. The work of a travelling carpenter for British Rail, with hindsight, is a far more obvious and detailed possibility than I would have dared to propose in those early days of our work, but the general tone of my suggestions was close enough for police investigators to see the logic of it.

Duffy also used a unique method to kill: he tied a tourniquet round his victims' necks which he then tightened with a large stick taken from the scene. He used this brutal garrotte to kill all his victims yet such a method had never been seen before in a British murder. I had taken it as an indication of planning and forethought but I had not been able to interpret this dreadful signature. Carpenters learn about tourniquets, though, most frequently in first aid. First aid manuals point out the dangers of this method of stopping the flow of blood from a wound: 'If digital pressure will not stop the flow of blood, it may be necessary to apply a tourniquet but this should be done as a last resort. The tourniquet is a dangerous instrument. The tourniquet should be applied between the wound and the heart (but not around the neck).'

Such innocent instructions could easily have been read in a very different light by a man intent on murder. Other martial arts and survival books found in his possession could have served to reinforce his awareness of how to despatch his victims.

The arrest of Duffy and the details that subsequently emerged about him helped to fill in the picture we had formed to draw up the profile. Some of the other questions we had been asking during our discussions at Guildford police station also began to be answered during the trial. On one occasion, his former wife told the court: 'He said he had raped a girl and said it was my fault.' John Duffy had found out that he was infertile and some of his most violent assaults took place after he discovered that his ex-wife had become pregnant by another man after she had left Duffy. So anger and frustration could be seen as triggers for his actions.

But why did he kill? Why did a man who had avoided capture for at least three years when raping his victims and letting them live go on to kill? There was some possibility that the Hart investigation had so run out of steam that if Duffy had not murdered he would have escaped detection altogether.

It turned out that we had the answer to this central question all along, embedded in the ideas inherent in the profile. As the *Daily Telegraph* reported:

> In December 1985, his fifth rape victim was taken to Hendon magistrates court, where Duffy was appearing on an assault charge brought by his wife.
>
> Although she failed to recognise Duffy, he recognised her as she peered at him. He came to a decision that any future women that he raped would be silenced.
>
> He killed Alison Day 27 days after his court appearance.

It all added up to a remarkably clear account of a man increasingly caught up in violence, entangling himself in crime. The more he tried to shake off detection the tighter he pulled the net around himself. Swimming through the murky waters of violent crimes the ill-formed silhouette of the criminal turned out to have an even more interpretable shape than I had hoped. It was much clearer than I had any right to expect for my first involvement in a major crime investigation. The outline provided by the profile became a silhouette that needed very little adjustment to contain the full image of the perpetrator.

There is a well-known principle that is seen as the foundation of forensic science, first formulated at the start of this century by Edmond Locard: 'Every contact leaves a trace.' He was thinking of the physical, biological traces that criminals leave from their clothing or where their bodies have touched the scene. Our work, leading to the arrest of Duffy, suggested that there was a more subtle meaning to this notion. The contact that an assailant has with his victim leaves a trace of the sort of person he is. There is the possibility of a behavioural strand to forensic science as well as a biological, chemical and physical one.

When the court proceedings were over, the full significance of our work began to become apparent. The Surrey police investigation team had a special tie designed to commemorate the case. It had the small image of a bluebell woven into it, a salutary reminder that a schoolgirl had been viciously killed one spring day. If it had not been for the time it takes a complex police investigation to unfold, her killer might have been arrested before he had been able to kill again. Rupert Heritage, an experienced detective who had never operated a computer or worked with a professor before, neither would he claim any knowledge of psychology, was convinced that we had opened up a new way forward for criminal investigation. He asked to study with me at the university. I saw that his experience would enrich our work and together we might have a chance of opening up the study of criminal investigation. That was the point at which I realized that some discovery or breakthrough had been made, but I was still not sure what we had done or how we had done it.

Certainly, the help I had given had not emerged from detailed experience of violent criminals and their crimes; nor would I claim any subtle intuition. I tackled the problem posed by the police as I would any other research question: I collected all the relevant information that was available and attempted to tidy it up in order to see what central themes it would reveal. The computer had certainly helped in imposing some order on the unruly data. The sequential maps had also been of great value. But neither the computer analysis nor the maps, or any of the other tables and lists that we prepared, would have told us anything more than the charts that filled the walls of the Hart inquiry at Hendon, if I had not had some systematic way of interpreting them.

Forced to peel away much of the overload of psychological complexity that emerges when one psychologist talks to another, in my discussions with Rupert and his police colleagues I was pushed back to identify the central perspectives within modern psychology. I came to the conclusion that there were two opposing themes running throughout the academic debates about the nature of people. One was a person's quest for identity and the explorations of what makes each person distinct. Here it was ways of dealing with other people which seemed central. In the acts of rape and murder Duffy had shown a style that combined a recognition of his victim's likely reactions with a total disregard for their feelings. This gave a social context to the description of him. He was a man who could relate to others but often abused that relationship; a man who had the intelligence to think and plan his crimes so their locations would therefore be far from random.

The contrasting psychological theme was the one of development and change. Like themes in a piece of music that vary and evolve as the music unfolds, revealing unexpected configurations while still holding on to the same central sequence of chords, Duffy's violent discords became more strident as his crimes progressed while still showing the same underlying interpersonal themes. I discovered that these developments themselves were reflected in where he raped and killed as well as how he did it. The reflections led us to the man.

When I was given that tie with the bluebell on it I could not be sure if my contribution to the arrest of Duffy was a freak instance, or whether the psychological principles on which I had drawn could be turned to detailed, consistent procedures with known evidence to support them. There was the open question of whether such contributions to police investigations would also be possible in other cases, or if they would be needed.

I knew that FBI agents had produced similar sorts of 'profiles' with apparently great success. Had they got far enough along this scientific path to be able to learn from them more directly? Or were their activities based upon a different approach? I presumed they had a basis in their experience of many crimes, but it was not clear to me whether they had derived from that experience an articulate set of principles, hypotheses and testable theories, or whether they had used their situation at the heart of the investigation of violent crime in America to develop further their own insights and personal skills. A subsequent visit to the FBI academy outside Washington enabled me to see that in fact their own studies drew on both the scientific and the intuitive, but with a definite bias towards personal insight and away from detailed analysis of data.

Chapter Three

ENRICHING INTUITION

When I now read accounts of my involvement in the Duffy inquiry I can see what young Arthur might have felt when he absent-mindedly pulled the sword out of the stone, looking up with surprise at the astonishment of those around him. Overnight I was regarded as an 'expert', hounded by journalists for opinions on any form of human depravity, sought after by police investigators. Even my stock as a professor of psychology seemed to have risen, with invitations to lecture to university departments and learned societies as far afield as the Punjab and Newfoundland. But as a professional I knew how little I could defend the opinions that had been so helpful to the police. One successful case certainly did not create a new area of applied psychology. I needed to meet the people who had cleared the path for systematic study of offence behaviour, the people of the FBI Behavioral Science Unit. The interest that surrounded my involvement in detecting the 'Railway Rapist' ensured that I was invited to the FBI academy in Quantico, Virginia.

Jodie Foster, in the film of *The Silence of the Lambs*, portrayed a new FBI agent trying to apply what she had learned about profiling at the FBI academy. Since then, it has become common knowledge that the major impetus for using profiling as a tool for detection came from where the character portrayed by Jodie Foster, Clarice Starling, was supposed to be undergoing her training, the Behavioral Science Unit of the Academy.

The Behavioral Science Unit is one, relatively small, part of the FBI academy which provides training in most aspects of law enforcement for the FBI and for the Drug Enforcement Agency (DEA) as well as other city, county and state police agencies. Topics as diverse as predicting future patterns of crime and forensic photography are explored and taught in a large complex of interconnected lecture rooms, offices, residences, laboratories and sports facilities. Programmes are intensive and all-embracing. They include sending in a team to counsel staff after one of their number has been murdered, and re-acclimatization procedures for people who have been living under cover for long periods of time; there are programmes on crimes against the elderly, weapons training, computer literacy and a fitness programme that leaves the students more athletic than they will ever be again. Lecture courses have a credit value at the local University of Virginia so each has a syllabus and recommended reading lists and all the paraphernalia of an academic subject which can be presented in digestible chunks to keen students. But the lifeblood of the Behavioral Science Unit is murder and violent assault, threats and abductions. Those students who come to take the courses become part of a team of active practitioners who are trying to find links between violent crimes across the United States and to give guidance to law enforcement agencies the length and breadth of the land and beyond.

'Hi, yes, I'm with the BSU. You're welcome to attend my class on threat analysis,' is a snippet of conversation that might readily be overheard in the academy bar, revealing the charged mixture of serious study and criminal detection that gives the place its excitement. The bar itself, somewhat whimsically called the Board Room, is not unlike a German Bier Keller. Staff and students happily get together there for extremely noisy discussions about the topics they are studying. What makes it especially different from other colleges is that, in the tradition of police forces around the world, teaching is done by people who have had direct experience of criminal investigations. They continue to extend that experience as a major part of their jobs.

For a number of the staff, their dominant task is to provide an advice service unlike any that could be created anywhere else in the world. As many as a thousand violent crimes a year are sent to the BSU for dissection and analysis. Any law enforcement agency can ask for assistance from their special agents who will respond to most requests with a description of the likely perpetrator. Investigative support and training activities are run on a large scale. Well over 100 FBI agents and thirty-two police officers worldwide have been trained with them. Many return annually for refresher courses. In terms of the number of committed, experienced people that are part of their network they have considerable resources on which to draw.

The federal nature of the United States means that the FBI can contribute to violent crime investigations only by invitation, unless the crime is a federal one (such as kidnapping or a series of related murders) that crosses a number of state boundaries, or is on federal property. Their role in the courts is also very different from what might be expected in Britain; they can be brought in as experts quite separately from the evidence of the police investigators. All this puts the special agents at Quantico in a unique position. They are the back-room boffins, the consultants to criminal analysis. They really are like Special Agent Cooper in *Twin Peaks* or the earlier film incarnation of Sidney Poitier in *In the Heat of the Night*, the outside expert from the big city who can see what the locals cannot, except that black faces are still quite rare at the FBI academy.

Quantico is in the most rural of settings, deep inside a military base, at least a ten-minute drive from the Washington freeway, through deep woods with glimpses of marines on manoeuvres and the distant sound of automatic weapons. The academy is housed in a spare maze of beige brick, fastidiously built at the stage when modern architecture was beginning to lose its rough edges and soften up. The buildings are sealed to maintain their air-conditioning so that the inviting countryside all around is everywhere seen through plate glass but never smelled or felt. If this building complex houses the intelligence of criminal investigation, nestling within the military might of the vast marine base, then the Behavioral Science Unit is quite literally deep inside this brain, reflecting the destructive urges that boil just below the surface of America.

To enter these fluorescent caverns that host the records of the male id at its worst, you must walk through the armoury-cleaning room, past men in fatigues cleaning their assault rifles, to an unmarked, grey, goods lift which travels to the concrete bunkers below. Never really strong enough to provide protection for the seat of government against nuclear attack (the purpose for which it was built), in the unknowingly appropriate ways of bureaucracies it was designated as offices for the Behavioral Science Unit, forcing the special agents to be rather like Plato's slaves chained to the floor of their cave, able only to watch the shadows flickering on the wall opposite, unable to turn and look at the figures walking past on the road above.

This warren of pictureless, flatly-lit white corridors houses the offices and trophies of the continuous quest to turn back the tide of crime that washes through the cellars in the form of reports and photographs, dossiers and telephone calls. From time to time the agents surface into the Virginia landscape and out to scenes of crime, but more often they go to lecture theatres and law courts.

The tasks of these labourers in the dungeons of the American psyche are difficult indeed. The USA is enormous and mobile, with greatly varying resources devoted to law enforcement. In Los Angeles a police officer may have to deal with a handful of homicides over the weekend, and if he cannot resolve an investigation in a couple of days it will just have to be filed. By contrast, the sheriff of a small town in the Midwest may never have investigated a murder in which the culprit was not immediately known. These differences have direct implications for information-collection procedures as well as the skills and technical resources that are locally available. A central advisory agency cannot therefore rely on the provision of information about a case or local expertise. They are required to provide guidance which will enable neighbours and acquaintances, or police officers who knock on doors, to recognize the person who is being sought.

In Britain, full central records on known criminals are kept. These are much more detailed than the fingerprint records that the FBI keeps in Washington of all people who have been arrested. Contrary to the fictional creations of Hollywood, Britain has a much better organized and far more centralized police investigative process. In Britain there is less need to be able to describe an offender so that neighbours and friends will recognize the description; it is more helpful to say where the offender can be found in the criminal record system, or the approach that will be most fruitful in furnishing possible suspects for closer analysis.

In contrast to Britain the distances in the United States are so great that visiting a crime scene and discussing matters with local police are tremendously time-consuming. At one stage the special agents at Quantico turned this into a virtue, saying that keeping away from the scene ensured that they were not contaminated by local ideas. When an FBI employee was murdered, bringing the case directly under their jurisdiction, the BSU agents reluctantly took the opportunity to become directly involved in the investigation and visited the scene.

The fact that crimes may be in different time zones, climates and types of urban development also means that the central experts have to create rather general approaches to the help that they give. One of their reports may say that the offender lived within a mile of the first crime in the series, but when I write a report for an inquiry in London I have the luxury of being able to say that an offender may live in the Tottenham area or within an area bounded by Streatham and Tooting High Streets. One consequence of this is that the assistance given from Quantico aims at providing general descriptive characteristics of offenders that paint a broad picture.

The work of the FBI as advisers to all comers is also complicated by the knotty problem of jurisdiction and the associated number of people investigating any major crime. To take just one of many possible examples: a man who committed a number of rapes across Boston, a city which is not very large by US or international standards, had managed to commit crimes on the patch of at least seven different law enforcement agencies, each of which was keen to catch him but for whom co-ordination posed some difficulties. In the United States as a whole it is reported that there may be as many as 15,000 different law enforcement agencies. The complexities of this become apparent when it is realized that each has its own records and forms of record-keeping, as well as its own investigative procedures and management structures. Each will contain people whose career progress depends upon solving their local crimes.

The conflict of interest inherent between people and jurisdictions emerged very clearly in a review of the introduction of computerized police information systems in

Chicago. In the patois that is *de rigueur* in academic books, the authors from the Center for Research in Law and Justice wrote: 'The integrative aspect of computer-combined data helps to overcome one of the most counter-productive aspects of detective work, lack of sharing of information.' This 'lack of sharing' is only partially a problem of procedure. Officers may withhold information from others in order to increase their own chances of making arrests. After all, salesmen will keep details of good customers away from competitors; university staff will jealously hide from each other the directions for research that are proving productive; guidebook writers will keep secret their very favourite restaurant so that it will not be overrun by tourists. These are all understandable human foibles that are in conflict with the more general benefits to the world at large. Effective managers constantly try to reduce the destructive consequences of personal ambition, but the balance between lack of personal motivation and too much is a difficult one to achieve. Why should the police be any different?

Technical advice that could not be expected to be within the abilities of the investigator does not pose the same threat to his aspirations. Quite the reverse: if he does not take advantage of the scientific resources on offer then he is failing in his duty. Contact with an external agency can help to give focus to a mixture of investigations and help to overcome local jealousies. But such advice must be authoritative. The people who give it have to have the knowledge to draw upon as well as the professional distance of objectivity. Otherwise they become just another jurisdiction to get in the way.

When the much-maligned J. Edgar Hoover set the FBI in motion he was aware of all these problems and was determined to create an intellectual élite. His agents all had to have university qualifications and preferably some other career experience. Furthermore, quite unlike British police training establishments, those who train agents have to have a higher degree and to have proven intellectual credentials. Besides the aspiration of creating a mindful, thoughtful, central nervous system to law enforcement it became clear that with so many different agencies some common memory process was also needed. An attempt was therefore made to create a national record of all violent crime. Quantico was the obvious place to do that.

With criminals roving freely across the wide roads and flat plains of America and a profusion of police forces, each with its own crime files, the task of central record-keeping is a major one. Police officers are not obliged to provide information or use the service any more than for any other aspect of FBI activities, but it has one central provision that clearly has a value. A centralized computer system, based in Washington, stores the information derived from the lengthy forms which appear to be the US approach to any collection of data. When a new crime is noted a simple computer search matches it up with crimes already in the records and then one of the bright-eyed, determined female assistants who keep the Quantico Academy moving checks through the computer output of similar crimes and decides which cases to pass back to the officer in the field as possibly linked to the ones he is already investigating.

Drawing upon the wide range of material available to them, and appreciating the need to give their trainee agents access to as many approaches to solving crimes as possible, class discussions in the early 1970s about ongoing cases evolved into an awareness that the expertise of the FBI agent lecturers offered a perspective that was not available in any other context. It was, therefore, in the deep passageways of Quantico that special agents began to realize that if they were directly to assist investigators on the job, they needed a new technology, an erudite and preferably arcane process that would be attractive to field officers; a process that the latter would select as a service they wanted. It had to be an inviting product, not easily available from their local store. A system, a bundle of skills based on special knowledge, would have to be fashioned then the world told about it. Out of these aspirations the Behavioral Science Unit was born.

Most visitors to the Behavioral Science Unit have to master a new and macabre vocabulary: vampirism, cannibalism, satanism, autoerotic fatalities, equivocal death syndrome, threat analysis, sexual sadism (by comparison, well-known terms like 'masochism' and 'bondage' seem benign). This vocabulary has been created to describe the stock-in-trade of the special agents and their instructors. Here, words like 'horrific' and 'appalling' quickly lose their meaning to be replaced by a sanitized jargon that allows crimes more brutal and vicious than any fictional conceptions to be discussed with calm enthusiasm by virtuoso investigators.

One such is Roy Hazelwood, Supervisory Special Agent Instructor, a small, precisely-featured man who orders his steak very well done and cuts it into many small shreds before he starts to eat it, almost as if he were making sure that it did not contain any hidden forensic material. It is not at all difficult to imagine him imposing hygiene and good order on a red-light district in Vietnam as he did as part of his military service. He was our mentor and guide when Rupert Heritage and I visited the FBI academy in January 1990. By then we had established our credentials well enough, from involvement in a number of cases, to be welcomed to a refresher course (or as they call it 'retraining') for graduates of the academy, all of whom had spent a year at some point in the previous decade studying with the master 'profilers'.

The style and details of the profilers' approach emerged as we sat in on their discussions of ongoing cases. It seemed like the epitome of detection, doing a Sherlock Holmes on a set of photographs and very little else to say whether a hanging was a suicide or not; what they call an examination of 'equivocal death'. Comments come with confidence and precision: 'Drug pushers do not hang their victims, they knife or shoot them'; there was no sign of trauma, therefore no support for murder; the complexity of the knotting was best explained by a number of attempts to carry out the suicide; the car found with the keys in the ignition, but locked, explained by the victim wanting the car, rented by his girlfriend, to go back to the rental agency without her getting into trouble; a place near where he worked so he would be familiar with it. 'I like it,' Roy shouted, when he was told that the man had previously attempted suicide. Forming a view of the event became a battle to defend an idea.

As a teacher myself I know how distant the enthusiasms of the lecturer can be from what students really take up. That great testimony to the power of debate between students and pupils, the Talmud, points out that you can get to understand a teacher best by getting to know his students. One evening Rupert and I were taken to a very pleasant restaurant by the 'students' on the course we were attending. Because the FBI academy is set within a military base it was no surprise, but a little disquieting, to see that the restaurant was frequented by senior Marine officers, their short-cropped hair and crisp military style making the FBI agents seem, by contrast, quite casual in their immaculate sweaters and brown suits.

The FBI agents started talking about the video Roy had shown us that morning of an autoerotic fatality. They had all been shown it at one time or another as part of a training session. It seems that to gain some sexual arousal a man had been filming himself in the act of self-strangulation, but he had slipped and accidentally hung himself. The notion that an activity such as this could be erotically arousing to anyone rather surprised me and that it should be filmed even more bizarre. Its ending up as a training film discussed by students over dinner, like any other lecture demonstration, perhaps captures most directly the mood and character of Quantico. Even scurrilous jokes about the film, which had obviously often been repeated, went round the table. These asides showed that they, like most intelligent students, were critically perceptive of those who taught them – the experienced FBI agents who had put 'offender profiling' on the map. They regarded these senior agents as having a 'seat of the pants' partyline, accepting that their approach is broadly intuitive.

The cases they had described to us earlier in the day were off the scale of my experience and well beyond anything Rupert had come across; murders encompassing vampirism and cannibalism, in which parts of the victim are eaten and their body fluids drunk; sexual sadism with extensive bindings and torturing of victims; a number of autoerotic fatalities. It was a new world, or abyss, of criminal horrors that were so distressing that when I now recall the images projected on to the lecture-theatre screen, of mutilated bodies, of scattered human remains, of bound and murdered victims, the memory alone still brings the nauseating taste of blood to my mouth.

The Fellows, as the refresher students are called, seemed much more human about it than their teachers. Perhaps that is the real contribution of John Douglas, Bob Ressler, Roy Hazelwood and the other experienced agents who teach what they now call Criminal Investigative Analysis: the cold look at mutilations and bodies. They show their students the value of a controlled emotional response to the crimes they explore, making sad, ironic comments.

Understandably, with their more limited experience the students are much more emotional about it, talking of leaving a room at the horror of listening to tape-recorded screams, wincing at even the thought of the teenager who filmed himself hanging himself and the mother who was filmed discovering the body. Fellows showed more distress at these horrors than the grand old men, and they certainly changed my view of US law enforcement officers, especially FBI agents. They listen and have a curiously liberal attitude which contains tough undertones.

Round the table in the restaurant the Fellows revealed themselves as pleasant, intelligent people whose minds were certainly more open than those of many British policemen. They spoke of racial violence breaking out in America and their role in curbing it, of their delight that the mayor of Washington had been finally caught for drug dealing. Yet they accepted that demand had to be stopped to curtail drug use. Their abhorrence of local police who abused citizens' rights to harass black minorities was genuine.

None of the people I met looked or sounded like the media image of agents. The character that Jodie Foster played in *The Silence of the Lambs* has no real counterpart. More typical was an overweight middle-aged man who admitted that adrenalin no longer rushes when he hears there has been an armed robbery.

They found me something of a curiosity with my academic background so sheltered in comparison with theirs. Bob Ressler in particular seemed to enjoy the notion of getting me to fire a round from an automatic weapon when I told him that I had never held even a handgun before. Much to my relief, he was called away on an urgent case before he could put my mettle to the test.

It was the intelligent amassing of experience that the students valued in their supervisory special agents. There was very little of what I could recognize as research. For them, research is collecting interview material, but little systematic use is made of it. It is another notch on the belt. For instance, Roy mentioned in passing that black murderers do not mutilate or go in for necrophilia, but he did not take this one step further and make a general statement about white murderers being more bizarre, nor did he feel the need for any detailed evidence or back-up data. Bob Ressler said he had a bunch of statistics somewhere but he clearly did not give it much credence or significance. His own extensive, direct experience was far more important to him. Like the gifted practitioners they are, they wish to be evaluated on the effectiveness of what they do, their recommendations to ongoing investigations, not on the richness of their conceptualizations or the statistical significance of their background evidence.

Detailed knowledge of devious criminals is the basis of the special agents' understanding. For example, the obsessionality of many violent offenders came through again and again. In one case, a shoebox was found in a garage, which contained every bit of paper on which the woman of the house had ever written a note to the murderer, whom she employed. This collection alone revealed how besotted with her he was. There were also a few photographs he had managed to get of his victim. The nursing of his fixated passion for the woman was an exaggerated version of a secret desire that unfolded into a series of attacks on many others, including other couples. Also in this same box was an ordinary women's magazine advertising clothes as well as a mildly erotic picture of a pair of legs used to advertise tights: one of the most striking illustrations of how turning women into objects, even for other women, feeds the fantasy life of men who turn to murder. That seemingly innocuous photograph in the shoebox said it all.

The importance of considering victims' responses was also a stock-in-trade of their investigations; the strength of will of ordinary folk dealing with violent crime. The students in class showed their warmth of feeling towards the victims and their admiration of how determination can be fired by the injustice of an assault. One particular victimized couple had them cheering when the husband described how, after he had been stabbed, his ire against the assailant increased when 'he wiped the blade on my shirt'. Although the wound was near fatal, after that insulting act the victim was 'determined to get him'. So although his wife was strapped, spreadeagled by a man who had already killed eight women, the husband struggled successfully to overpower the killer. Roy said laconically: 'We call that the will to live.'

The central discovery made by the FBI in their development of 'profiling' was both more profound and more direct than their writings indicate. They found that there was a pattern, a shape, to the actions of violent criminals; a shape that was overt enough for some criminals to be aware of it themselves. They did cast unique, identifiable shadows, not random markings as might have been expected. Becoming aware of the essence of their discovery, I was reminded of what atomic weapons experts said about the espionage that transferred the weapons secrets to the Soviet Union: the spies may have speeded up the process of the Soviets building an atom bomb, but the real, critical secret was the *possibility* of building such a bomb. Once the scientific community knew that a bomb based on nuclear fission was feasible, then appropriately trained scientists could work out for themselves how to make such a weapon. The critical secret was revealed at Hiroshima.

The FBI demonstrated with many highly-publicized examples that 'offender profiling' *was* possible. Once I knew that it was possible, I knew that the tools I had at my disposal could probably do the job too. If you are told that shadowy ciphers are the letters of a language then the task of interpreting them is made considerably easier.

Roy Hazelwood was particularly clear in highlighting the probability of continuity or consistency in a criminal's behaviour from non-criminal situations to criminal ones. He pointed out that if a criminal had been successful in having the victim feign passion or involvement, he would have believed it was due to his ability to arouse, and thereby control, women – a characteristic of the offender that would also be found in his non-criminal associations with women.

The same principles apply to the primary distinction that Bob Ressler drew up between organized and disorganized murderers. It is a simple idea once you spot it. A man who plans his life and thinks things through, who holds down a job which makes some demands on his manual or intellectual skills, will go about the business of murder rather differently from the casual, confused ne'er-do-well. An organized crime scene will be produced by an organized criminal. The person who leaves his victim in a hurry with no attempt at concealment is likely to have left many difficult situations in his life in a hurry and be known for his haphazard ways.

The BSU focused on what actually happened in the crimes, not on the introspections of the criminal. That was the FBI breakthrough.

In the subterranean depths, the Behavioral Science Unit has a separateness that gives objectivity to its perspective, but its staff needed to turn their insights and experiences into teaching programmes. In doing this they faced the problem many practitioners face: a teacher cannot spend the whole time recounting anecdotes of his own successful activities.

Occupational psychologists call the approach to training on the job the 'sitting next to Nelly' technique, a time-honoured procedure at least as old as indentured apprentices and their crafts guilds. Most detectives around the world learn the practicalities of their trade in this way. But as much as there is to glean from the many valuable insights and experiences of experts such as Hazelwood, Douglas and Ressler, students require a system or a framework in order to feel that they are working from established principles rather than trying to emulate the twists and turns of the minds of their teachers.

There is an inherent conflict here. The expert investigator draws upon his years of experience, particular foibles and ways of seeing the world, his heightened intuition, to think and act as the material he has in front of him demands. As John Douglas says: 'You don't learn this stuff in college.' Yet on the floors above him, beyond the maze of corridors, are high-tech lecture theatres, libraries and rooms for study.

If intuition does have roots in knowledge and experience then it should be possible to polish and enhance it. But where can that enrichment come from if what you are looking at is rare, hidden from view and difficult to explain? To build up his knowledge and help him to see critical patterns the expert needs a very special expert. FBI agents realized, as many police officers had before them, that the criminals who had committed the crimes were probably in the best position to increase their understanding. Here were people who had a wholly different perspective on the crime, experts of a different ilk.

The character of Hannibal Lecter, the gruesomely brilliant multiple murderer created by the novelist Thomas Harris and interviewed by a novice FBI agent, draws on the interviews that were conducted by real FBI agents with murderers and rapists, but the fictional creation has as much to do with reality as the fictional Dr Jekyll and Mr Hyde of a previous century.

The real agents needed to know the crimes of their interviewees in great detail so that they would not be misled by criminals wishing to show themselves in a light that was more heroic or less invidious. This shadow-boxing had the primary aim of finding out exactly how violent crimes were committed, what criminals were aware of about police investigations and what they did to avoid detection. Far from the intense intellectual games that make such a good basis for a Hollywood movie, these interviews were more typical of a detective closely questioning a suspect. One example that FBI agents delight in quoting is illustrative. Initially the FBI were rather coy about who the serial killer being interviewed was, but in his autobiography Robert Ressler makes it clear that it was Ed Kemper:

On returning for a third session of a particularly violent serial murderer who had killed nearly one dozen victims, a veteran FBI interviewer was about to conclude a final four-hour visit. As previously instructed by the attending guard, the agent pushed a button to alert the guard outside the room that the interview was over. The agent pressed the buzzer to summon the guard three times over a period of fifteen minutes: it became apparent that the guard was not responding. The offender, six feet nine inches in height and weighing 295 pounds, told the agent to 'relax' because it was shift change time and also because the guards were feeding the inmates in the secure areas nearby. The murderer further indicated, with a note of intimidation in his voice and with a facial grimace, that it might be fifteen to twenty-five minutes before any guard would respond.

Noting the discomfort of the agent, the offender mused, 'If I went ape-shit in here, you'd be in a lot of trouble, wouldn't you? I could screw your head off and place it on the table to greet the guard.' (The man's crime patterns included the dismemberment and beheading of most victims.)

The agent stated that such actions would cause him difficulty by landing him in more trouble. The inmate was then serving a sentence for seven counts of first-degree murder. The offender indicated that the status he would gain by killing an FBI agent would more than offset the punishment. The agent responded, 'Surely you don't think we come here without some method of defending ourselves!'

The inmate in obvious disbelief, said, 'You know as well as I weapons are not authorized in here!'

The agent then focused on self-defense and martial arts as a topic of conversation designed to stall for time, a method he had learned from his hostage negotiation training. The stalling technique worked, and the guard appeared at the door. As agent and inmate left the interview room, the offender placed his arm on the agent's shoulder and said, 'You know I was just kidding don't you?' He winked.

'Sure,' the agent replied and let out a deep breath.

Robert K. Ressler et al, *Sexual Homicide*, 1988, pp. xii–xiii

During the late 1970s interviews took place with thirty-six convicted murderers, all in prison. Twenty-nine of these had been convicted of killing more than one victim. All the crimes had some sexual connotation. Some of the offenders denied the crimes for which they had been convicted and indeed wished to be interviewed in order to demonstrate why they could not have committed them.

The reports on this project never give the full details. I

remember, after my meeting with Vince McFadden, study-ing a television documentary made about these 'mind-hunters' to see if there were any computer print-outs in the background or any terminals from which we could glean a hint of the large-scale research programme on which 'pro-filing' had reputedly been built, but nothing was to be seen. By judicious detective work, it would seem that in the region of twenty convicted serial murderers had been prepared to talk to FBI agents about their crimes. An interesting collection of material but hardly a vast scientific project.

The study of serial rapists was on somewhat stronger grounds. Forty-one imprisoned men were each inter-viewed for between four and twelve hours by special agents from the BSU. The taped and transcribed interviews were then used by the agents to complete a seventy-nine-page questionnaire. Each of the interviewees had been convicted of ten or more rapes, so a vast amount of information was collected, both on the crimes and the perpetrators. The interviews were complemented by accounts from the victims.

However, like the investigation of serial murder that preceded it, the rich pool of information on serial rape was not systematically analysed in great detail. Only a few, limited publications provided glimpses of the facts and figures inherent in the mound of material. When, in 1987, Hazelwood came to publish an account of 'Analyzing Rape and Profiling the Offender', he said his approach was 'the result of reading; attendance at seminars, lectures, and courses; exchanges with others' and his own twenty-six years' experience of law enforcement, covering contact with 'over 1,000 rape cases'. He makes no reference to scientific or statistical analysis of the seventy-nine-page questionnaires.

The interviews with rapists appear to have been used to

provide teaching material; illustrations of the details of what exactly happens in rapes; descriptions of the sorts of people who commit a number of rapes; as well as summaries of the rapists' own accounts of how they see their offences and what they did to avoid capture. Of course, criminals do not know what the investigators did when trying to catch them. They may get a glimpse of how close the police came, but it is a rare offender who can recognize the patterns he leaves in his crimes, or understand how they will be interpreted. What a criminal can report is his perception of what happened and why. This opens up the prospect of seeing the reasons for the assaults from the offender's point of view.

An interview may, therefore, provide an FBI agent with an example of a person similar to the one he is looking for. Like a dramatist who feeds off the people he knows in order to create a fictional character, an FBI agent can draw upon many criminals to enrich his or her own imagination. For example, this is Hazelwood's description, as graphic and confident as any novelist could wish, of an offender he had never met. It is derived entirely from details of what happened when a schoolteacher was raped in her apartment late one night:

> [The assailant's] work performance will reflect an attitudinal problem, and he will complain of being bored. His supervisors will report frustration with his performance because of his potential for excellence. He is frequently late or absent and takes offense at being chastised. His employment is a front, and his primary source of income is from the sale of narcotics or other illegal activities.
>
> In keeping with his lifestyle and image, he will operate a two-door vehicle, 2 to 4 years old. He spends a great deal of time in his car and loves to

'cruise'. He is strongly associated with his car, and his friends would describe him and his car as inseparable.

He is a very neat individual whose normal attire is contemporary, with designer jeans at the lower end of his dress style.

Robert R. Hazelwood and Ann W. Burgess,
Practical Aspects of Rape Investigation, 1987, pp. 197–198

The published account of this description covers a number of pages, all in the same sort of detail. Hazelwood reports that when the offender was arrested he was found to fit about 90 per cent of the characteristics. (British police records would not contain enough information to check how accurate the description was. They may record that the convicted man sometimes wore jeans, although that is unlikely; they would certainly not record his dress sense or that 'designer jeans' were typical of his lifestyle.)

There are now enough anecdotes to confirm that such descriptions sometimes have an uncanny accuracy, although Hazelwood himself is at pains to point out that they can also be very inaccurate. As he put it to me: 'When we do a good one I tell them to put it in the bank so that we can draw on it the next time we get it wrong.'

Although criminals as experts on crimes, teaching special agents how to catch other criminals, is the stuff of thriller fiction, it is a much more feasible prospect than might at first seem apparent. Some criminals, once incarcerated, are looking for an easy time in prison and like to break the boredom by talking to interesting visitors. But this does not apply to all convicted rapists or killers. FBI reports on their studies give very little information about the people who were reluctant to be interviewed or exactly how their sample was drawn. In personal discussion, though, they indicate that surprisingly few people did refuse to talk to them. Not all the people interviewed were able to give much useful information, either because they wished to hijack the discussion to achieve their own ends, such as an appeal against their sentence, or because they were so wrapped up in their own fantasies and hallucinations that they could not answer questions coherently.

The people who did talk to the BSU interviewers, like those who happily take part in social surveys, were fluent, intelligent people. Certainly, the FBI respondents were different from the 'typical convict' captured in the pages of learned journals. The latter are below average intelligence, inadequate people who appear to stumble into crime because of circumstances. The existence of intellectually capable people among those who commit a series of murders of strangers is itself illuminating, but it does have to be set against the reluctance of many violent criminals to talk to anyone about their actions.

So, what can be learned from these helpful, expert criminals? The main thing they can reveal is the thought processes associated with their crime: whether there was any planning, if or how they selected their victims, what they did to evade capture and other technicalities on which they have a unique perspective. In the absence of the type of central records available in the UK, access to the criminals allows much more background information to be collected about their lives and what had led them to their crimes. These interviews also become trophies for the agents, scalps showing their valour in battle. Moreover, they are also of assistance to the interviewer when considering another crime. The agent may remember how one interviewee told him of returning to the grave of his victim on the anniversary of the murder and so recommend surveillance of the graves of victims of other murderers. A convicted killer might delight in describing how he deliberately laid out the bodies of the victims to imply sexual assaults where none had taken place, so the detective would become more alert to the 'staging' of a crime scene at other murders he visited.

Particular details may be relevant, but how can the expert go beyond the individual case? How can he go beyond 'sitting next to Nelly'? Even when 'Nelly' is a hardened criminal who has committed many murders, his experiences will be limited and idiosyncratic. How can this experience be turned into a marketable system or, more importantly, become the structured basis for a training scheme? If you teach you have to impose a system; it cannot be a personal exploration like a novel. Where could such a system come from?

Paradoxically, the scheme which FBI agents developed to summarize their experiences owed more to the similarities between their interviews of incarcerated men and the processes of therapy which many convicted sexual deviants undergo, than to the hard-nosed experiences of fighting violent crime.

A clever detective coaxing details out of a man who has killed or raped, may easily slip into the guise of a therapist listening to a client. If the criminal had had any form of therapy, more of a possibility in the USA than in Britain, then he may even have the vocabulary to feed the detectives with motivations recognizable from the clinical textbooks. If the convicts are involved in sexual assaults, then they will talk to their therapist about the anger that impelled them to rape and mutilate, or the feeling of power that so excited them, or how their desire to talk to the girl had got out of control. FBI agents were probably given similar explanations in the interviews they conducted and recognized that the mixture of motivations that clinicians had harvested over the years could be related to characteristics of the individual of use to police investigations.

The task of creating a framework that would provide an

outline of different types of rapist was facilitated by contact that the BSU had with Ann Burgess, a psychiatric nurse. By the late 1970s she had already published, with Dr A. Nicholas Groth, a leading forensic psychiatrist, a theory of the role of power and anger in rape. So, when the FBI needed to present their own account of rapists, a wardrobe of types already existed for them to use.

There is a fascinating contradiction here: investigators drawing upon their special intuition and experience to identify vicious criminals yet needing to turn to therapists and their psychological accounts in order to present their experience as a package. Yet the paradox is more apparent than real. Both systems of explanation come from talking to the criminal and getting his account of the events. They have the same roots and so come to similar conclusions.

FBI agents accepted the view of psychotherapists that the variations between crimes is due to differences in the type of psychological disturbance that the criminal is suffering. They see their accounts of the offender as growing out of the psychopathologies that are revealed within the criminal's actions. It is these different forms of mental disturbance that they use as the touchstone for diagnosing the criminal's 'profile'.

In the examination of sexual assaults attention is drawn to the relationship the assailant does or does not attempt to develop with his victims. Does he reveal that he is the type of assailant who is fiercely angry with his victim and women in general, or is he by contrast one of those looking for reassurance that what he is doing is not really coercive, that the victim really wants to be raped? The extreme form of anger is revealed when the assailant gains gratification from the victim's response to pain; the inflicting of pain being his sadistic objective.

Sitting between the two extremes of sadism and reassurance, the suggestion is made that there are some types of rapist whose desire is to exert influence and power over their victims, to make them experience fear and realize how 'significant' their attacker really is. This four-way split between sadism, anger, reassurance and power has become the dominant way of thinking about sexual assaults, assigning each assailant to one of four possible categories or types.

In an investigation each of the four types of motives behind an offence is assumed to relate to identifiable characteristics of an offender. The sadistic rapist, for example, is expected to be married, whereas the reassurance type is predicted to be single, living with his parents. The anger type is believed to have an action-oriented occupation, and the power type to have a history of property crime. Yet as attractive as this prospect is – using a typology as the basis for deriving profiles of rapists – it does have many problems.

The FBI approach to classifying types of murderer is rather simpler than their approach to rapists, but none the less fraught for all that. This framework owes most to Robert Ressler, a confident, hard-talking square-jawed foil to Roy Hazelwood's intense precision. As already mentioned, Ressler suggested that the major distinction between serial murderers is in their 'organized' or 'disorganized' style of attack. The former plan and restrain their victims before carefully hiding the body; the latter, by contrast, carry out an impulsive attack, fleeing the scene with little attempt to move the body after death. Characteristic criminal behaviours here are thought to reflect aspects of the offender's personality. The organized offender is expected to be intelligent and socially competent with a reasonable work history, whereas the disorganized offender is the opposite.

Hazelwood's rape typology and Ressler's murder dichotomy, like all attempts to assign people to types, have the problem that the boundaries between the categories are extremely broad and ambiguous. Many individuals are clearly a mixture of more than one type. Furthermore, even if assailants could be assigned with confidence to a 'type', the relationship between such types and offender characteristics is far from precise. Such a classification can therefore act only as the most general guide to an investigator, a hook to get him started, but it must quickly be modified by experience of other similar cases and other rather more vague notions of how offenders act. This is often called a hunch or intuition.

FBI instructors are all happy to admit to the power of their own hunches and intuitions. They experience a sudden insight, an awareness, that appears to come from nowhere, yet they know it is based on their earlier experience. There is a Talmudic discussion which illustrates the essence of this experience. The rabbis of old asked each other why, in the opening sentence of the Bible, the word 'create' is used to describe God's activities, why not 'make' or 'shape'? They decided that the profound difference between creating and making the world is that 'making' implies a putting together of existing components whereas 'creation' speaks of invention from nothing. Intuition feels as if it comes out of the blue. It gives a God-like sensation of contact beyond the immediate here and now. Those who are seen to have it appear to have powers beyond the human. It therefore gives them an authority that might be challenged if their abilities were shown to have recognizable, common roots.

I discussed this at some length with Roy Hazelwood, hoping to convince him that such powers are no less impressive if we understand them. He described the sensation he had when he entered the apartment of an FBI employee who had been brutally murdered. Almost immediately, he says, he knew that a black assailant who lived in the vicinity must have done it. It took some probing on my part to extract from Roy what he had been aware of when entering that room. He spoke of the violence of the offence and its somewhat haphazard nature, the type of victim and location.

This questioning revealed that, as in all intuition, there are recognizable sources that can be brought to the surface for examination and development. First there is Roy's particular sensitivity to detail: he noticed that there was soil near the base of a flowerpot by the broken window through which entry had been gained. This indicated that the assailant had, probably unthinkingly, lifted the pot back up again after he had knocked it over when climbing in. Roy's attention to such details comes from considerable experience of looking at crime scenes and selecting which apparently trivial details will turn out to be important.

The second component of intuition is the ability to perceive patterns. This applies to all virtuoso performances. Expert musicians see chord sequences in the music where the beginner is looking at one note after another. Roy Hazelwood could read the whole scene as one that was violent and disorganized but not frenetic or overtly destructive for the sake of wreaking havoc. Many individual details, where the body was left, the bloodstains showing where it had been dragged, the indications of sexual activity around the time of death, all indicate to an experienced investigator a style of attack.

The third constituent of intuition is background knowledge with which patterns can be compared. Here the major differences between science and craft emerge. For the craftsman like Roy, it is the particular, personal set of experiences on which he expects to draw to interpret, assess and develop the patterns that he perceives. Roy's examination of many violent murders had led him to the view that this particular pattern of unthought-through violence without the indication of really bizarre, ritualistic aggression was typical of black offenders who perpetrated almost casual crimes in the area where they lived.

For the scientist, Roy's ideas are interesting hypotheses. I would be unhappy espousing the relationship between particular criminal behaviour and ethnicity without knowing the data that supports it. Of course, if I present the ideas as personal intuition based on years of experience then it is unlikely that I will be challenged to present the data. Without the data and a clear articulation of principles, it is difficult to know how to evaluate the suggestions made by the expert, or how to calibrate their applicability in different settings. FBI agents have, for example, often said that serial white rapists typically attack women of the same race as themselves, although black rapists will attack black or white victims. But without knowing the details of how they form that judgement its use can come unstuck. From data we have in Britain we know the proposed relationship between the colour of the victim's skin and that of her assailant does not hold. This leads inevitably to the question of whether it actually holds as a reliable general principle in the United States.

For Roy Hazelwood or his colleagues to be successful in helping police investigations it is not necessarily of importance that the principles they write about or use in lectures are firmly established. The richness of their experiences is likely to mean that when it comes to an actual case they will deal with it in terms of what occurs to them at the time rather than drawing on any general, published principles. But this does not mean that their approach is casual or fundamentally outside the realms of science. Quite the reverse, they are creating hypotheses, ways of thinking about violent crime. Their experiences provide a rich soil from which systematic tests of scientific research can grow.

The thesaurus captures a common misunderstanding about the relationship between science and intuition, or similarly between reason and feeling, by listing them as opposites. This reflects the stereotype image of the scientist, recorded perhaps most strongly in the image of Madame Curie wearing a pinafore like a scullery maid and stirring great vats of tar in the search for radioactive elements. The dogged amassing of facts, to make discoveries that are often presented as flashes of insight or tests of well-established hypotheses, is contrasted with the work of the much more 'attractive' creative artist who follows his inner inspiration, who must be true to himself and for whom external criteria of the worth of his creations are irrelevant and often inaccessible.

Creative artists are adored. Leading scientists are admired. The person who painstakingly reveals ways of reading the impressions left on sheets of paper will be highly regarded, but the person who intuitively knows where a killer will strike next will have a film made about him. Detectives are steeped in this mystique, much influenced by the popular fictional portrayal of cops. One experienced detective close to retirement gave me a potted history of the styles of clothing he and his colleagues had worn over the years that had followed directly media portrayals of heroic detectives; trench coat and homburg hat in the 1950s, giving way to natty suits in the 1960s and then on to the jeans and bomber jackets in the '70s. More importantly, though, the media image had one common theme. In order to keep the plot going, a sudden break in the investigation is needed. A brilliant, unexplained intuition from the star actor is a time-honoured way of moving the film forward.

It might be thought that a house-to-house inquiry is far removed from the 'inspiration' of the TV series, but many officers have told me: 'When the villain answers the door I will "know" whether I've got the right man or not.' They put the word 'know' in inverted commas, or use a range of terms like 'I have a hunch', 'I've got a gut feeling', or the term used by an older generation, 'You feel it in your water'.

This approach may also be revealed in direct action. The impact of this trust in personal judgement is well illustrated by one case in which I was tangentially involved. The police were looking for an unknown man who had committed a number of rapes at night, breaking into the victims' houses. All these attacks happened within a few hundred yards of each other, the assailant managing to escape quickly each time the alarm was raised.

A special watch of police officers was put in the area at night to try and apprehend the man after his expected next attack. Careful instructions were given to all the police officers involved that, the next time a call came in that the man had just attacked, they were to surround the locality and move in slowly and quietly in a coordinated fashion, making a note of everyone they came across. It was thought that the man must know the area well and would therefore be able to slip away if he suspected the police were moving in to arrest him. Hence the need for a cordon around the area that would systematically cut off all his escape routes.

As expected, a subsequent assault took place and the call came through, but the local policemen did not follow their instructions. Those nearest the scene of the offence thought to themselves, 'We're very close to this one, let's go and nab him.' They rushed to the scene, alerting the offender before they got there and opening gaps in the cordon. The assailant escaped without being seen by the police. All they found was the weapon he dropped in haste as he fled. Later, door-to-door inquiries led to the identification of a strong suspect which was confirmed by DNA, leading to conviction and a sentence of eight years' imprisonment.

The police officers at the scene felt that by acting on their hunch they would get to the offender before he got away. As in all gambles they experienced a feeling of certainty that can be called intuition. They felt they knew the right thing to do despite the instructions they had been given.

Scientists, though, need intuition too, but they are afraid to take it at its face value. They defend themselves with their methods and laboratories against too personal an involvement in an idea. They can be capricious lovers of any particular representation of reality and so save themselves from a relationship that might demand too much of them, but they can never be free of intuition. The whole basis of the scientific enterprise is faith that patterns will be found, results will be forthcoming from ideas that have never before been asked to stand up to test. This is especially true in psychology where it is believed that ways of thinking about human behaviour and experience will reveal shapes and structures that will increase our understanding. The FBI Behavioral Science Unit strengthened that faith: there were patterns there; the shadows cast by criminals were not arbitrary; they could be read. Even more important was the fact that Roy Hazelwood and his colleagues had indicated the directions in which to look, the sort of patterns that might be expected.

I came to realize that what I particularly had to offer, steeped as I was in psychological research, was a more thoroughgoing scientific approach, derived from a desire to develop the psychological way of thinking about 'profiling'. This was really a longer-term objective. I wanted to establish some of the principles from which a psychology of investigation could evolve; I was not necessarily interested in devoting my life to solving crimes. There was a need, I saw, for someone to go beyond the enrichment of intuition so that the expertise could become more readily accessible. I suppose I sensed within myself more of a commitment to science than to detection.

Part Two

◄━━━━►

APPROACH

Science is not esoteric.

Professor L.S. Hearnshaw

*This statement is true to the best of my
knowledge and belief and I make it
knowing that if it is tendered in
evidence I shall be liable to prosecution
if I have wilfully stated in it anything
which I know to be false or do not
believe to be true.*

Official opening of
victim statement to police

Chapter Four

WITH SCIENCE IN MIND

Detective work is essentially no different from solving any other of the problems with which we all have to deal. Perhaps this is the appeal of detective fiction. The lone detective resolving a complex riddle of life-and-death significance is a potent metaphor for each of us trying to find our way through life's maze. The investigator is trying to resolve a problem, making important decisions without complete information, like most other people have to do in their professional and personal lives. In this light, criminal investigations are just extreme examples of coping with being human. Therefore, all the ways people have found of coping with difficult or intractable problems are also going to be drawn upon by detectives.

For some detectives the idea of approaching a psychologist for help hardly differs from approaching a psychic or astrologer. It might work, so where's the harm in trying? To my mind, the harm comes if there is no accumulation of tested and proven logic. If an astrologer comes up with a proposal that has any success, can that success be reproduced from known principles? Could another astrologer produce the same results? Even a casual reading of the star fortune columns of a couple of newspapers will show that this is not the case.

Few people outside the corridors of science have a very clear idea of how scientists work and why their approach has had such an impact on the world. The picture is confused even further when it comes to all those sciences that relate directly to our own experiences, psychology being the most vulnerable. Talking to criminals about their crimes is not psychology and is certainly not science, although it can contribute to scientific study. Journalists, whom I had expected to know better, frequently ask me if I put the information I collect into a computer. Indeed, even quite intelligent civil servants seem to think that building up a 'data base' (although many of them are not really sure what that is) is all that is needed to turn observations of crime into a systematic science of criminal investigation. Computers, as useful as they are, are not the hallmark of science either.

Science is the development of theories, generalizable principles, and the testing of them against reliable facts. It is a fundamentally creative process in which the invention of ways of thinking about what is observed is the *sine qua non*. The amassing of information may be a starting point for suggesting hypotheses and their grouping into theories; or theories may evolve from the careful checking of speculations against verifiable facts. Facts on their own never made a science. Assumptions and conjectures may be the first steps in the emergence of scientific explanations, but they fizzle out if they are not consistently supported by the solid fuel of data.

In the book, *A Brief History of Time*, that led the way for abstract physics to become part of the bestseller list (much to the surprise of many publishers, schooled as they are in the traditions of the arts), Stephen Hawking describes a scientific theory as 'just a model . . . and a set of rules that relate quantities in the model to observations that we make'. He goes on to emphasize that this model 'exists only in our minds'. No theory can claim to describe any objective truth. All it can do is summarize relationships found between ways of thinking about the world and ways of observing it. Working in the realms of physics,

Hawking's ways of thinking about the world can often be presented as quantities. His observations are of radiations from remote galaxies or emissions from particle accelerators, but his description applies just as well to the science of psychology. The only substantial difference is that, unlike particle physics or astronomy, psychology deals with concrete, immediately perceptible aspects of our experience. It is more down-to-earth. This tends to mean that the quantities we derive are much more crudely conceived and measured, but none the less psychologists try to build models, representations and theories of the way people feel, think and act, and experience the world. They test the validity of those models against accounts of what people say and do.

As a psychologist I might propose that the mutilations to a murdered body are unusual. This description assumes a theory in which some wounds are normal and some not, just as astronomers talk about some stars being hot and some cold. With the careful definition of terms it is possible to put more precise labels on different degrees of heat for stars. In principle, it is similarly possible to define degrees of 'normality' of wounds. Those inflicted in the course of trying to control a victim who was fighting back may be regarded as more usual than those inflicted after death, for example. Those produced as a means of inflicting pain to control the victim, may be thought of as somewhere between the two extremes of 'normal' and 'bizarre'. In the early days of physics there were heated arguments about the most appropriate quantities to use. The same has always been true of psychology.

Assigning quantities to observations in a systematic way, however, is not the essence of science. People who read tea-leaves may be able to agree on when a particular pattern shows a ship on the sea and when it is a person running (although it is rare indeed for such consistency to be demonstrated), but any such reliable categorizations, or measurements, are only the first essential step before a science can evolve. The futile practice of alchemy gave way to the far more productive science of chemistry only when clear definitions could be given to the compounds that were being studied. The essence of science lies in establishing coherent relationships between sets of measurements, or categories, as predicted by the model.

Producing a reliable classification of how bizarre the wounds are on a body is only one side of the detection equation. The other side may, for example, be a classification of how bizarre offenders are. These two sets of classifications, or measurements, become part of a scientific process when two things happen (often it does not matter in which order they happen). One is the demonstration from a number of observations that there is a consistent, predictable relationship between these two sets of measurements: in other words, when abnormal wounding is found, the culprit tends to be a person who is assessed as bizarre in areas beyond his actions in the crime. This finding on its own, though, makes a *technology*, in which relationships are established but the reasons for them not understood. For the activity to be scientific some explanation, theory, model or framework also needs to exist, from which the predictable relationships can be derived.

My awareness of these subtleties came from Leslie Hearnshaw, head of the department of pyschology in which I first studied. A children's storybook professor, thin and stooped, with thinning grey hair and a careful and considered mode of speaking, he had started his studies as a historian and his view of science as an unfolding history of ideas never left him. He pointed out that medieval studies were fundamentally unscientific in that they 'looked for symbolic resemblances rather than causal connections'. In *The Shaping of Modern Psychology* (1987), he gave a fulsome and thorough description of science: 'Knowledge that is abstract, generalizable and based on principles, that is public and tested, and not esoteric, that is organised and coherent, open-ended and subject to correction, and, when possible, experimentally and mathematically grounded.'

It is the *combination* of all these properties of science that make it so useful and successful. If we really can establish a general relationship between forms of attack and forms of attacker, which can be described independently of any specific crime, then we have a tool that can be used to work directly on some future incident that we currently know nothing about. By being abstract the knowledge is generalizable, provided the principles on which it is based are open to public scrutiny and therefore are subject to correction.

The wonderful paradox of science is that it uses theories derived from past correlations, tested on current associations, to predict future relationships. It really is a form of time-travel in that the trends which support systematic models allow us to know what will happen in the future. My early contact with police officers revealed how little some of them understood this. When I asked for details of solved cases so that I could look for possible relationships between offence details and offender character in the material, their reaction was that this must be some form of cheating. They were interested in currently unsolved cases, not in history. Of course, the strongest test of a scientific theory is when it can predict relationships before they occur, but this test is so significant because it is a replication of previously established associations. Replication is at the heart of science, showing that a logically organized set of principles when applied to known circumstances consistently predict the same correlations.

Science is not esoteric. It is not essential to scientific

activity to have arcane, little understood terms comprehensible only to the initiated. The opposite is the case: clarity and accessibility to facts and concepts are indispensable. Precision is necessary, too. Terms, evidence and data must be as overt as possible, and one must be able to consider and evaluate all these components. Vocabulary therefore has to be developed that will enable these discussions to be productive.

Only the most rigid of disciplines, with centuries of training and close to the martinet of mathematics, can hope to keep their terminology under strict control. Those whose area of concern is more recently developed and closer to everyday experience, notably psychology, have a continuing battle to keep their terms precise. Words such as 'intelligence', 'personality', 'habit', 'behaviour' and many, many others are constantly harnessed to scientific psychology only to break free from scientific constraints when nobody is watching. This makes the task of really understanding what psychologists mean especially difficult.

Modern, scientific psychology, some would claim, had its origins in the distrust that the astronomer royal had for the measurements that one of his assistants was making. Initially the chief astronomer thought that his assistant was careless because when he measured the movements of the stars he obtained different timings than those of his boss. Eventually, however, it became clear that individuals differed in the time it took them to look at a cross-hair down a telescope and then look at the clock. This time interval became known as the 'personal equation' and had to be added to the very precise measurements of astronomy.

It soon became clear that the time interval was a function of physiological processes which later became known as 'reaction time', but the idea that we all have a personal equation that describes the distortions between what we see and the sense we make of it is a central theme of psychology. A totally clinical, undistorted reflection of objects, people and events would be possible only if perception were not shaped by what we know or do not know. What we see is rooted in what we have learned about the ways of the world. Painters struggle for years to learn to look at objects as mere shapes. If they succeed in producing images that bear no relationship at all to anything we know or feel, then those images will be dead and uninteresting. Seeing an action as a threat or a challenge is a parallel perceptual process, shaped by our internal psychological processes.

We cannot be aware of everything in our surroundings. We have to select what we listen to, look at and think about. That much is obvious, but the extent of this selectivity and the ways in which it is channelled by our expectations and knowledge is much greater than most people appreciate. Senior investigating officers will say, 'I have an open mind on this one', but no one can act with an open mind. There has to be some shape, some direction, to make thought and action possible.

The shape itself makes the experience seem complete and full, but it is very difficult to know what we are not aware of. It has been shown on many occasions that the confidence with which a witness to a crime reports the details of an event bears very little relationship to how accurate that report is. The view they had of the incident, what they were able to pay attention to at the time and how familiar they were with the setting and type of people involved, are all far better indicators of the accuracy of their report than the confidence with which the report is given. What is true of a witness to a crime is also true for anyone attempting to make sense of complex events.

Scientific psychology has the complex task of trying to avoid these distortion processes while often at the same time studying them. Attempts to keep the personal equation out of the scientific equation are never wholly successful, but that is the constant and paradoxical quest for those scientists who are devoted to understanding other people, using psychology like the mirror that protected Perseus from the gorgon. Directly facing the gorgon of experience is too open to distortion. The mirror of psychology frames and tames experience just enough to make it watchable and so eventually manageable.

The distinction between psychology and psychiatry also helps to clarify how scientific psychology can be developed for use by investigators. Clinical psychologists train first as general behavioural scientists. Their specialization in psychological problems as they relate to mental and physical health comes *after* their primary qualification as scientific psychologists. So, typically, clinical psychologists end up working in health-care settings, sometimes with psychiatrists (whose primary training is in medicine). As physicians, psychiatrists specialize in the cure of mental disease after becoming qualified in general medicine. Putting it at its essence, clinical psychologists are first and foremost students of human action and experience, 'behavioural scientists'; psychiatrists are primarily physicians. This does not stop clinical psychologists being trained in how to treat people using therapies derived from psychological research, nor does it stop psychiatrists doing valuable scientific research on the causes and cures of mental illness. Both professions are likely to call their treatments psychotherapy, although psychiatrists are more likely to supplement 'talking cures' with medication. If either group uses psychotherapy which is heavily influenced by the work of Sigmund Freud or his followers, they may call their treatment psychoanalysis.

The distinctions I have described may be illustrated by considering the case brought to me of a woman in her late thirties who was anorexic. She had spent some time in a psychiatric hospital. Her body was discovered by the fire brigade when they were called to a fire at her small stone cottage. The murderer appeared to have set fire to the house after the killing, but it was put out before it had taken hold. The body was found up a twisted flight of wooden stairs. The most unusual feature of the crime was that knife wounds were inflicted on the body after death.

A psychiatric textbook view on knife wounds, based in part on a number of interviews with patients undergoing therapy for sex crimes, is that the use of the knife is a form of sexual penetration: 'The patient becomes aware that a knife, unlike his anatomical "weapon", would never lose its erection, would always elicit fear, and would never fail to penetrate.' The psychiatrist may think she is being scientific by giving an account of the inner motivation of the assailant, a motivation he may not be able to express himself. But this cannot be used directly to help identify the perpetrator.

How can we ever know what the symbolic implications of the criminal actions were at the time of the offence? It may be helpful in a therapeutic conversation with the criminal as a patient to explore with him the metaphor of a knife as a penis (although many would question even that utility). This may give the patient new ways of thinking about his reactions to sex and sex-related acts. It may be a way of helping him to recognize his own fears about his sexual competence and give him new ways of thinking about his actions that will help him to change them. But such ideas will become part of a science of criminal behaviour only if, for example, the model that a knife wound represents phallic penetration can be taken beyond the bounds of metaphor and shown to predict relationships, say, between the inflicting of such wounds and sexual dysfunction (one technical illustration of this would be 'erectile insufficiency'). More overt consequences of the model would need to be established as well, such as the lack of a long-term sexual relationship with a woman. Now, however, we are no longer discussing the power of the knife-as-penis metaphor. We are developing a theory, loosely linked to this metaphor, that predicts relationships between certain classes of action in an assault and testable characteristics of the assailant. That is the basis of science. It is also the basis of intelligent action.

The comment made by a police officer was in some ways more helpful than the knife metaphor: 'He's a nutter.' That, implicitly at least, hypothesizes that the behaviour in the offence reveals some general characteristics of the offender that might be available to public scrutiny. A scientific theory would require more detailed specification of how 'a nutter' would be recognized, say by having had a history of in-patient care in a mental hospital, together with evidence to show that such patients do indeed carry out acts of this sort.

A suggestion by another police officer that it was 'burglary gone wrong' is even further away from a scientific theory on which criminal investigations could proceed. It postulates what the offender was trying to do, but does not make any obvious predictions about what sort of person the offender was. Is this the action of an experienced burglar when surprised by an unnaturally thin, possibly slightly deranged woman? Or is this the hallmark of a very inexperienced criminal, possibly young and with a police record? By asking these questions a model is evolving, looking at actions in terms of what they might reveal about a person's criminal history, whatever we guess about their 'motives'.

Unfortunately, in the above case of murder and arson the test of any psychological hypothesis was not conclusive. A man was identified by the police, fitting a general description I had prepared, but detectives felt there was not enough evidence to charge him.

Lack of evidence with which to convict (and the consequent scarcity of details on the offender) is only one of the problems of completing research into criminal behaviour. Every theory requires data. It has to be tested against relevant information. Access to the information I required was difficult because it was carefully protected from curious eyes in local and national police records. Such information is made available only to people who are regarded as being of direct assistance to the police. Although my credibility had increased after the arrest of John Duffy, 'profiling' was still regarded with suspicion by most police officers. Furthermore, the material the police have is not in a form that is immediately open to systematic analysis. The uniqueness of every crime further challenges the prospects for research. In order to find a way through these problems I had to draw on my earlier experiences of studying what people did when caught in a fire or similar emergency.

My desire to explore how people deal with adversity had been stimulated very early in my career as a psychologist. As a student I was given the opportunity to go to an international conference of applied psychology in Ljubljana. One paper on the programme was an account of the Skopje earthquake which had happened a few months earlier. Being, even then, a little jaundiced at the lack of contact with reality of much psychology, I thought that here at last was a topic of some significance and substance that would do justice to the huge intellectual effort that people all over the world were putting into the study of human mental processes. My disappointment in the paper was profound. First of all it was actually dull; it was a topic of such import, such intensity and misfortune, yet it was tedious to listen to. It was reduced to a few percentages that lost any contact with what people had in fact done, how they had coped, what they had experienced. I was convinced that scientific psychology did not have to alter what it was examining beyond all recognition. When I later had the opportunity to study behaviour in fires, that resolve was tested many times over.

I discovered that I had to become a behavioural archaeologist, gathering information from any available sources, cross-checking them with each other to build up the best possible approximation of what actually happened. For example, on one occasion I was able to speak to Ron Lipsius who had been caught in the King's Cross underground fire in which thirty-one people died in 1987. He was an American in his late twenties, resident in Britain where he played guitar and composed music. His hands, I remember, were deeply wrapped in gauze, one fastened to his thigh in a skin-grafting operation. It did not take much imagination to feel the anger and distress caused to this musician, his career just developing when, on an ordinary daily journey, he was caught in a fire that might have destroyed everything.

I recorded Ron Lipsius' honest, harrowing account of his contact with the fire and transcribed it. Like all free text, it appears almost seamless. It is also relatively free of emotional reaction partly because I asked him to tell me what happened. This direct instruction to give an unfolding account put Ron in a position of the expert on his own experience. It gave him the opportunity to tell the story in which he played the central role. Allowing the person who is the focus of the interview to tell his story in his own words permits things to emerge that the interviewer might never have thought of asking about.

Journalists take first-hand accounts and turn them into

readable, graphic descriptions, drawing out the central themes and often commenting on them. For example, the lack of preparedness of the fire brigade and ambulance service, illustrated by Ron's having to search for help when he escaped the fire, might become a topic that a journalist would pursue. Dramatists might highlight the tragic personal misfortune, Ron's separation from his travelling companion and his own feelings, possibly of guilt and confusion, about that. The subsequent implications for his life of the experience would be another dramatic issue to develop. In a clinical setting, where Ron goes for help with the reconstruction of his life, these personal feelings would become paramount, especially any blame and anger he attaches to himself for what happened, even though he has nothing to blame himself for.

How is what I was trying to do different from all these reasonable, laudable and often very important issues? I wanted to find some general consistencies that could be relied on to help us understand what people did when faced with a fire. To discover these trends I needed to explore whatever examples I could get hold of, dissecting them (in much the same way that later was so fruitful when looking at Duffy's rapes) in order to reveal their central themes.

The basic social nature of human actions was shown in the common experiences revealed in the individual dramas of people caught in fires. The logic that underlies a person's actions is derived from their contacts with others: travelling companions, other passengers, the uniformed staff, anyone that the person comes into contact with has a significance. There are always others, and what they do is relevant. They may be part of an existing organization or social structure. Reactions to them may involve acceptance of authority, or reaction against it, but they will always involve an individual's interpretations of the social rules as they see them.

Above all, the fire research taught me to respect the details of what people say and do. Odd phrases can carry deep significance. General patterns grow out of a sensitivity to each individual's plight, rediscovering the insights of the dramatists, creating an awareness of the power of the social matrix. Such patterns show in high relief the processes that are relevant to all human experience, whether it is conventional day-to-day activities or on the outer reaches of criminality. We all experience this directly as being part of an entangled web of causes and effects. By harnessing our skills and abilities we attempt to utilize the opportunities provided by our friends and family, the people we work with, or we strive to overcome deficiences in ourselves or our surroundings. Like a spider who must walk carefully on her own web lest she stick to those strands she has woven to catch flies, some of the strands in our life are helpful and some are dangerous. Yet it is not always easy to tell which is which because every part of the web has connections, even if only indirectly, with every other part. Some strands may be broken, as when friends go away, or we fail an examination. New strands are added from time to time, say in the discovery of a new talent, or the emergence of a job opportunity, but there is no way any one of us survives independently of the web.

Even if we are hanging by the slimmest thread, we are still only able to demonstrate our independence by the length of our connection to the web, never by getting away from it entirely. Some psychologists say that we are a point in the web, no more no less, claiming that we are defined by the strands of the web we have climbed upon. They argue that the separateness of our existence is a myth we invent to maintain our sanity and give us a necessary fiction for guiding our lives. Although that vision may be extreme, it does have value in drawing attention to our need to create some sense of our selves by carving a personal life story out of the many differing experiences we have. Just as I had to create an understanding of what happened in a fire and the way in which the individual actions formed a coherent narrative, so we all must make some sense of the sequence of events in our lives if we are not to lose contact with reality.

The personal narratives that criminals live will be explored in some detail in later chapters. The need to make sense of the lives of violent criminals, from an examination of the details of their crimes, emerged as a requirement for the scientific theory that would be at the heart of offender profiling. Such a theory would have to get close to the inner narrative that reflects the criminal's interpretations of his actions.

When studying actions in a fire I had realized that the forced neutrality of the psychological perspective had provided a different way of thinking about emergencies from that held by firemen and engineers, whose main concern was with the physics and chemistry of fire growth and spread. My involvement with police investigations began to suggest that there was an analogous contribution to be made. The criminal storylines that are dominant in police circles are those drawn from legal considerations. Most criminals are described in terms of the legal definition of their actions. For example, because a sexual assault on a pubescent girl is legally closer to a sexual assault on a young boy than to the rape of an older woman, the assaults on young boys and girls will tend to be considered together in police discussions. Recognizing the assault on the young girl as a form of rape may have much more psychological credibility.

From my earliest contact with detectives it had seemed possible that psychology could make a fundamental contribution to criminal investigations by replacing the legal perspective on the narratives of crimes with the inner narrative that shapes the criminal's own actions. Criminals give sense to the web of actions and experiences of which they are a part by writing their own stories. The task of the psychologist is to help to read those stories in the records, and discover traces of the actions that occur before, during and after an offence. This will be an account that covers much of the interacting web of experience, not just single criminal strands. Such accounts, though, can be derived only from detailed study of many different aspects of many different crimes.

The phonetic experts at Leeds University were given just one strand when they were used in the 'Yorkshire Ripper' case. In my involvement in the Duffy case I was integrated into the investigation, even if it was at arm's length. I had all the facts and was able to develop an overall picture of the actions of the killer. The very precision of the analysis of the dialect on the tape led to inappropriate exclusion of possibilities. If the experts had been less precise and more able to comment on all aspects of the offender's behaviour in a full knowledge of the investigative options, then they might have given guidance that could have been integrated into an appropriate investigative strategy. But to do that they would have needed research results that could come only from analysis of many solved crimes.

Consider one example of the need for research: the seemingly obvious conclusion that Duffy was out of a job because he attacked during working hours. He may have been working shifts. He may have been a travelling salesman, or a driver like Peter Sutcliffe, whose absence for a few hours would not be missed. If it is concluded that the offender does not have access to a vehicle then the traveller inference may be ruled out. If the timing does not fit well-known shift times then that possibility may be reduced. But there will always remain the open question that many people could skip work for an hour or two without being missed. A general analysis of solved cases to see if offenders with jobs tend to attack at different times from those without would be one step in testing the robustness of even such an 'obvious' inference. That type of test is the cornerstone of turning profiling into a science.

In order to develop any theories I needed data, examples of solved cases, to analyse and explore. My contribution to the Duffy case meant that I was not considered just another academic curious about criminals. Senior police officers and one or two civil servants saw that there might be some value in allowing me access to information about crimes. But Rupert Heritage and I knew that support for our research would be maintained only if we continued to help in ongoing enquiries. We therefore slowly amassed some basic data while also advising, as best we could, on the basis of the little we already knew.

Part Three

DEVELOPMENT

The sexual assault squad profiles all sexual assault occurrences in the same manner as does the FBI, i.e. psychological or behavioural profiling. We have found that physical description is the least accurate in sexual assault occurrences. The actual behaviour of the suspect during the sexual assault is the most accurate descriptor.
METROPOLITAN TORONTO POLICE FORCE

Chapter Five

CRIMINAL MAPS

The interpretation of the series of maps of Duffy's crimes seemed obvious at the time, but one clear set of results does not establish a scientific principle. Since then we have looked at the geographical distribution of many series of crimes and none of them shows the distinct pattern of Duffy. His turns out to be the classic shape that helps us to understand other more subtle variants of it.

When dealing with violent crime, the shadow that it casts over the victim, and often over a community, can be so horrifying that there is a tendency to focus on the particularities of the case. It is unusual to take the more distant perspective of seeing what general principles may be applicable to finding the perpetrator. Until we look for such principles we will not be able to establish which ones are valid and under what conditions their validity breaks down.

The scientist's task is to derive principles that will consistently predict observable relationships. What principles are available to predict the relationship between where a criminal lives and where he commits his crimes? About the only rule of thumb that FBI special agents have ever been prepared to offer concerning the possible residence of a serial attacker is that, in some cases, particularly where the criminal appears not to have planned his attacks very carefully, he may well live near the location of the first assault he carried out. This is the nub of the plot of *The Silence of the Lambs* after all, that the serial murderer can be found close to his first abduction and killing. As is the way with the FBI, no published evidence really substantiates this idea; it was a throwaway remark attributed to the light of experience. But the direct logic of this suggestion appeals to me. It seems reasonable to assume that in the early stages of a person's criminal career they may be rather impulsive and somewhat amateur in their approach, wandering out at night, for example, without too clear an idea of what they are going to do, and seizing what they perceive as an opportunity.

The key to solving a series of crimes may be found in working out what happened *before* the first crime rather than in establishing where the offender went after the most recent. A criminal is more vulnerable in his history than in his future. Before he committed the crime he may not have known himself that he was going to do it, so he may not have been so careful as he would have been afterwards. Duffy left few traces at the crimes far from his home, but carried out his early crimes close to home – this fact of closeness contributing to his detection. Is that the basis of a generally applicable principle? If we can find where the criminal shadow comes from, will that pinpoint the culprit?

A chance to carry out the first serious test of the geographical logic of crimes came in the form of a lively, decisive student, Mary Barker. She showed great enthusiasm for my work with the police and wanted to do a project to follow up some of the ideas. Getting details on a number of serial rapes and murders did not seem too easy, or really appropriate, for a psychology student's exploratory project, but there are plenty of burglaries around and it seemed to me that the general principles ought to apply to them in broad terms. So Mary contacted a local police force that was both involved in crime prevention studies and prepared to tolerate the presence of a university psychologist and give her access to records of crimes and convicted felons.

It is some indication of how far our relationships with the police have developed to recall the hard time that Mary was given by some of the local police officers. Crime prevention was all right but this 'profiling stuff' was to be avoided at all costs. Ever the diplomat, Mary managed to get details on thirty-two burglars who had committed anything from five to seventy burglaries each before being caught. She made a note of where they had lived at the time of their burglaries and of the addresses of their crimes. She wanted to see what geographical patterns emerged for each criminal.

I asked her to get maps for the area and draw out separate sheets for each offender, marking the location of the burglaries and the burglar's home. At that stage it was not at all clear to me how difficult or time-consuming this task would be. The locations, for example, may have been so scattered that it would not be easy to identify them all or find maps to include them all.

A week or two later Mary turned up for a supervisory meeting looking rather despondent: 'I've put them on maps like you said. It took ages, but I don't know what to make of it. I don't think it shows anything.' She was holding a neat pile of sheets of A4 paper on which were drawn dots to represent crimes and a cross to indicate where the offender had lived. Confidentiality had been ensured, at some cost to clarity, by having a code number at the top of each page and no indication of the page from the local street atlas that had been the original underlying map. Only the locations were marked on the white sheets of paper.

'Are these all to the same scale?' I asked, not quite believing what she had discovered.

'Sure. They're all the usual few inches to the mile. That's what you wanted, isn't it?'

'And you got them all on to the same sheet of A4, the crimes and where he lives?'

'Yes, except for the guy who did seventy burglaries, I needed two sheets for him.'

I told her that I thought her results were amazing: all the crimes were surprisingly local to where the offender lived.

Mary was still not convinced that this had any significance. I had the impression that she thought that science could not really be as simple as that, but I was not aware that anyone had done any work quite like this before. I had certainly not come across anything published. I told her that, at the very least, if we could establish general rules relating a criminal's residence to where he commits his crimes it would give the police more of a system for how and where to look for burglars. More important at this stage, this A4 effect would make further analysis quite feasible. If we can get each set of crimes on one sheet it makes sense to start making measurements to see if we can find any trends to summarize it all.

The next step, then, was to see if there was a further structure to the patterns on the sheets of A4. The most simple question I could think of was to ask if the crosses usually sat inside the dots. In addition, some of the distances could be measured.

This A4 effect, as I like to think of it, that without a lot of modification of map scales most burglaries can be put on the same sheet of paper as the burglar's residence, seemed to work for the thirty-two felons in the small town in which Mary did her study. There are many conditions under which I would not expect this relationship to hold: where there was a good transport system, for example, or if a burglar was looking for special objects and had his own car. But the run-of-the-mill burglaries Mary was looking at hinted at something beyond the one-off vicious rapes and murders of Duffy.

Mary did the further analysis and we came up with what we rather grandly called the 'circle hypothesis'. This is the idea of putting on a map all the crimes thought to have been committed by one, possibly unknown, individual and identifying the two crime locations furthest apart from each other. Using these locations as the diameter, a circle can then be drawn that includes all the offences. The hypothesis is that the criminal will be found to live inside that circle, possibly close to the middle of it. I always take pains to emphasize that there are many known factors that would destroy the power of this hypothesis, but that, none the less, in some samples of rapists as many as 80 per cent have actually been found to live inside the circle and over 60 per cent in a central area half the radius of the large circle.

John Duffy had not been so unusual in this regard. The contribution to that inquiry, presented in the newspapers with all the glitter of a Sherlock Holmes deduction, can now be presented as a general principle with some of the elegance of a Pythagorean theorem. The ideas that gave rise to the 'circle hypothesis' also seemed, from the studies that Mary and subsequently other students did, to be relevant to more common crimes such as house-breaking and burglary. In some samples the great majority of burglars do have a fixed abode within a circle covering all their known crimes.

As valuable as such direct findings are in opening up new ways of thinking about detection, they are of little long-term, scientific value unless we have some framework or explanation for them. Without a 'theory', the findings cannot be developed or tested, or the conditions under which they operate clarified.

In order to see how the 'circle hypothesis' might be explained, let us start from the privileged position of knowing where a criminal lives, or has some sort of base relevant to his crimes, and imagine that location being marked in the centre of a blank sheet of paper as, say, a small, shaded red square.

An assumption has already been made with this first stage. We are proposing that the people we might be looking for do indeed have a fixed abode. Well, that is open to test. A surprisingly high proportion of the criminals we have looked at, involved in serious crimes like rape and murder, have a permanent base of some kind; it might be their own home or a girlfriend's place. Very few of them are described as 'of no fixed abode' on the criminal records at the time of arrest, probably less than 10 per cent.

Accepting, then, that the criminal does have a base, let us assume that he is determined to carry out a crime, but also wants to reduce the risk of being caught. To keep it simple, let us assume that the possibilities for committing the crime, the opportunities, are evenly distributed around his base. Where is he likely to go to perpetrate his first crime?

In a sense we are trying to learn to think like a criminal, seeing the location of his crimes as derived from the simple logic of maximizing the opportunity for them while reducing the risk. If we assume that the criminal has a base, then he is likely to have some degree of familiarity with the area around that base, but he is unlikely to carry out a crime very close to home for fear of recognition, or because of the risk of getting drawn into police inquiries. As one police officer put it to me in the succinct way that police officers have: 'Oh, you mean dogs don't crap on their own doorsteps!'

The optimum distance from the base to the first crime could be indicated by drawing a small circle, say, at the top right-hand corner of the sheet of paper. Let us think of this small circle as being labelled 'first crime'. The idea here is that in this simple world that I have created for the criminal he cannot travel very far without getting into unknown territory. Too far and he may not know his way around and be unable to escape easily. There may be other risks that he is unaware of as well. The imaginary distance between the 'base' and the 'first crime' may be regarded as an optimum one, from the criminal's point of view; just far enough to be safe, but not so far that unfamiliarity provides its own risks.

This is a simple, logical argument for how far he would travel to commit his first crime in an area in which there are ample opportunities. But after his first crime the criminal may become aware of new threats to his safety. If he wants to keep the same optimum level of risk, the area in which he attacked is probably no longer safe. People may be more vigilant there. He may be recognized. It is no longer the sterile, unsullied zone it was. If he is to keep his optimum distance the criminal has to go elsewhere, at the same distance from his base but in a different direction. Assuming the opportunities are the same in every direction, then, for example, up in the top left-hand corner is as good a place as any. We can, therefore, draw a further circle in the top left-hand corner of our sheet of paper, and mark it 'second crime'.

What is true of the location for the second crime is true for the third, which he must locate at the same sort of distance, although in a different direction, and also for the fourth. The four notional crimes would be arranged on the blank sheet of paper in the four corners like the dots on the number four on dice cubes. Of course, in an actual example we would not expect the dots to be quite so evenly spaced out because the actual layout of streets would produce distortions in the pattern.

Once you have committed four crimes, if you want to continue, keeping the same optimum distance from home, then you must return to the vicinity of earlier crimes. A fifth crime, therefore, could be located between the third and fourth, or anywhere else that the criminal felt he was least vulnerable. In fact, the power of this geometry would have been understood immediately by Pythagoras. To maintain the optimum distance that balances familiarity and risk you would have to commit your crimes in a circular region around your home: a band of criminal opportunity.

The problem for the police is that they would not have the location of where the offender was living marked on their map. All they would have would be the locations of the crimes reported to them. They would have the equivalent of our sheet of paper with the red square for the base removed, leaving just the locations of the five crimes. In my example these form an irregular circle of points with a large blank white space in the middle. So, as you can see, in this simple example, if the police had a map of offences sitting roughly on a circle like this, it would be reasonable to take as a starting assumption for any investigation the possibility that the offender lived near the centre of this circle.

The simple, direct logic, derived from as few principles as possible, leads to the 'circle hypothesis'. In order to keep the principles as simple as possible in this elementary illustration, we have assumed an even distribution of both familiarity and opportunity for crime. We certainly know that such assumptions are unlikely to hold for many people, but I find it fascinating that even a model as simple as this can apply to some criminals who have committed a series of crimes; including, I believe, perhaps one of the most notorious of all.

By assigning the name of a victim to each of the five crime locations, our hypothetical example can be turned into a real map of the murders attributed to the Whitechapel murderer, 'Jack the Ripper', over a hundred years ago. In the top left-hand corner for the second crime we can put the name Chapman, and just below it for the fifth, Kelly. In the top right-hand corner, the location of the 'first crime', the name Nichols can be written. The bottom two names at the left and right of centre are Eddowes the fourth victim and Stride the third. Diagonally across the sheet of paper we can draw the Whitechapel Road, turning the exercise into a specific set of places in Victorian London.

There may be a simple logic guiding the actions even of crimes as strange as those that held London in thrall in the last century. Whatever the outcome of historical research, or the new documents and evidence that will undoubtedly emerge in the future to keep alive the search for the identity of 'Jack the Ripper', the geographical pattern of his attacks does indicate some important points. One is that his killings were clearly circumscribed within a limited area. This suggests both that he was very familiar with that area and that something kept bringing him back to the same limited locality. The most obvious reason for this is that he lived within the neighbourhood circumscribed by the location of the murders, but if he did we will have to discover why he did not spread his crimes further afield, as did Duffy. To answer such a question a lot would need to be known about available victims on the streets of the East End of London in the 1880s, and about available modes of transport. If it was an area where he lived, then the centre of that area has to be a reasonable guess at the position of his residence.

It is interesting to test ideas about the residence of 'Jack the Ripper' against the best documented arguments about likely suspects. Perhaps the most convincing proposal at present is the suggestion, by the historian Paul Begg, that Aaron Kosminski was the 'Ripper'. Kosminski was an expatriate Polish Jew who worked as a barber in the

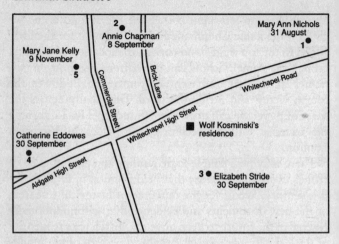

Map ii: Whitechapel in the 1880s, indicating the location of Jack the Ripper's victims and the possible residences of two prime suspects Kosminski and Maybrick (numbers indicate sequence of offences).

Whitechapel area. A team of FBI agents and other US experts examined all relevant material and agreed with Paul Begg's view. Some authorities have even suggested that Aaron Kosminski confessed before he died in Colney Hatch asylum in 1919.

Although Paul Begg did not know exactly where Aaron Kosminski had been living at the time of the murders, he did establish where Kosminski's brother was known to be living. This brother had taken responsibility for Kosminski in the mental asylum and probably looked after him before that. It also seems likely, according to Paul Begg, that Kosminski had lived a few doors away from his brother in what was described by the Assistant Chief Constable at the time, Sir Melville Macnaghten, as 'the very heart of the district where the murders were committed', at the top end of Mulberry Street. The likely residence of Kosminski was more or less where the 'base' would be marked on our original sheet of paper.

A very different suspect is James Maybrick. Diaries discovered in Liverpool, where Maybrick lived, are claimed to have been written by him as an account of his crimes. The readiness with which many experts accepted these diaries as genuine ignored the important question of why anyone should keep such a potentially incriminating diary, especially someone who had taken such care to avoid capture. Maybrick's residence in Liverpool would also challenge the circle hypothesis.

The debate over Kosminski and Maybrick is of more than historic significance. It illustrates a distinction between a person who used a permanent base as a starting point for his crimes, as Kosminski might have done, and the 'commuting' proposed by the writer of Maybrick's diaries. These are two very different theories of how the location of a crime relates to the residence of the offender. In studies we have carried out, the 'commuters' have been very rare. As a consequence we have not obtained enough examples to establish whether the distances between crimes would enable us to tell if the offender was 'commuting' into an area. For example, it might be hypothesized that commuting criminals would commit their crimes in a smaller area than those who are based in that area. The people based in the area might have more time to travel and also wish to keep some distance from their home to avoid the risk of being recognized. How the distances of this hypothesis would translate to Victorian London, though, is a difficult question to answer at present. However, that Jack the Ripper was a local resident of the Whitechapel area has got to remain a strong hypothesis in the light of the clear pattern in the sequence and locations of his crimes.

A further point about both Kosminski and Maybrick is that neither of them was free from mental illness. Kosminski ended his days in a lunatic asylum, believing that his movements were controlled by 'an instinct that informs his mind'. Maybrick is reputed to have indulged in a variety of drugs and was violently jealous of his wife (who was convicted of his murder). Yet despite the extremes of mental instability typical of both these men, it seems quite feasible that during the commission of the murders the attempt to avoid capture had an identifiable logic to it. Thus, although there may be many strange qualities to violent acts there will still be aspects of those actions that reveal processes that are overtly logical.

It should not be assumed, however, that these actions indicate some conscious process of which the criminal is aware and therefore could easily hide. It seems more likely that these patterns are a product of habits of thought and behaviour rather than conscious choices.

There are many habits that relate to how we use spaces; even though most have no implications for violence, they reflect the fact that violent actions have common roots with many other aspects of daily behaviour. I have found a frequent illustration of actions that are unknowingly tied to spatial patterns in the public lectures I give. The next time you attend any sort of talk, make a note of where the people who ask the questions are sitting. People who have studied this systematically will predict that question-askers tend to sit towards the front and towards the middle of the audience. In my own experience, questions are most likely to come from people sitting in the first few rows towards the side of the room which contains the main entrance.

The fact that there is even the merest hint of a trend here is curious. It suggests that the asking of a question is not a simple, direct result of a particular person wishing to have the answer to a problem arising *during the course* of the lecture. At least two processes seem to be at play. One is opportunity, or technical possibility. In some positions it is easier to catch the lecturer's eye, or to judge when an interjection is feasible without being impolite. The second is individual predetermination. A person who is keen and especially interested in a topic, or in taking part in discussions of it, will tend to place themselves in a seat from which sight and sound of the lecture is clear, also making catching the lecturer's eye or asking questions easier, probably arriving a little earlier to get a 'good seat'. This keenness may not reach the level at which the person is aware of what they are revealing. Typically it is part of implicit habits that we take for granted and notice only when someone mentions them.

Similarly, a serial killer or rapist will put himself in locations where victims are available and undetected crime is possible, even though he may not realize that that is what he is doing. Like the member of the audience who gets a good seat without intending, necessarily, to ask a question, so the rapist will go to an area where he knows there are vulnerable young women without specifically planning to attack one. But if the opportunity arises to ask a question, or to carry out a crime, the person is well placed to do so.

This may seem a curiously unemotional way of mapping the logic of a violent criminal. It certainly does not fit in with the notion often portrayed in newspapers, and apparently accepted by some judges, of rapists as sex-crazed beasts who cannot resist the temptation thrust in front of them. Most people can understand a bank robber planning his raid carefully to avoid risk, but surely a sexual assault or a murder is a much more impulsive act? A loss of control?

It is certainly the case that bank robbers plan to avoid risk, as do hired assassins. One of the consequences of this is that they may travel a great distance to commit their crimes. There is reasonable evidence that the more emotional the crime, the closer to home it is. What the police call 'a domestic', the assault of a husband on his wife, or the not uncommon assault of a wife on her husband, typically takes place in their home. They don't usually travel a great distance to thump each other.

Some studies have shown that rapes are typically carried out nearer to a person's base than many burglaries, especially burglaries requiring real skill, such as theft of antiques, where the burglar must know what he is looking for. So the minimization of and optimization of opportunity may be directly reflected in the distance over which the search for a target takes place, rather than reducing the balance of familiarity with distance from home.

The indications are that many rapists wander around exploring areas where they hope to see women of interest to them. They put themselves in situations that have particular possibilities, as does the person selecting a seat in a lecture theatre, or the film director I know of who will leave his hotel room door open to increase the possibility of something of interest happening.

This creating and opening of the opportunities for criminal actions often goes to remarkable lengths. One man, who was eventually convicted of murdering his wife rather than let her divorce him, and who had a history of sexual assaults, was found after his arrest to have kept the most remarkably detailed little red notebook. In it he had recorded, with obsessional precision, a list of women he had seen, where he had seen them and the time to the nearest minute. The notebook records their estimated age, hair colour and style, what they were wearing, their car if they were driving, including its registration number.

A chilling spectre is conjured up by this seemingly inoffensive little red book, showing as it does that this criminal shadowed many women, perhaps not even knowing himself that he was identifying potential victims. His notes, though, show the extent to which he had systematized his obsession: '29.5.85, blo 30' (presumably, a blonde, thirty years old). A later entry is 'Pink/pony. 6.15 pm got on 718 at Bloomsbury St, 6.32 pm got off 718 at Arundel Road.' The notebook also contains a strange list with the date of sightings and descriptions of the women summarized with a set of numbers on each line, mainly 8s and 9s. I suppose these are his personal ratings of desirability.

The horrific intrusiveness of this criminal's mind-games gleams through this neat little red book. Here was a man so out of touch with his own emotions that he was compelled to keep a log of potential targets, women he passed in the street, people he had no contact with yet recorded day after day as part of the creation of his private world. The fantasy of having sex with any attractive woman who passes by is not of itself unusual. It is not necessary to have men in the privacy of the therapeutic confessional in order to find examples of this type of mental undressing. Whether it is the mass appeal of James Bond or the highbrow deliberations of Hermann Hesse, the collecting of women as targets for sexual acts is expressed commonly enough. But within the bounds of literary playfulness, despite the outcries from time to time, many people accept this form of male delusion. What makes the example of the little red book so appalling is the knowledge that it goes beyond the bounds of playfulness and was undoubtedly linked to subsequent destructive behaviour. Rather than revealing what some would call an understandable interest in women, it showed a distorted, obsessional involvement in women as objects. With each note he took he was removing himself further from real experience of women as people, feeding the vicious cycle.

Here is impulse and obsession all right, but it has a form of planning and study to it that is completely in accord with the geographical 'circle hypothesis' I have outlined. The circle is just a way of representing the domain, the geographical repertoire over which the criminal operates. Where he lives is often part of that repertoire because it helps to define it.

This cognitive, rational model of the criminal presents him as little different from other men. It does not indicate any qualitative break between the criminal and the ordinary male member of society.

A significant point, though, is that although the *type* of fantasy that this murderer exhibited was possibly no different from that of many men, the *amount* and *intensity* of it was very different. Doubtless its intensity increased as it fed on itself. This may have led to his day-to-day dealings with other people not being regarded as normal, although of course he did marry and in that regard may have passed unnoticed. Possibly his obsession slowly changed with him. His notebook also shows a frantic preoccupation with the stages of his divorce, the dates and procedures. But in regard to what might be called his geographical activity, he could only be in one place at one time and the places and times were shaped by the normal limits on human activities.

Criminals exist in normal society, limited like everyone else by available jobs, working hours, bus routes or the costs of running a car. The degree of the limitation depends where they are in their criminal development. A young lad who breaks into the electricity meter may well do it next door, but the same man ten years later may have graduated to stealing antiques and travel twenty miles to find good pickings. In the early attacks that Duffy and his accomplice carried out close to home, he appears to have been a relatively passive observer. His later murders many miles away were carefully planned.

This view of a rapist's development suggests that rapists, like most criminals, go through stages that are not dissimilar to what would be expected in a conventional career. A number of researchers have pointed out the broad similarity that many rapists have to criminals in general. Most convicted rapists have previous convictions for other offences, usually not sex-related crimes. The only broad differences between rapists and other criminals is that sexual assault does tend to be committted by older criminals. Where the average age for all crimes is in the mid-teens, sex offenders tend to be in their early twenties.

These figures, and the overlap between non-sexual and sexual crime histories, add some weight to the arguments of Diana Scully, an American sociologist, who derives from her interviews of incarcerated sex offenders the view that sexual assault is just an extreme example of men's general reactions to women. In considering this view it has to be remembered that the people I have been talking about are not average individuals; they are violent, often long-standing criminals, still a minority of British citizens. There *are* differences between criminals and the population at large, whether it is the cause or the consequence of their criminality.

This may appear to contradict the suggestion made earlier that there is an everyday logic to even the most violent crimes. I am not really contradicting myself, however, because it is true both that criminals are typically different from the non-criminal population in many ways, and that their actions are often shaped by the same forces that shape everyone's lives. In terms of their activities, their carrying out of actions that are explicitly criminal, they can be understood as part of the criminal fraternity. But when we consider their actions in time and space, then, unless they are very bizarre indeed, they must be influenced by the same processes and limitations as any other citizen.

Many people will claim, though, that, criminal or not, they do not plan their lives within a circumscribed circle. Yet although it is true that there is no such conscious planning, the piece of geomancy of drawing a circle was a systematic device for proposing how police investigators could assign priorities to the areas in which they would search for possible villains, say by looking at the details of known criminals' places of residence. It was a geometrical summary of a set of interrelated psychological processes.

There are really two principles underlying it. One is the fact well known to criminologists, but sometimes ignored by the police, that many criminals commit their crimes near to where they live. As long ago as the 1930s, sociologists in Chicago pointed out that crime and criminals were unevenly distributed on the maps of large cities. There were concentrations where most criminals lived and where most crimes occurred, so in general terms it was clear that criminals did not travel very far to perform their crimes.

The second principle comes from the studies of how people make sense of and learn to cope with their surroundings, the area of study that has come to be known as environmental psychology in which I did research before I moved into crime.

To illustrate the relevance of environmental psychology, when we were making a television film about my work with the police (called 'Helping Police with Their Inquiries', shown in 1991), I asked one of my colleagues, Sean, an easy-going, affable chap, to draw a map of London under the all-remembering gaze of the film camera. He did it without any rehearsal, and I was surprised by how well his drawing illustrated the point I wanted to make. He started drawing a sketch map, putting a few names to the locations so that it was clearly a map of the area around Covent Garden. I was curious that he had chosen to draw that particular area and asked him why. His immediate answer was that he had lived around there and so he always thinks of London with that area at the centre. Environmental psychologists have carried out many studies of this process of sketch mapping and how it reveals the internal representations, or 'mental maps', that people have of an area, trying to find out what leads to accurate and what to inaccurate mental maps. Their conclusion is as significant as it is obvious: familiarity with an area is the biggest influence.

So, although we don't plan our activities to sit inside a circle, we do operate over an area of familiarity. It is probably quite a complicated patchy shape, this area. The circle is just the simplest shape to take as a starting point. A personal experience illustrates how surprising the obvious can be. I once startled some overseas visitors who had heard something of my work with the police. They turned up early one summer's evening, when I was not expected back until much later, so my wife took them and the dog to a pleasant country pub a couple of miles away. When, a little later, I turned up at the pub, my friends were convinced it was a piece of subtle detective work, knowing that no message had been left at home. What they had not taken into account was that I knew that there were only one or two pubs that my wife would be prepared to walk to with the dog, and where there was somewhere to sit out on a pleasant summer's evening.

We are all constrained in the choices of locations we go to by where we know. This may be true of where we look for a place to live, where we go shopping, for entertainment, or to commit a crime. We may read about places or talk to friends, so our familiarity can, in effect, be extended indirectly. We may work out what must exist between two places we know and so extend our knowledge in that way. But the primary knowledge, like that revealed in Sean's sketch map, is determined by where we spend most of our time, typically where we live and work. The criminal who perpetrates a set of crimes in a particular area is telling us something about his familiarity with that area. This familiarity may be entirely a product of his criminal activities, but often it will be influenced by the same limitations that influence us all, where he has his base. Shadows do not float free of their origins.

What of the criminal who deliberately murders strangers at different points in time, the serial murderer? The media image of the travelling loner moving across the freeways of America does not accord with the more structured world I have been describing. But like many media images it is not deeply embedded in the real world. In the most thorough examination of serial murderers published so far, Eric Hickey, an American criminologist, studied over 200 such men and women who had been convicted since the end of the eighteenth century. He looked especially closely at sixty-three serial murderers who had been active since 1975. Only about a quarter of these could be classed as travellers. Two-thirds operated in the area close to where they lived. So even for these most threatening and apparently abnormal criminals, some of the general geographical constraints that we have seen in other people may well be relevant.

'Familiarity' and the 'circle hypothesis' are all very well as slogans for people to take home with them, but like all slogans their advantages are outweighed by the over-simplifications they enshrine. The outline of the geographical mind world that a criminal uses is shaped by subtle processes that might not be immediately available to detectives or obvious even to people who know the offender.

If you ask a Londoner the direct, crow-flight distance from Piccadilly Circus to the Elephant and Castle and then compare how accurate his response is with an estimate of the distance from Soho to Buckingham Palace, you will find that, typically, the first distance, which is across the river Thames in a broadly southerly direction, is overestimated much more than the second distance which is roughly east–west, not crossing the Thames. The river acts as a mental barrier that may be more powerful than its impact as a physical barrier. Even London taxi drivers with all their detailed knowledge of London's geography are not much better at estimating crow-flight distances than other Londoners. The river, in particular, seems to fill mental space in people's minds, expanding the map that people draw for themselves. Parks and major roads are other typical examples of buffers that lead to distortions in the way people represent the world to themselves.

These distortions in the way we represent the world in our minds are not just mental buffers, they are reflected in how we act. Many London police officers will tell you that villains who live north of the river rarely carry out crimes south of it. 'Living on the wrong side of the railway tracks' is a cliché that encapsulates the association between locations and the meanings that those locations have; a meaning that is usually a product of a lack of any direct experience. North Londoners who rarely travel into the unknown territory of South London think of it as distant and unfathomable. Large cities are especially prone to the creation of such distorted images because travel around them can be surprisingly limited as well. Many youngsters in North London have never seen the Thames. I once met an elderly lady in Central Park, New York, who was very worried because her grandson had just gone off to a summer camp less than a couple of hours drive away on the Atlantic coast. She had never seen 'the Ocean' herself and it was linked in her mind to such overwhelming images of huge seas and breaking waves that she felt she had to ask an expert (who could be more expert than an Englishman who must have crossed that ocean?) whether it was really safe for her grandson to be near something as awesome as the Atlantic ocean.

A carousel of influences holds these tendencies together. Where we go depends upon what we know to be available. What we know depends on where we go. Over time in an area we slowly evolve our understanding of what is where from the contacts we have. Someone who moves to London may know the area around the tube station where they work and around the tube station where a friend lives. One day, taking a wrong turning by accident, they may discover that the two locations are much nearer than they had realized because, being on different tube lines, their closeness had never been appreciated.

Ask someone who regularly drives through Birmingham, but has never shopped there, how to walk from the station to the Bull Ring roundabout. He will probably have great difficulty telling you. The Birmingham of the regular driver and of the walker are virtually two different cities in the minds of residents. Two quite different sets of navigational skills are necessary to find your way about each of these cities. So, if I asked you the walking route or the driving route and checked the accuracy of your response it would not be difficult to say, from this information alone, whether you were a walker or a driver. Perhaps a not very impressive party trick. But what of its value to a police investigation?

It is possible to walk around the Whitechapel sites related to the 'Jack the Ripper' murders in an afternoon (about a quarter of a million tourists do each year). There will never be such tours of Peter Sutcliffe's 'Yorkshire Ripper' murders or of the scenes associated with the 'Railway Rapist'/murderer John Duffy because the scenes are too far apart. Many of Sutcliffe's crimes are over twenty miles from each other and some of Duffy's have over forty miles between them.

The very distances over which crimes are committed tell us something about the individual who perpetrated them. In Victorian Whitechapel it is not surprising that 'Jack the Ripper' moved around on foot, but if he left the area in a horse-drawn cab why was the farthest distance between any two attacks still within an easy walk? Whitechapel was not the only area of London with narrow streets and many potential victims. The most parsimonious assumption to make is that the scenes of his crimes were within walking distance of each other because he walked to them from where he lived.

Car tyre markings were found at some of Peter Sutcliffe's murder scenes. The distance between his killings therefore accords well with the assumption that these tyre markings were produced by a car he was driving. But the possession and frequent use of a car could have been taken by the police to suggest that the person they were looking for was not a complete down and out. Indeed, the cost of keeping a car on the road may even be taken to indicate that he has some sort of regular income. If you accept that he has a car then you have to ask why all his attacks were in a circumscribed area of Yorkshire. The answer you are likely to give yourself is that he was familiar with that area and possibly lived within it and travelled around it.

Duffy travelled even further, but the location of some of his rapes and their closeness to railway stations enabled British journalists, without detailed knowledge of the crimes and confused by unrelated crimes, to spot the link to the railway line and dub him the 'Railway Rapist'. The increasing distances he travelled out from a central point certainly fit with a person going to a railway station and then choosing to go off in any one of a number of directions, but this use of the railway system also suggests

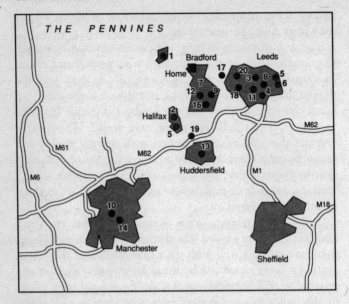

Map iii: Locations of Sutcliffe's murders and his residence (numbers indicate sequence of offences) (Derived from Kind, S.S., 1987).

rather more knowledgeable experience than the average traveller would have. Knowing what the main routes were north, south, east and west would be unusual, I would think, for most local railway users. A person employed as a carpenter by British Rail, as Duffy was, would have the rather more specialist knowledge that his pattern of behaviour suggested.

The power of this way of thinking can be gleaned from a couple of further cases to which it has been directly applied with some real benefit. One was the investigation of a series of vicious attacks, robberies and rapes carried out near the southern area of the M25 ring-road that circles

London. Apparently under the influence of drugs, a gang set off in a stolen car, ransacking houses. Eventually, as many as ninety-two assaults on houses in the stock-broker belt may have been committed by a gang of at least three men, all in their early twenties, although accomplices are also known to have been involved. During the course of these attacks one man was kicked to death, another stabbed and a woman raped.

The chief investigating officer on these cases was Chief Superintendent Vince McFadden, the man who called me in to help with the Duffy inquiry. He told me that when he started to lead the investigation he determined to use what he regarded as the profiling approach. At an early meeting reviewing the available material, he examined the location of everything associated with the incidents being investigated. This included where cars used in robberies had been stolen from, where they had been left later and all the minor offences that were suspected of being linked to the major crimes in question. This meant that when the £25,000 reward led to a number of tip-offs, it was feasible to identify quickly which potential suspects most closely fitted the geographical and behavioural profile that Vince McFadden had built up. Chief Superintendent McFadden told me that the account they had been able to build up was so clear that they knew when they arrested the first group of suspects that their 'leader' was not among them and further investigation was necessary to catch him.

If it is true that all actions are shaped by the same environmental psychology processes, and that therefore criminal and domestic actions overlap, it will be true for trivial aspects of behaviour as well as for the major deeds. A bank robbery may be planned to take the person beyond his normal area of activity, but where he steals a car from in order to carry out the robbery may be much closer to home. The 'trivia' may therefore turn out to be more indicative to an investigation than the scene of the crime itself. Unfortunately, police records may not store minor offences in a way that will enable them to be accessible to a major investigation. In the case of the M25 gang, such details were available and without doubt helped the police to locate the gang quickly.

The second case was also a series of assaults, this time sexual assaults on elderly victims in an area of the southern Home Counties. The distances between these assaults suggested that the offender had used transport. No obvious rail links existed and the times of the attacks, anyway, ruled out trains. Anyone living in this area of Britain will also tell you that buses cannot be relied on for shopping trips, let alone planned late-night sexual assaults. So, we concluded he had a car. This opened up other possibilities. The costs of running a car suggested that he had some sort of job, but the times of day and variety of locations did not accord with a very skilled, reliable form of employment. Any job was therefore not likely to be well paid. So we considered it unlikely that he had a very new car. The MOT test puts three years as the difference between an 'old' and a 'new' car, so we could take as a starting point that his car would be at least three years old and probably older. When a suspect who was forensically linked to the offences was found to have a five-year-old saloon, no one was more impressed by the power of scientific logic than Rupert Heritage and I.

Where a criminal operates is one of the most distinctive features of the shadow that he casts. It gives a hook of enormous value for any police investigation. It can direct house-to-house inquiries, narrow down lists of suspects drawn from criminal records or provide guidelines for surveillance operations. There is no secret to this. The travelling criminal is potentially far more difficult to locate; on the other hand, he can leave a trail that assists his identification, but this requires that the trail is readable. Through small British towns this might be so, but across the vast expanses of America it is a different matter. The distances travelled in the United States by some criminals who commit a series of crimes are so large that the FBI reports on profiling rarely consider locational material in detail. (They have, however, carried out studies of serial arsonists which show that very simple calculations of the geographical centre of a series can, on occasion, indicate the arsonist's place of residence.)

This idea of a geographical 'centre of gravity' was also used to good effect in the 'Yorkshire Ripper' investigation. Stuart Kind, Director of the Home Office Central Research Establishment, joined an advisory team set up in November 1980 in response to a request by the Home Secretary to assist the Chief Constable of the West Yorkshire Metropolitan Police in finding the 'Ripper'. It says something of the British valuation of experience over direct, systematic expertise that Dr Kind was the only scientist on this advisory team and that the other four members were senior police officers. Why have four officers? Would four consultant brain surgeons be brought into an especially important piece of surgery? I think not. If a profession has clearly established principles, then any one expert ought to come to the same conclusion as the others. The fact that the Chief Constable of West Yorkshire was deemed to need help and that not one but four other senior officers should help him is the clearest indication that the Home Secretary did not think that there was any consensual expertise in the senior levels of the police force. The later inquiry into the investigation by Biford serves to support this argument.

The value of an alternative perspective can be illustrated, though, because of the involvement of Stuart Kind. In a subsequent account of his involvement, the reticence of which reveals his years as a cautious civil servant, he describes the value of considering the murders linked to the 'Yorkshire Ripper' in terms of what he calls their 'centre of gravity'. He summarizes this idea neatly by referring to a map on which the seventeen 'Yorkshire Ripper' crimes have been marked.

> If we mark each of these positions with a map pin and tie a piece of thread to it we are then in a position to consider the following question: 'At which single location on the map could be placed an eighteenth pin, such that if we stretched the seventeen threads and tied each loose end to the eighteenth pin, the minimum total amount of thread would be used?'
>
> Stuart Kind, *The Scientific Investigation of Crime*, 1987, p.377

'Near Bradford' was the answer a computer analysis gave to this question. This solution was of value, not least because it conflicted with tape-recordings reputed to have been sent by the killer and established by phonetic experts to indicate a Geordie, not a Yorkshire, accent. Stuart Kind's other considerations had a similarly systematic quality to them that all added up to the 'Ripper' having a base near Bradford. These included a careful examination of the sequence of offences which led Kind to conclude that the criminal was at pains to avoid returning to the towns of recent, earlier crimes.

The region Peter Sutcliffe roamed over was very unlike the Whitechapel of the original 'Ripper'. Small towns are dispersed across the countryside between large but not enormous cities. The fact that some of Sutcliffe's victims had the same trade (prostitution) as those of his London counterpart is testimony to both the resilience of that trade and the enormous physical risks associated with it. The distances that Sutcliffe travelled therefore also illustrate what a number of criminologists have emphasized: that the distribution of possible targets for crime will influence how far criminals travel. Our own studies with burglars illustrate this quite graphically. Burglars operating in the semi-urban county of Surrey on average travel over seven miles; burglars in the small, readily demarcated town of Cambridge travel on average less than two miles.

The mental map a criminal draws upon is not a fantasy created in the imagination which has little contact with the real world. It is a distillation of his own particular transactions with his surroundings. If we can find out how to interpret the wake left behind by a criminal when he plunges through a community, we can understand those special qualities of his transactions that will lead us to him. The directions and distances he travels are one important indicator of his personal silhouette. This silhouette may change from one set of opportunities to another.

A man was recently arrested in America for attacking a woman in the block of flats where he was staying. During the course of investigations it became apparent that he had been sexually assaulting women in South Wales, where he lived. He was on the other side of the Atlantic to visit a friend. In South Wales he had assaulted women in an area close to where his friend lived, often on the way home from visiting him. He would knock on doors of houses in which previous watching had revealed that single women lived and, having gained entry by asking directions or for a glass of water, he would then attack them.

Blocks of flats have often been seen as streets in the sky. Each block acts like its own neighbourhood where people are strangers to each other, habitually seen without being noticed. In the large cities of the New World they are direct translations of the urban streets of Britain. The symmetry of the assailant's behaviour seems almost inevitable. A comfortable distance from his friend's house he has noticed a potential victim. Eventually he knocks on her door. In Britain this is down the street; across the Atlantic it is a few floors away. In a tower block, though, the population is more clearly defined, so the police could launch a search more speedily and identify their suspect more readily than in Britain. By not taking account of this aspect of the translation of his actions, he was caught.

A man who sets out on a train to look for locations in which to commit a sexual assault, and possibly a murder, is telling us something about himself that is different from a man who wanders down the street to knock on a door behind which he knows there is a lone woman. Both of these men are clearly different from Sutcliffe who set off in his car looking for women on their own walking the streets. They are all acting within the confines of their own knowledge and awareness. Even when they break out far beyond the bounds of morality they are still constrained by their own experience and habits. Like a beggar who makes the same protestations to every passer-by and who always approaches people in the same area, or for that matter like a lecturer who uses the same joke to make his point every time he gives a particular lecture, these habits and constraints grow out of the full panoply of dealings that the person has. Through their actions criminals reveal more than just what they are familiar with; they tell us about other aspects of their lives. We have to learn how to listen.

A special example of the way rapists have remarkably consistent habits occurred to me quite early on in studying men who had carried out a number of sexual assaults. The first few cases I read were of men who attacked women in their own homes. In subsequent cases the men had attacked women in streets or public parks. I started to wonder if a distinct style was being reflected here. So we set about examining systematically what proportion of serial offenders were erratic in their choice of venue. Once again I was excited by the shape revealed in the actions of these criminals. In our first sample of sixty serial offenders, attacking strangers, only five showed variations in types of venue. Thirty-eight had always attacked indoors; seventeen had always attacked outdoors. Subsequent material has confirmed this general trend to venue consistency.

What is this telling us? Well, it could be what researchers call artefact. It could be an accident of the way in which the information is collected. Think of it this way. If police officers use the type of venue selected for an assault as a criterion in deciding whether offences are committed by the same person, then they are less likely to link an outdoor assault to an indoor one. Someone called in as a suspect might therefore be charged only with crimes that have taken place either indoors or outdoors. If he kept quiet about any other crimes that did not fit his known predilection, then the records would show a neat and tidy consistency that was a product of what police officers assumed to be invariable rather than an actual account of a criminal's habitual attack location.

Such artefacts are difficult to challenge directly. All that can be done is to check out the implications of this hypothesized process and see if there is any further evidence for or against it. A starting point, though, is to make sure that the finding is as consistent as the assumed actions of the criminals. Other sets of data that became available to us were explored, and contacts with the FBI academy were asked to check their own data set. All of these showed the majority of offenders to be consistent. The proportions of erratic offenders varied from sample to sample, so that this variation alone emerged as an interesting topic for further examination.

The continued support for these consistencies in different data sets requires the artefactual argument, the self-fulfilling prophecy, to take a very strong form. The implication is that the criterion of type of venue is a very clearly conscious one that police officers regularly use. Two bundles of questions would follow from this. Had police officers ever told us about their use of this principle, or, by contrast, did they express surprise when told about our findings? That is the first bundle of questions. The second bundle has to do with the origin of any beliefs in consistency that the police held. If the origins were based in the collective experience of the police force, then all that I was doing was adding systematic support to facts that the police had discovered for themselves. The self-fulfilling cycle could, in this light, be seen not as an artefact but as an implicit hypothesis based on experience.

Discussions with police officers revealed the 'now you come to mention it' syndrome. They expressed initial surprise at the findings but then, thinking through the cases they had direct experience of, they said that with hindsight they had always been vaguely aware of such consistencies in particular individuals. Seeing this as a general principle went rather further than they would have been willing to go on the basis of their own direct experience. So there may be some artefactual component in the results. The consistency we have found may be rather higher than is actually the case, but not low enough to dismiss.

When I first realized that these consistencies were worth taking seriously, I thought that a quite simple explanation could be given for them. 'How about this possibility?' I said to any colleague who would listen. 'Those guys who start off as house-breakers, get used to finding their way around houses. They feel comfortable in that sort of setting. Then if they graduate to rape they carry on with the same habit, attacking indoors. But your street muggers are the outdoor types. Their violence continues in the sorts of venues it started in.'

We tested these possibilities against actual examples. Like most elegant ideas in psychology the truth is rather more subtle and complex. We did not find that our outdoor attackers had no history of burglary or that our indoor attackers had never committed crimes outdoors. As I write we are still trying to tease out exactly what the differences are, but there does appear to be a tendency for the insiders to be the more devout criminals with a longer history and more experience of crimes like theft and burglary. The outsiders are more likely to have a history of sexual deviance and relatively little previous criminal background.

With hindsight this does make sense. Going into a stranger's house for whatever reason is a determined criminal act. A person would need some experience of what it feels like to creep through another person's rooms. He would also have to be prepared to deal with any occupant he came across, unless he was very careful to make sure the property was unoccupied. Many convicted burglars when interviewed about their choice of targets have said that their main concern was to make sure that there was no one in the house at the time.

The burglar who cautiously avoids contact with an occupant is rather different from one who climbs into a house and sexually assaults the person found there. Such an assault can never be totally impulsive. Nor can anyone caught by an occupant convincingly argue that committing a criminal act was no part of their intentions. Jumping on someone in a public place has a quite different psychological feel to it. It could be more obviously thought of by the perpetrator as an impulsive, opportunistic act. It is both more risky in terms of being caught and less demanding of any criminal skills or preparation.

There is some sort of difference between offenders who choose one location or another. But it will be subtle. Let me remind you of the person who asked for a glass of water and, once inside the house, attacked. His behaviour is very different from that of rapists such as Tony McClean, who terrorized Notting Hill over a number of years. He waited indoors for the victim to return home. Gaining entry by subterfuge implies both a readiness to talk to the victim and a lack of experience of entering a house by illegal means. It seems unlikely that such a man would be a burglar-turned-rapist. By contrast, as some of the detectives on the case realized, McClean showed all the hallmarks of the experienced burglar he was.

Distance from home and crime location, venue, mode of transport, all are overt, direct characteristics of a crime. They can be derived, with some effort, from the available police records. No in-depth analysis of criminals in a caring, non-judgmental relationship is necessary. Yet these conspicuous aspects of what offenders *do* add up to show us that they differ from each other in important ways. Against the similarity in the processes we can see the behavioural styles that distinguish criminals from each other. How much further can we shine a light down this dark tunnel to help us identify in more detail what is casting the shadows on the wall?

CONSISTENT CLUES

Looking at solved cases, or even unsolved ones such as the Whitechapel murders, and seeing what relationships between offender and offence characteristics are embedded in the known details, is as close to my other, everyday, behavioural science as my work with the police has taken me. The facts are there to work with, not unfolding as detectives uncover further information or related crimes. There is no time constraint set by the possibility of another serious assault before the results can be gleaned.

Our early work on the distances that criminals travel showed how fruitful looking at solved cases could be, helping to clarify the very real limits to the actions of many criminals. Reflections on the 'mental map' that a criminal draws upon evolved into the rudiments of a theory which saw an offender's actions as relating to his familiarity with his surroundings and his attempt to minimize the risk to himself with as little inconvenience as possible; a simple, logical theory that somehow loses the emotional charge of rape and murder and hides something of the determination, often becoming an obsession, that is central to any series of violent offences.

An active contribution to an investigation puts the victim and her suffering in high relief. That is the starting point for the police work and for the request to me for assistance. The information that is collected during a police inquiry is often more detailed than that distilled out to keep in later records. The culprits' own accounts and the court proceedings around cases in which I have been involved also provide a rich, close contact. It is this intense material that reveals the significance that the crime has to the offender, from which we may be able to build a further, more detailed understanding of what shapes the actions of a criminal and how those shapes can therefore be interpreted.

My attempts to strike a balance between distant, academic analysis and involvement in current investigations always create a tension within me. Should I be offering the best guess I can come up with, like a paperback Poirot, or should I follow my own scientific inclinations and wait for more data and clearer results before making suggestions to detectives?

This tension was particularly acute when I was asked to help in the investigation of a series of sexual assaults by an athletic young man on elderly women living in tower blocks in a very limited area of Birmingham.

It was a couple of years after Duffy had been arrested, and by this stage Rupert Heritage was ensconced as a student at the university. We were trying to pull together whatever research we could in order to establish some firm principles that tied offender characteristics to the style of their offences and to help answer the increasing number of requests from police forces to assist them in intractable cases.

Birmingham police officers approached us in the late spring of 1988. Seven attacks had taken place on elderly female victims in tower blocks in the Edgbaston and Druids Heath areas of Birmingham between January 1986 and March 1988. As the police report put it in an attempt at unemotional language: 'Three of the incidents involved genital intercourse or attempts thereat concomitant with the definition of Rape in legal terms. The others are serious sexual assaults in which activity is confined to non genital penetration which may have been due to victim resistance, outside interference or cessation of the attack.'

Women in their seventies and eighties, often infirm, were followed into lifts by a stocky young man who overpowered them and took them to the top floor of the tower block, sometimes carrying them up the last two flights of stairs to the landing near the roof. There he raped them and escaped.

In one attack he walked into the flat of a very frail, demented lady and sexually assaulted her. The victim was so disturbed that it was only the medical examination and reports from friends of her distress that brought the offence into the inquiry. The victim was unable to give any account of what had happened. Some of the victims never really recovered emotionally from these attacks, drifting into depression and senility soon after. At least one died a number of years earlier than she might have hoped, virtually giving up the desire to live after the assault.

The reaction of the local community, not renowned for its cohesion, showed how affronted people were by these crimes. Newspapers reported that at one stage local vigilante groups were set up to patrol the tower blocks, although police officers deny that these ever actually existed.

There was little difficulty in establishing that one person was responsible for all these crimes. Again, to return to the more formal police report: 'There are strong Modus Operandi links within this series. The consistent use of High Rise buildings, Lifts within, and the removal of the elderly white victim to the upper stairways, all the actions of a black male, have a strength in themselves which would support the treatment of the series as a whole.'

Unlike Duffy, then, whose spreading series of crimes initially made linking difficult, yet whose very spread helped to identify where he had started from, this offender was operating in a very small area, in very similar settings, acting in very consistent ways.

The local newspaper had quickly elicited a response from a professor of psychology at York University. This enabled them to produce the headline: 'Sex Monster Could Kill in the Next Attack.' The paper cited Professor Be-nables (his name is actually Venables, presumably the interview was done over the telephone) as saying: 'This man is clearly a psychopath and sensation seeker, the more danger he puts himself into, the more fun he gets.' In one assault he had told his victim that his name was Leroy. Professor Benables is quoted as saying: 'He may have given this information to increase the risk of getting caught.' Without the benefit of access to the full police dossier, apparently, Professor Benables saw this psychopath as getting thrills from sexually assaulting defenceless old women. He also is said to have proposed that the offender 'may have sublimated anger against his mother, and is now punishing older women whom he sees as authority figures'. But other, equally feasible, alternative hypotheses are possible. The offender may have given a false name to mislead investigators. He may have found older women sexually attractive. Perhaps these alternatives were dismis-sed because Professor Benables shared with the police and the journalist who questioned him a difficulty in relating such actions to his personal experience. The fisherman has to be careful not to cast his own shadow on the water. In this case it is not frightening away the fish that is to be avoided, but confusing his own shadow with the one he is trying to interpret.

The tower block attacks also had a very curious style to them. The offender was strong and determined, but never overtly vicious. In some cases the victims complained about how cold the concrete floor was when he forced them to lie on it naked. He showed an unexpected, minor consideration for them by putting some of their clothing underneath them. He later remembered this, when questioned by the police, saying with apparent disinterest and acceptance: 'There's been one or two like that, says it's cold. Well I don't want them to be cold do I?'

Police officers expressed special difficulties in understanding these assaults. As one policeman put it, not realizing how much he was assuming about men's attitudes to women: 'We could understand it if he were raping young attractive women, but frail old women, I can't see what he gets out of that.' He was reinforcing the stereotype of human sexual aggression as having a 'normal' form that involved conventionally attractive women, and all else being distorted and bizarre. The conventional fitted in with his own experiences and was therefore understandable, the bizarre was beyond his comprehension.

The separation off of unfamiliar sexual behaviour implicitly leads to the search for some kind of a monster, a person who would be noticeably different from other people and recognized as such by those who knew him. The police felt they needed our help to understand this 'monster' who was so far beyond their own comprehension. Yet precisely because his actions were so apparently bizarre they presented a challenge to our emerging theory of rational, risk-reducing criminals who could be detected by simple logic. Could we wait for a thorough study of sexual attacks on the elderly and do nothing to help reduce the risk that he would kill one of his next victims before the police got to him? He had already attacked so many women that he would certainly not stop until he was caught.

A further problem was the traumatic nature of the assaults and the difficulty of investigating especially vulnerable victims and making sense of their accounts. This was brought home to me by the suggestion from some policemen that one victim might have been lying about a second assault by the same man. They thought she might have invented this to try and speed up her move to other housing. Yet the account this woman gave of what had happened to her the second time included being forced to fellate the assailant, an act that had not occurred the first time. Other victims had reported similar actions to the police without it ever becoming public knowledge.

Such doubts expressed by the police are echoed in their popular distrust of what children say in criminal proceedings, although there is growing evidence that children's accounts can often be trusted. The elderly victims were sometimes confused and this threw a general unease over the investigation. Police disquiet was strengthened by the fear that one of the attacks would lead to the death of a victim, for although the attacker was not overtly vicious, the force of his assaults on such frail people was feared.

It is possible that these fears and confusions kept the investigating officers too closely involved in the case, and reduced their capacity to give a more dispassionate consideration to the facts. Perhaps the report we produced had its main value in helping them to see that the peculiarities of the cases were indeed their distinguishing characteristics and ought to lead us to the offender.

The psychological principle I was exploring was that the many similarities in his overt behaviour should tell us something about the offender. He had a limited repertoire of locations, victims and actions. This was a limited man operating in a constrained world. What were the implications of those constraints? Perhaps the police get used to so many different places that they can lose the sensitivity less experienced people have to the peculiarities of any particular setting.

My feelings about the special qualities of the physical

setting of these crimes were clarified after the culprit had been convicted. The concentration of the attacks in tower blocks on the edge of Birmingham's city centre had always struck me as revealing something curious about the attacker. His familiarity with tower blocks had been recognized, of course, by police investigators long before they approached me, but why these particular tower blocks? It was only when I was involved in making a television documentary dealing with these crimes that it was brought home to me how much these particular tower blocks captured the communal anonymity of Britain's second largest city.

The director of the film, Patrick Fleming, had wanted some dramatic shots to capture the abstract notion of the 'mental map' that the criminal must have been working with. He wanted to show, with visual immediacy, that there is an internal template that everyone carries around with them for choosing what they will do where. Patrick came up with the idea of putting me into a small, four-seater helicopter to fly over the tower blocks in which the assaults had been committed. My task was to be filmed pointing at the city below, explaining how this bird's-eye view revealed the likely inner workings of the rapist's personal geography.

From a helicopter Birmingham emerges against the horizon like something left over from a failed attempt to ape Manhattan on the Warwickshire plane. At 15,000 feet, a couple of miles away, the tower blocks scattered around the outskirts of the city centre look like the remnants of children's blocks used to build the office towers that are crammed together in the middle. They give the impression of a determined youngster who had started on an ambitious project systematically enough but eventually lost interest, shoving the pieces down wherever they would fit. This creates an incomprehensible bundle of offices and shops that fade off into the miles of semi-detached sub-urban residences, punctuated with asides that are the high-rise council towers. Confused streets in the sky, they are not sure whether to throw in their lot with the megaliths of the city centre or to huddle together on the scarred lawns and pretend they are part of the suburbs.

Air traffic regulations kept us above 1,000 feet, which is the height from which you can recognize that each back garden in a housing estate of semi-detached houses is unique, but it is still not close enough to distinguish what it is that makes each garden different. Flying at that level I could see quite clearly the desire for each household to express their uniqueness, but it is equally clear that they can never succeed.

As we came in lower and closer to the edge of the city centre, the shaping was increasingly provided by the dual carriageways and railway lines. The helicopter pilot navigated by the roads towards the tower blocks in which the attacks had taken place. It was then that I became aware of just how distinctly those clumps of tower blocks stood between the offices of the city centre and the residential sprawl beyond it. At the time of the investigation I had been given aerial photographs and maps of the area and the separateness of these particular blocks had been apparent. But from the air it seemed even more plausible that locations for the majority of attacks had been selected because of their distinct separateness. Shouting over the noise of the helicopter I showed how I had formed the view that the major dual carriageways that surrounded the tower blocks acted as mental buffers. They made the attacker feel that the blocks of flats were a secluded island.

He had moved about this island with confidence and there had been no sign of a vehicle; he had even mentioned the use of a bus to one victim. There was the possibility that he lived in among these buildings, but it seemed unlikely. He was not recognized by anyone and had made little attempt to wear any disguise. He was confident and familiar with the scenes of his crimes, but was he alien to them? This was certainly a challenge to the elegant logic of the 'circle hypothesis'. What of the idea of an offender choosing locations that would reduce the risk of him being known? Is that still a viable possibility in this setting?

The anonymous concrete towers on the edge of Birmingham must have many strangers passing through. They are close enough to the city centre to attract many friends and relations, salesmen, casual visitors on their way in or out, but large and anonymous enough for a lone black man to go unremarked by the victims until he assaulted them. The victims' acceptance of an unknown man asking for help to gain entry was apparent from their statements. The distinctness of the island in which the blocks of flats sat would not be so apparent, though, to the casual visitor. Only someone who had day-to-day experience of tower blocks close to the city, probably close to these, might be expected to take for granted the ease with which strangers can come and go in such places. But, would coming from close by not have risks?

When police officers brought us maps of the area of the assaults, we asked them to describe the characteristics of the inhabitants of the different areas around the offences. They produced an account that indicated distinct regions: areas that were known to be frequented by prostitutes, others that were known to be predominantly black, regions with an ethnic mixture, and so on. The suggestion emerged that perhaps the offender was as aware of these different types of area as were the police officers. Perhaps he and they shared a sort of communal mental map. If that were the case, he might think that he reduced risk to himself not by moving a great distance but by moving from one territory to another. In the helicopter I could see

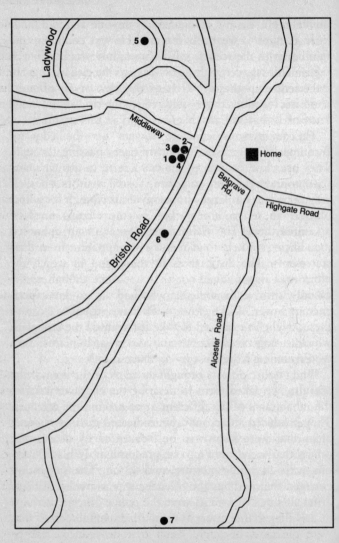

Map iv: Edgbaston, indicating the location of Babb's rapes and residence (numbers indicate sequence of offences).

even more clearly than on the maps how this all made sense. Against the backdrop of the centre of the city with its complex network of roads, the only pattern that can be gleaned is made by the busy arteries streaming out from the centre, creating zones that are physically close but none the less distinct. By crossing a road one could walk into an almost alien location, but still be close to home territory. The conclusion I drew from this was that he lived near by and probably in a similar sort of tower block.

These considerations led Rupert to study the aerial photographs the Birmingham police had brought us. One tower block seemed to fit all our discussions. 'He must live there,' Rupert said, mirroring my earlier confidence in the location of Duffy's home base. But Rupert experienced a conflict I had never had. The detective in him wanted to go to Birmingham and search for the rapist where he lived; but now he was a university researcher and that was not really an option. He had to wait for more detailed considerations and an extended police investigation before we found out how accurate his suggestion had been.

Although the helicopter ride had helped me to see more clearly the impact of the geography of these locations than I had gleaned from the material supplied by the police, and as dramatic as such a bird's-eye view is, it does not indicate how people live. The possibility of a man hanging around blocks of flats on many occasions, unnoticed yet living a short distance away, can only be garnered at grass-roots level. An understanding of the context in which the crimes occurred, and of the different domains through which the offender moved, reveals the rules of anonymity that guide the lives of the people who live in these tower blocks.

The idea of a 'territory' as a distinct, protected area to describe parts of a city, like an area defended by an animal, was given credence by the films made in the 1950s and '60s about the emerging 'concrete jungle'. (*West Side Story* glamorized the idea with the Sharks and Jets patrolling their protected areas of New York.) These strange parallels with the actions of animals were convincing because, despite all the evidence showing that animals do not behave in the way humans are said to, high-rise housing in Britain has created a remarkably anti-human environment.

Wandering around the edge of Birmingham city centre it is easy to tell that the great boom in building came in the late 1960s and early '70s. The architecture is uncompromising. People have to be housed, so what is the simplest way to do it? Not for these designers the flippancies of the 1980s, no post-modern frills. But these tower blocks and slabs were not thrown up in the flush of enthusiasm that destroyed parts of major cities such as Liverpool and Glasgow. These have a gesture towards play spaces on their roofs and locking systems on the entrance doors that parody the private penthouse towers in which a concierge makes sure that the locking system is effective. The towers built by the corporation for its tenants do not have the maintenance funds to keep the roofs clean or to fix the doors that are so regularly vandalized. Where a private block of apartments would have a welcoming entrance hall, the high-rise council flats have dark alleys, approached through broken doors, smelling of urine. Hoping the lift is still working, residents rush through these uninviting entrances, heads averted, to the comfort and comparative safety of their flats. There are no garden fences over which neighbours can get to know each other or corner cafés where friendships can develop over a slow cup of coffee. This is a planned world where people are placed in accommodation on the basis of the number of points they have on a form. They will be shuffled into a tower blck without fear or favour, concern for colour or creed, creating the type of social pot-pourri that private, unplanned housing never produces, where salary and choice often lead to people with similar tastes and lifestyles picking similar localities in which to live. Local authority tenants do slowly manage to swap and change so that clusters of similar people begin to drift together, a black area emerges or one with many old folk. These are unwanted changes, so little effort is put into providing special facilities to support the various, distinct groups that evolve.

I remember one local authority housing officer who telephoned me to ask if by painting the walls in his office a different colour he could reduce the violence and complaints he got. He thought the problem was external to the system he was part of. In a situation like that, when an old lady complains of being attacked and raped for the second time the police and housing officers think it may be just another ploy to get reallocated. The bureaucrats know that if residents do not have the financial resources then other leverage will be used. A general mood and quality of life unfolds around these insensitive controls on people's lives: violence in the office for allocating accommodation; residents inventing crimes to move on; a network of people treating each other as instruments for personal benefit. That was the world the rapist seemed to be part of.

The world created by council tower blocks is very different from that created by street-level estates; it has different rules and expectations associated with it. The illusion is given to the outsider that the corridors, lifts and stairs are private places where everyone is known, but in fact they often operate like the hidden cul-de-sacs of Victorian cities, anonymous networks used mainly by local residents but none the more private for that. This mixture of the open and the private produced an ambiguity in understanding the assaults that took place within them. Was the offender a person used to going into other people's private realms, like an experienced burglar would be? Or was he an impulsive attacker, like someone who would grab at a victim in a public place because the opportunity is seen to present itself?

So although the early considerations of geography and territory gave rise to some intriguing suggestions about the offender, there was still the central question as to the type of criminal that he was. To form a view on that, a closer examination of the details of the assaults themselves was necessary. A composite statement drawn from a number of different victims gives the harsh reality of these assaults.

I am seventy-two years old. I have never been married. I have never had sexual intercourse and I was in fact a virgin. I had gone into the block of flats where I live. The external door leading to the block was open, just pushed to. I know that the door at the back of the block was open, just pushed to. I saw no one. I pushed the button for the lift to come. After a while the lift came and the next thing was I was pushed from behind into the lift. I was pushed against the side of the lift. I saw a West Indian male about twenty years old. He was holding me against the side of the lift. I had one of these buzzers in my pocket so I sounded it, but he just took it off me. He told me to be quiet and I wouldn't be hurt.

He held me with one hand and started to press the lift buttons. I kept struggling but he was still holding me. The lift went up and down a few times before it eventually stopped.

He had his sports bag on his left arm.

He pushed me through the doorway leading to the stairs and said we were going up the stairs. I told him I couldn't get up the stairs as I was an old lady.

He then picked me up in his arms as if I was a baby. He then ran up four flights of stairs with me in his arms. He then stopped and put me down and told me to walk up the rest of the stairs. I again refused and he grabbed hold of my left hand and started dragging me up. We went up two flights of stairs to the eleventh floor. I knew it was the eleventh floor because I could see the roof area through the glass.

There was a door there which he kicked open and pulled me through, on to the roof.

He pushed me on to the floor on to my back and told me to stop shouting.

I can remember seeing him holding a knife, when he told me to stop shouting. He held the knife to my breasts. I could feel the knife in the middle of my chest. He pulled my skirt and underskirt off.

He pushed me down and sat on my chest, his legs either side of me with his back to my face.

I said, 'You're crushing me', but he only said, 'I will crush you'. Whilst he was sitting on my chest he started to push my woollen tights down. He then pulled my pants down. Then my bottom touched the cold concrete. I told him it was cold and moaned.

He then said, 'Lift up, I'll put this under you. It'll keep you warmer' and put my underskirt under my bottom.

I said, 'Have you got a mother?'

He said, 'Yes.'

I said, 'How would you like somebody to do this to your mother?'

He said, 'I wouldn't.'

I said, 'Well, what are you doing this to me for?'

He said, 'Cos I like women's bodies.'

He told me to relax and said, 'I'm not a rapist.' He tried to get his hand between my legs. I couldn't see what he was doing, but because I kept struggling, trying to breathe, he couldn't get his hand into my privates. I don't know which hand he used.

He pulled my legs open with his hands. I felt his finger go into my privates and it hurt. I was crying. I felt so helpless. He was so heavy. I could feel his finger moving about inside. He did this for about ten minutes.

I screamed and he stopped and grabbed his bag and ran away down the stairs.

With some victims he was even more determined than indicated in this statement, forcing them to fellate him and completing sexual intercourse, although he never appeared to have ejaculated.

Some points could be assumed in preparing the report for the police. The victims had given similar estimates of age with appropriately younger estimates being given for the early offences than for those eighteen months later. There was a general agreement that the offender was black, although some disagreement as to exactly what his racial origins were. His athletic build was described directly by some victims, but could also be assumed from the ease with which he apparently carried one of the heavier victims up two flights of stairs. In common with many sexual assaults there was also no indication of alcohol or body odours. Here was a clean-living, athletic young black man. On some occasions he actually carried a sports bag that was certainly in keeping with the athletic persona. He was not reported as having an accent that would have distinguished him locally.

Contrary to some people's expectations the attacker was not a drug-crazed Rastafarian, but neither was he a violent assailant demonstrating anger or particular delight in controlling his victims. So where should we begin to make suggestions about this case? Intensive police inquiries had revealed nothing, even with a photofit picture and extensive coverage in the city's newspapers. I was sure he must be local, but how? Why? Where?

Possibly the easiest place to start was to come to some conclusions about what sort of a criminal the assailant was. Here the matrix of behaviour, the patterns that had emerged from earlier cases, were invoked to help lay this shadow to rest.

The criminal who sees sex as just something else to take for himself appears to be rather different to the person whose inner drives lead him to this distorted form of sexuality. The age of the victim does not appear to be an obvious distinguishing characteristic for these two styles of offending. The basically anti-social offender, though, is more likely to be involved in a range of criminal activities, to have committed thefts and possibly burglaries, whereas the more clearly deviant offender is more restricted to sexually-related deviant activities.

Was this man a confident indoor attacker, used to taking advantage of domestic privacy, a hardened thief, turned to raping weak victims? Or was his behaviour more impulsive, more an attempt to get sexual satisfaction where he could, in hidden but public places? Some shape came into these answers by considering what he did *not* do. Many attackers of weak victims knock on their doors and talk their way in. Others force an entry into the private realm, then use the privacy as a protection from being disturbed. He did none of this. He followed his victims into lifts then overpowered them. Theft or burglary appeared to be no part of his actions. Here was a man more like those we would expect to attack outside, seeking the opportunity to find a victim. The streets in the sky were just that.

It was not just his knowledge of tower blocks but his confidence in moving around them, his awareness of what to expect where. He knew that he could kick open a door on the roof and get access to a secluded area from which no one would heed screams. He knew that the possibility of a lift opening at a floor with someone waiting there was very remote indeed. There is no indication in any of the statements that there was ever any doubt in his mind about the way of living in a tower block. His pressing of the lift buttons to go to the top floor and then confidently going up the further stairs were as much indications of his special characteristics as knowing what music he liked or whether he would prefer to read a book than go to a party. This personal level of knowledge goes beyond what could be gained from delivering milk or fixing the heating. It requires at least having lived within places very similar to those in which the attacks took place, probably as a youngster at the age when exploration would reveal their hidden secrets.

After the first offence he made no attempt to disguise himself; so he had no fear that he would be recognized locally. Here was a potentially very helpful paradox: deep familiarity with confidence in anonymity. He operated in a clearly defined area, bounded by main roads, when there were many other potential, similar targets nearby. The marauding pattern, moving out from a base into ever wider localities where the residents may be less alert, is a more common and indeed more understandable pattern. What does it mean when a person deliberately chooses not to do that, even though the targets and opportunities are so obviously there?

We concluded that it must mean that the terrain in which he chose to attack felt safe to him. It provided him with a security that any of the other obvious targets would not. From the aerial photographs and the descriptions of the localities given to us by police officers it was apparent that the target tower blocks were all separated from other tower blocks by major roads. A city that has no natural topographical landmarks such as parks or hills has to rely on man-made features to give it shape in the minds of its citizens. In such a city the roads take on a special significance. Just as the helicopter pilot used them to navigate because they were the main distinguishing features, so pedestrians are likely to have their mental maps shaped by these dominant features. When the police officers told us about the different areas of the city and the sorts of people who lived in each area, they used the roads as boundaries for defining the different domains. There is no reason to suppose that other people would not do the same.

There was at least one assault that happened some distance away from the main group of attacks. After there had been a number of attacks and a lot of public attention was focused on them, a mile or so away due south a different tower block was the scene. Here perhaps was an indication of the start of the marauding activity, although in later assaults he returned to the area of his initial attacks. But if this isolated incident was true to our theory, it indicated the direction *away* from where he lived. He must therefore live north of the main roads. The distance he travelled was also of interest because it suggested that he felt safe at that sort of distance. Perhaps we could also use it to estimate how far north he was living from the primary sites.

There were not many tower blocks similar to those in which he attacked at the appropriate distance, so our hypothesis revealed very few places in which he may have lived, or could still have been living. (Hence Rupert's confident identification of the most likely tower block.)

Beyond these important conclusions about the focus on the locality and the security the assailant felt, is the significance of his chosen victims. We could have followed a sort of Freudian interpretation, taking tower blocks as the most obvious of phallic symbols. The forcing of his victims to the top would have metaphorical significance, reflecting his lack of ejaculation during the assaults. (Such an explanation would not have got us any closer to working out where he lived.) So we could also have focused on the frailty of his victims, his curiosity about their genital area and the sexual exploration that characterized many of his attacks. These were important points, suggesting a man who did not have a lot of sexual experience and was unlikely to be married or have had a lasting relationship with a woman.

Here also was a very clear indication that the victim was a special type of object to him. 'I like women's bodies,' he said in a distant way, as if these bodies had little contact with the people who inhabited them. This awareness had a remarkable superficiality to it. He knew he could over-power them, but did not especially want them to be uncomfortable. He was curious about their scars. On one occasion when a victim said an ambulance was coming to take her for a regular hospital appointment he was at pains to say that she would make her appointment.

Here again, like the paradox of the locations, was a strange mixture that must hold a clue to his lifestyle. He was showing through his actions with the victims some-thing about his daily life. If only we could read the patterns of his actions we would understand a lot about him. The victims were objects to him, but not distant objects, ob-jects he was used to handling. Were these crimes his attempts to explore objects that he had seen only from afar, or had had passing contact with but which he wanted to get closer to? Was this the way he saw them? Did he have some regular contact with women in their seventies? Was that part of his world that he was showing to us in these attacks, possibly even a caring, supportive but distant contact?

From his first attack, though, he knew what he wanted to do. The exploration was determined and extensive. Most of the rapists we had looked at had some criminal history. Our matrix showed that the bizarre outdoor attackers were more likely to have previous convictions for sexual crimes than for other sorts of crime. These attacks in deserted streets in the sky indicated a prior sexually deviant, possibly criminal history.

Our report to the police developed these ideas:

In this series the use of aggression appears to have been no more than necessary to force the victims to comply. Some of the elderly victims were, within the bounds of their age and ability, quite resistant to the offender. In these instances there was ample opportunity for the offender to retaliate and cause some physical damage and yet he did not. He was probably non-profane in his language and in some cases conversed with the victim in a style which may be seen as indicating a need to relate in some way to her. Overt anger, then, in physical and verbalized form, appears to be absent in these attacks.

The sexual acts performed against the victim were mixed and although resulted in degradation of the victim the question to be answered is whether that was in fact the intent of the offender. Fellatio, vaginal manipulation and penetration are present in the various incidents. It is in the examination of sexual acts together with conversation that enables a hypothesis to be formed. In most cases where fellatio has been required, the conversation had been more reassuring to the victim; in two of the four cases some personal conversation is reported and in all cases conversation of some sexual content was reported. It may be that degradation therefore was not intended and the early anal interest were exploratory acts on the part of the offender. In either case anger is not noticeably present.

Examination of the offender's activities and physique can be extrapolated to a finding which has been noted in other cases. In the fourth and sixth attacks the offender picked up and carried the victim up flights of stairs to his selected scenes. Not an easy matter, particularly in the case of the victim who is described as of heavy build. Solitary sports interests have been noted in other sexually motivated offenders, body-building, swimming and the like as compensatory activities to reaffirm masculinity. Tattoos were noted in a similar vein but general experience suggests that in the event of a West Indian attacker these are unlikely. Together, the muscular interest, cleanliness, dress and description of hair style may be seen as significant. Coupled with the predominant selection of scene and victim the indications are possibly that the offender is obsessive. This would not be uncommon in people with sexual disturbances.

All victims who have reported the sight of the offender's exposed penis describe him as being fully erect. The sexual acts committed against the victim would appear to be directed at sexual gratification. However, no seminal discharge seems to have occurred. On one occasion the offender told the victim that he had a handkerchief, which would appear pointless unless it was an indication of his preparedness to ejaculate into it. It cannot be confirmed that this happened. Therefore it is probable that the offender suffers sexual dysfunction in his ability to ejaculate. This is not unusual in sexual offences.

In previous work connected with this research it had been noted that levels of forensic interference can indicate the experience and history of an offender. Used together with the development analyses the existence of such interference can be revealing as to the probability of an offender being 'in the system'.

This series had no indications of forensic awareness on the part of the attacker. There would appear to be no attempts to avoid fingerprint evidence being left at or near the scene, and generally no more than an average lay knowledge of such forensically important matters as fibre transference and the like.

Time patterns were revealed by a simple table containing details of day, date and time together with descriptive particulars of the offender. Those descriptions are drawn from the witness statements and show consistencies and patterns over time. The offender was predominantly a weekend attacker at the start of this series changing to weekdays at a time around May/June of 1987. The weekday incidents also occur at a different time of day and in the fifth incident coincide with a change of clothing. On three occasions, each on a Sunday afternoon, the offender has attacked whilst in possession of a sports bag. The consistently later time of day is associated with incidents closer to, and within, the area of the initial attacks.

Development over time was of interest too. Unfolding changes can indicate experience, history and other aspects of an offender's changing situation. Unlike Modus Operandi which seeks similar activities over a series, the assessment of development allows inferences to be drawn from a common view that humans learn from experience and mistakes.

In January 1986, in the first incident, the offender was described as being disguised by a scarf over his face. This action can possibly be seen as a means to avoid identification which is no more than any inexperienced offender might use. As the series continued the offender abandoned disguise and was more prepared for the victim to see him before as well as during the attack. Seen with the complete disregard for forensic matters, the indications are of an attacker whose level of experience is low at the start of the series, but develops both in confidence and approach.

Further evidence of development can be seen in the type of control exercised on the victim. Physical control of the victim was apparent in the first, second and fourth incidents wherein she was held but not gagged. The fourth incident however, resulted in the victim making considerable noise, screaming and kicking out at the attacker, who fled without pursuing any overt sexual attack.

The fifth incident some weeks later, was the first of a change in control where the victim was gagged by the offender's hand until he could subdue and remove her to the scene of the assault. By the sixth assault a weapon was being displayed and the knife was mentioned again in the seventh attack. The overt possession of a knife, particularly at an incident removed by some four miles from the starting area of the series, may be significant in that the offender felt less secure in that area and required additional means to reinforce his threat. It may also indicate more conscious planning, taking a knife with intent to attack. In the same incident, it appears that the offender fled as the result of the victim screaming despite the presence of the knife. This also may be indicative of the offender's desire not to harm the victim.

Other than the developments already discussed, there was little evidence to suggest that this offender had come to the fore as a viable suspect in the inquiry to March 1988. Although his details may be within the police record system, it is possible that he has not felt the threat of suspicion associated with an interview concerning these attacks.

The series considered commenced with the first four assaults committed in a particularly small area circumscribed by Wellington Road, Charlotte Road and Ryland Road. The main routes of Ladywood Middleway and Bristol Road formed the boundary to the north and east respectively.

This starting area is clearly defined as a group of six high-rise multi-occupancy dwellings. The attacked buildings are in the centre of the small group. Within the circle of high-rise dwellings are other multi-occupancy buildings and the area is surrounded by a mixture of housing. The estate probably has an identity which is recognized by both residents and non-residents.

Following the fourth incident, of October 1986, the first newspaper report appeared in the Birmingham *Evening Mail*. Later newspaper reports indicate a vigilante presence around the starting area. Should that presence have been instigated overtly after this attack, then either the activity of such a group, the police presence on inquiries, or the news story may be seen as likely to influence the offender to move further away from where he is comfortable.

The development of offender movements through a series of crimes also interlinks with what is happening to him, and around him, and therefore if discovery or detection avoidance is considered he will move offence locations to a place, and at a distance, in which he feels secure to carry out a further attack.

Seven months after the third attack, and following at least press and police activity, the next assault occurred approximately one mile north of the starting area. Six weeks or so later the fifth incident was committed approximately one mile south of the starting area on a direct north/south axis.

The last known offence was committed in March 1988 and the scene was close to the initial area of the attacks. A matter of a few hundred yards from the first four incidents. The return to that area is significant. The movement in and out of an area has been seen before in other cases, not least the case of the 'Yorkshire Ripper'.

The last incident also contained an action by the offender in the stripping of his victim which he is reported as having said was to facilitate escape. The possible significance of this is an indicator of the offender's insecurity in that location, which is possibly closer to his base, and where losing himself in the anonymity of a larger area is more difficult.

Further consideration of the neighbourhood of the attack in the light of information from local police officers makes it apparent that the offender attacks in areas where black youths are not unusual. For example, the fifth assault, although in an area described as being predominantly white, involved a victim who was approached by the offender in a 'confidence trick' to gain access to the building. She did not report anything unusual in a black youth seeking entry to that particular block.

The early abandonment of disguise and the subsequent attacks are indications that the offender attacks where he expects not to be recognized. He is likely therefore to travel into the identifiable areas of the various attacks rather than live in the same neighbourhood. Because of his knowledge of high-rise occupancy and the fact that he feels safe and confident to carry out the attacks in the upper levels, there are indications that he possibly originates from a similar identifiable area of high-rise dwellings.

Should the distances between the fourth and fifth,

and the fourth and sixth assaults be seen as those at which the offender feels safe to continue attacks away from the starting area, then the distance of approximately one mile may be significant. This possible 'safety distance' may be consistent also in the move to identifiable areas of similar socioeconomic content in future attacks.

It is very likely that he has committed attacks against the elderly before this series. The very strong Modus Operandi links in this series are present from the first incident. The possibility of previous 'acting out' attacks in slightly different circumstances is present.

He is unlikely to have had relationships with a peer age female. He is likely to have distorted sexual adjustment for his age. Also he possibly had dealings with elderly people in a non-offence context.

To those who know him he is possibly not thought of as capable of such attacks. Cleanliness, and hair style with consistent selection of offence venue may indicate obsessional personality, which is possibly reflected in a controlled individual with a low impulse lifestyle.

He possibly had employment after October 1986. Changes in Temporal patterns between incidents 4 and 5 together with the noticeable change of dress may indicate a move from schooling or institution to employment.

He possibly lives or has lived or has connections in similar high-rise property not within the first attack area but at a distance within approximately one mile from it.

The indications of a local base, together with the race and population factors would indicate the offender possibly lives, or is based in the areas listed below.

Highgate – Probable
Bell Barn Road – Possible
Calthorpe Park – Low probability
Lee Bank area – Very low probability

This report was taken very seriously by the police. Intensive investigation had so far not met with any success and senior officers were looking for ways to encourage renewed interest among their colleagues. Investigating officers felt that the report could stimulate further attention to the crimes, not only because of its novelty but because it did provide a clear list of factors that could be used to eliminate suspects in the search for the rapist. It was now possible to add to the descriptions from victims of what the rapist looked like, his possible domestic circumstances and lifestyle, an indication of his previous criminal history and the area of the city in which he might live. The profile had been seen to reveal a person who was used to being with older women. Perhaps of even more significance to police officers was the realization that the victims were objects of almost conventional sexual desire. Their age was an aspect of their vulnerability and accessibility, not something that was particularly significant in creating sexual arousal.

Of particular importance was the suggestion in the profile that the offender had a previous conviction for a minor sexual assault. This should mean that there were police officers somewhere in the West Midlands who actually knew the culprit and would be able to recognize him from the profile. Yet inquiries in this direction had not produced any suspects who could possibly have committed all the rapes.

A summary of the key points of the profile was published in *Midlands Crime Informations*, a localized *Police Gazette*, made available to all police forces in the Midlands area. Officers were asked to consider the profile and make suggestions as to the possible identity of the rapist. Many suggestions were submitted, but painstaking inquiries led to all of them being eliminated. A further trawl was carried out by asking the Intelligence Officer assigned to each West Midlands police station to speak to each serving officer at the station about the profile to see if this more personal contact could produce suggestions. Again, a number of suggestions were received by the investigating team, but ultimately all were eliminated from the inquiry.

Detective Superintendent Frank Rawlings had not been directly involved in the inquiry, but he was the senior officer on duty with overall responsibility for criminal detection when, one otherwise quiet Saturday morning, a report reached him of a sexual assault in a tower block. An elderly woman had been carried to the top of a tower block and sexually assaulted. The assault bore the unmistakable signature of the 'Tower Block Rapist'. This brought the total to at least eight attacks. Even though many of his victims were disturbed and confused, they had given very similar descriptions of the offender. Rawlings shared with other police officers the fear that these attacks would continue and that future victims could die whether from the violence of the assault or the shock of it.

Rawlings was at his desk in the CID headquarters of the West Midlands police at Lloyds House in the centre of Birmingham, some distance from the scene of the offences and the incident room. But he did have on his desk the profile that had been circulated in the *Midland Crime Informations*. So he consulted that, trying to get some further understanding of the offender and possible lines of inquiry.

Rawlings was struck by the possibility of the offender having a conviction for a minor sexual offence. He therefore started to search the centralized criminal records held in the Central Information Unit in Lloyds House, for offenders who might fall into the appropriate categories. Early in the alphabet he came to Adrian Babb, who had been convicted for attempting to put his hand between the legs of a woman in the Central Birmingham Library. Although this offence was classified as an attempted indecent assault, it would not be regarded by most police officers as a precursor to violent rape, yet it did fit the sort of offence indicated in the profile, so Rawlings called for the actual case papers. He saw that the offence in the library had been committed against a sixty-year-old woman. Further, the twenty-year-old Babb lived in the Highgate area of Birmingham, that area specified in the profile as being the most probable residential location.

One point noted in the report to the police was the lack of 'forensic awareness', a term used to capture the difference between a villain who seemed to take account of police investigative procedures, who was aware of what forensic examination could reveal, and one who took no care over these matters. It had been predicted that he was so unaware of forensic possibilities, or paid so little heed to them, that he would eventually leave a trace. The most recent offence had left a fingerprint on the stairs, so it was not a major task to link the new fingerprint to the records of Adrian Babb. The link was incontrovertible and arrest followed shortly.

Once aware of the evidence against him, Babb cooperated with his police interviewers and, as became apparent in court, he spent a number of days responding fully to close questioning by police officers. These officers found our profile helpful as a benchmark to help them to test the logic and psychological validity of what Babb told them. His answers also helped us to test further the hypotheses we had formulated about his actions and what had guided them.

He said that he could not recall committing similar offences in any place other than in a block of flats, admitting quite clearly that he preferred to carry them out in blocks of flats because it was quiet. He was also quite open about the fact that he had never carried out a similar attack in or near his own tower block because of the large number of people who knew him, and because there were few elderly people in that area.

Seeing these direct answers, so obvious with hindsight, illuminates what a strange scientific quest we are engaged in. The bird's-eye view, seen from the helicopter, emphasized the focused and particular nature of these crimes, enabling us to formulate a strong hypothesis about what was giving shape to the culprit's actions. Looking on his actions from such a psychological distance we had to form a specific view of what was guiding events. There was no way of knowing if the offender himself was aware of what was shaping his actions, or even if he realized his actions had a shape to them. To find such direct confirmation of hypotheses in the answers a suspect gives a police officer, neither of whom knows of these hypotheses, is to my mind one of the purest forms of scientific discovery.

The answers Babb gave to his police interviewers also revealed a strange lack of personal involvement in the offences. He gave an explanation for them that appears almost trivial against the background of the terror and trauma that he caused.

The police asked him on a number of occasions throughout the days of interview what had made him carry out the assaults. He gave two different answers that were never linked by the interviewers or their connections explored. His earliest answer was, 'I think it was more of a confusion than anything else after losing the girl that I was with.' This referred to a married woman whom he claimed to have been seeing for five or six months, but who had left him for another extra-marital relationship. He also claimed that he had had another girlfriend for about four months before that. In police interviews both these women denied any close relationship or sexual activity with Babb. But whether they perceived a close relationship or not, Babb felt that he had been slighted and saw this as one reason for his attacks on elderly women.

Later in the interviews, when asked why he chose old women to attack he replied, 'Their age', saying he didn't know why their age made them targets other than 'maybe vulnerability', but he also indicated that it was possibly a sort of retaliation for 'getting done for the one in the library, could be sort of like revenge, don't know'. He was adamant that he had never assaulted young women and also that he never took much notice of the women he did attack. Indeed he simply described his victims as 'elderly', claiming he was 'no good with ages at all'.

During the detailed examination of the sexual events the police needed to establish if he admitted to rape, defined as vaginal penetration, or to an assault that the law regards as a less serious crime in which no penetration of the vagina takes place. This close examination revealed physiological characteristics that also add to our understanding of Babb's assaults. His response to questions about vaginal penetration elicited the response: 'No, can't remember it, but on occasions I've had sex with women before . . . I haven't really felt like, that it's penetrated. I know like it's there, like 'cos you can tell from the way the girls react but I couldn't feel anything.' He had no memory of ever ejaculating.

An only child, he was friendly with a nearby family of four sisters and had systematically collected their underwear for some time, although his collecting had stopped a little before he started the tower block assaults. The police found this collection neatly labelled with the owners' names, in piles at his house. He had a job as a swimming-pool attendant. The friends he remembered from the pool were young girls, nine- and ten-year-olds, not close adult male or female friends.

The pattern taking shape here fills in the details of the outline we had seen from the crimes themselves. But the reason why our research was necessary became more clear to me when I learned how the police officers were trying to make sense of Babb and his crimes.

'You see what puzzles me, Adrian, is that all I've seen of you you're prepared to be a perfectly pleasant intelligent man, that's the impression you've given me and I am quite keen to know what changes a perfectly pleasant, decent man into the sort of man who can do these things that you've done?'
(Pause)
'I honestly don't know.'

Of course he didn't know. If he had he would possibly not have continued doing it. By his own admission he stopped in the middle of some assaults and ran away because 'I thought no, forget it. Shouldn't be doing this then I just ran off . . . it's sort of like your brain sort of like saying shouldn't have done it, shouldn't have done it, sort of like wipe it from your mind.' He found it embarrassing and awkward to talk about these incidents. He said he was very shy and he would not be able to go to a nightclub or talk to women there.

The defence lawyer and the judge, at the close of the trial, debated whether or not Babb was in fact mentally ill. The report to the court from a forensic psychiatrist, Dr Bluglass, was unequivocal. In his interview with Adrian Babb, Dr Bluglass 'found no evidence at all of serious mental illness of any kind or disturbance of mental function'. The judge was clearly puzzled by this and checked that Dr Bluglass knew that Babb 'was stealing women's underclothes and attaching labels to them', which of course the psychiatrist did know. A curious debate then ensued in court in which legal precedents were considered for accepting that a man was sane who had committed such a series of strange, vicious crimes. The purpose of this debate was to establish if Babb should get a determinate, fixed-term sentence or be given an indeterminate sentence conditional on his improving under treatment. In effect, by assigning narrow bounds to the definition of sanity the defence sees it in their client's interest to get a fixed term of imprisonment. Such incarceration has little likelihood of any treatment or help to change whatever is at the root of his offending. An indeterminate sentence would be served in a secure hospital dedicated to attempting to help offenders.

On 20 December 1989 Babb was in court, charged with three rapes, taking into account another four, although the police said he had admitted to eleven. The judge in court, sentencing Babb to sixteen years' imprisonment, had said how remarkably accurate had been the profile we had prepared for the police prior to Babb's arrest. In fact, when the police charged Babb because of fingerprint evidence, they called us and said, 'Your report was so accurate we thought you had his name and address but were keeping it from us!'

Our report indicated the area in which Babb lived to one of four tower blocks. It suggested that he was used to being with elderly women and also that he was active in sports. His involvement as a swimming pool attendant, looking after sessions for the elderly, was a remarkable combination of these two predictions. The general description of the offender, his age and cleanliness, also turned out to have been of particular value to the police investigation.

Probably the most significant contribution was to suggest that he had had a previous conviction for a similar offence.

This was our fourth report on an investigation, having been completed eighteen months earlier on 27 June 1988. It was probably more detailed and accurate than the report that led to the arrest of Duffy. It was beginning to seem that criminal behaviour was penetrable. The distorted silhouette that is produced in a report could be matched, under the right circumstances, to one suspect.

With hindsight, there are some fascinating pointers in this report that we all completely missed. Why carry a sports bag with you when you go off to rape old ladies if you are not en route to, or from, a sporting activity? In either case you are likely to be near familiar territory. The sports bag was seen only on Sunday afternoons, the great British time for amateur sport. It turned out that Babb was on his way back from a football game, probably games that he had lost. (A Dutch serial rapist was a track athlete who attacked near the venue of his meetings, again usually attacking when he lost.) But perhaps the central point was that in the complexity of any investigation it is easy for the police to miss details. The police officers who had arrested Babb for his first assault in the library had never been shown our profile. He was in the records as we had predicted, but they missed him.

Babb contrasted with Duffy. Babb commuted a short distance into a particular area to find a very distinct type of victim. His narrow focus of action broadened my understanding of the variations between violent criminals. The tower block investigation in Birmingham taught me to beware of general rules of offender behaviour, to look cautiously at any geographical distribution of linked crimes. When Babb was arrested and I learned of his confessions, I became more confident that psychological principles and methods could contribute to many different sorts of police investigations, but I also saw more plainly the importance of understanding the significance of the variations in offenders' actions. It was not enough to recognize their shadows, we also had to make sense of them.

Chapter Seven

DISTINGUISHING ACTIONS

John Duffy had taught us that no matter how murky a shadow is cast by a violent offender, it is open to interpretation. It should therefore be possible to establish some general principles for offender profiling; a science could grow even in this dark and confusing area. Studies of the geographical patterns of persistent offenders had added weight to the argument that there were patterns to be found, if only we knew where to look. Even cases as old and overlaid with conjecture as the Whitechapel murders might be susceptible to behavioural analysis. Adrian Babb took us deeper into the examination of exactly what rapists and killers do, and where they do it. He showed us that the choice of locations and victims could reveal the inner world of the criminal even more surely than his own confessions.

Any confidence that these successes provided, however, soon evaporated with the realization that many different criminals act in remarkably similar ways. Disentangling crimes when behaviour is the only thing to go on can prove extremely problematic. This was brought home to us in the latter half of 1988 when a series of rapes of students in the Midlands threatened the whole lifestyle of a city that contains a large number of students.

These cases emphasized that a crucial part of reading the shadows a criminal casts is to be able to recognize which are his shadows and which are those of another, possibly similar offender. Making such a discrimination is often much more difficult than might be expected.

The task of linking crimes, as the police call it, is enormously important to their investigations in general. By tying a criminal to a number of crimes, more information becomes available about his actions. In addition, a significant management decision then has to be made as to whether or not to treat the investigation as one major, interconnected inquiry. That inquiry then becomes a magnet for resources, but also for attention from senior officers and the media. Careers are made or destroyed from effective involvement in a major inquiry. So the decision to link crimes is not taken lightly. Hard forensic information is the preferred basis for setting up an investigation of a series; this could be a shoe-print common to all the crimes, or detailed blood-typing showing the same blood-type at different scenes. These days DNA 'fingerprinting' is the ideal, but old-fashioned digital fingerprinting will do nicely too.

Specific linking information is often missing. Crimes may have been committed in different police divisions, so that details are not brought together, or are distorted by slight differences in the methods of collecting or recording them. The actions of the victims, or of other witnesses, may have been so different in each offence that it is difficult to tell if the same person was involved in each. Some witnesses may be very clear, others confused, making it difficult to establish if it is the witnesses who are different or the villains. DNA tests can also take months to come through, increasing the risk of more crimes and an escalation of violence before the criminal is captured. He may even escape completely. There are therefore many situations in which more general aspects of the offences are reluctantly used as a basis for linking them. These, typically, include descriptions given by victims (for example, a scar or a gold tooth), or very particular aspects of behaviour, the *modus operandi* (for instance, entering premises by removing slats from louvred windows).

The decision as to whether or not a number of crimes have been committed by one offender, and therefore deserve a special inquiry, is typically made by senior officers reading through the statements made by victims and witnesses, together with reports from forensic laboratories and the investigating officers. No statistical or probability analysis is brought to bear, except as it might apply to blood-typing or DNA. It is the considered opinion of senior officers that is paramount. The differences in these opinions can be gauged by the Canadian police statement quoted earlier that behaviour is a better indicator of similarity than descriptions given by witnesses of the physical appearance of the offender. This view would surprise many British police officers; but then they are also surprised by the well-established finding from the study of eye-witnesses which shows that a person's confidence in his or her testimony does not relate at all closely to how valid or accurate that testimony is.

When the details on which the senior officers are basing their decision are direct and clear, then there is little difficulty in deciding to set a major inquiry in motion. Yet often the actions of a criminal and the descriptions given by victims and witnesses appear to be so general that it is difficult for the police to tell whether there are several criminals at work in a similar way or one person committing many crimes.

It may be thought that a careful examination of the actions in the crimes, together with some general psychological principles about types of offenders, will reveal the distinctions. But even setting aside the rush and tension of a major investigation, this detailed consideration is not so easy for police officers, as we discovered when we carried out an experiment.

The experiment was run by Margaret Wilson, a colleague who had worked with me for a number of years on various applied psychology projects. She was assisted by Lynne Martin, a postgraduate research student for whom this type of applied research 'in the field' was still quite novel.

Five detectives were given summaries of statements made by twelve rape victims. These statements had been doctored so that any obvious links between the offences, such as descriptions of the rapist or the location, had been removed; all that remained were accounts of what the offender did and said – his behaviour. The police officers were asked to work out between them which of the offences had been committed by the same man. The information they were given was not at all unlike the material that would be available during an investigation, being drawn directly from existing police records. The task was certainly one that would be part of any major inquiry into a series of rapes.

However, this was a stressful situation for the police officers because it was the first contact they had had with psychologists and they felt that the two women were watching their every move. Despite Margaret and Lynne's protestations, and promises of confidentiality, they suspected a hidden test. Within the police force, accounts of most events find their way, eventually, to senior officers.

Margaret and Lynne were genuinely interested in how police officers would normally make such decisions, because they wanted to assess how computers could improve their effectiveness. The detectives, however, felt that they had to demonstrate their psychological sophistication. They were therefore relieved when one of their number, 'Paul', professed to knowing all about rape.

'Yes, I read a book on it. There's different types, you see. One lot's sadistic. They don't give a damn about the victim so they'll hang around after and may rape her a second time. All we got to do is find out which are the sadistic ones and that'll be the same villain. Then another lot is sexual rapists. They're perverts. They ask the victim sexual questions. They want her to talk. You often find dirty mags at their house. Another type is the angry rapist who has a grudge against women. They're getting their own back on women by degrading them and taking out their aggression. They often have a domineering mother.'

Another detective, wanting to give his support to the expert in their midst, said, 'Yes, his mother was probably a prostitute.'

Paul, encouraged, continued: 'One other type is the psychopath criminal. He's just a little toe-rag and so doesn't see rape as a crime. He doesn't really have a motive to rape but some other crime like house-breaking.'

Armed with this authoritative review, the detectives examined the statements closely. In one assault the offender had asked his victim if she was enjoying it. This was seen as a clear indication that the offender was trying to seek revenge and so must be the same criminal who viciously hit his victim when she would not cooperate. In a different attack, money was demanded. This was seen as the psychopath criminal who must also have done the crime in which the victim was beaten around the face and told not to tell anyone or 'he'd be back'; clearly a criminal worried about being caught.

Through such analysis the detectives eventually came up with four groups of offences. Margaret and Lynne studied these carefully. They found that every group contained a mixture of actual criminals; if they had been assigned randomly to the groups there could not have been more errors. The ideas that Paul had convinced the group were so relevant had completely misled them. This group had been less accurate than other groups of police officers who went on simple police experience, dealing with direct overt similarities without attempting to interpret them.

Margaret and Lynne's experiments illustrate only too well the special problems of most applications of psychology, showing how these problems are magnified when dealing with criminal behaviour without any other forensic back-up. The raw material of psychology is lying around everywhere to be picked up and fashioned at will. Human actions and experience are not restricted to the clinical realms, the laboratory or the consulting room. In crimes especially, where the culprit is not available for close examination, the material available is there for interpretation by anyone who is allowed to see it. Unlike the chemist or physicist who works with specially prepared materials and ponders on patterns that can be seen only with special apparatus, the student of human behaviour appears to have access to the same material as the non-specialist. So Paul felt confident in commenting on the actions recorded in a rape as if he were a trained psychologist.

Paul's confidence was brought about by the fact that he could relate the material directly to the book he had read. He would insist that we all know what violence is, or an act of theft. So when the witness statements recorded actions similar to those mentioned in the book, he felt on firm ground. He was also happy to pontificate because the book used words and ideas that have a common currency, such as sadist, pervert and psychopath. Paul did not realize that these words may have been refashioned to do a particular job. He took some ideas, which may have been more or less clearly presented to him, and absorbed them directly into his own experience without considering that they too might have limitations. He probably expected his obvious expertise to win the day.

'If you and me had got together, and ignored Paul here, we could have done quite well,' one detective said to his colleague with amused satisfaction.

Paul was not so amused. 'It can't be done with the little information you gave us. Have any other police officers been able to sort it out?'

Margaret tried to allay his anger without making matters worse. 'We've carried out exactly the same exercise in three other forces so far. In some cases the detectives doing it did get most of it right, but,' she continued quickly, seeing that this had not satisfied Paul at all, 'there are always some errors. That's why we are trying to develop a computerized system that would support police decision-making.'

Paul would not be mollified. How could a young woman really know more about the links between rapes than he did with all his years of detective experience? If he admitted that she did know better without any of his training or background, surely that would undervalue his own hard-won credibility. It is more comfortable to be convinced that some trick-cyclist sleight-of-hand had been performed to try and make a fool of him. The expert always poses a threat to local knowledge. Why bother with all this university stuff, when there are experienced officers doing a good job under trying circumstances?

Some senior police officers are fond of saying that they don't need computers or science to help them find the culprit. They will refer to their criminal intelligence officer and say, 'My guy can do it fine by the seat of his pants.' It takes a rather full understanding of how scientific psychology can make a contribution to see that it can go beyond an individual's experience and even beyond the collective expertise that the police believe they have.

Contact with forensic scientists has tended to confuse the issue. Give forensic experts a shoe-print and a shoe and they will be able to say within a known range of certainty whether the shoe is likely to have produced the print. The forensic service has therefore evolved to provide evidence to be used in court to challenge or support the case against the accused. It is not part of the forensic scientist's remit to say what sort of people buy shoes that leave that sort of print. Even such elementary relationships as that between shoe size and height are rarely offered by forensic scientists. It is the detective's job to find the culprit. The forensic scientist is then looked to by detectives to help prove in court that they indeed have the culprit.

A curious imbalance exists in this relationship between police and scientists. It is reflected in the difference between an incident room and a forensic laboratory. An incident room is usually an office that has clearly seen better days which has now had extra desks pushed into it. The walls are covered with boards containing names of duty officers, lists of crimes and actions to be carried out. There is paper everywhere and the only books are likely to be a dictionary and the police almanac. Here is an office where men of action, in their brown and grey suits and highly-polished shoes, make contact to get instructions for their next action and write accounts for their superiors of the actions they have already taken.

A forensic laboratory, on the other hand, is filled with equipment. White, formica-topped tables have low-slung fluorescent lights over them. Microscopes of many sizes and shapes, centrifuges and fume cupboards abound. Here many of the staff are women in white coats studiously looking at the objects brought to them by the police. Most of the scientists will have university degrees, many to postgraduate level. The police officers have mostly left school at the earliest opportunity and have little or no formal training in science.

The detective wants something that will help him identify the culprit that he can take to court. The scientist is concerned that her credentials as a professional are not sullied. Out of this emerges the language of caution that is · so characteristic of reports from forensic laboratories to the police. The favourite of detective stories, 'the blunt object', is a product of the forensic scientist being unwilling to go further than the generality that 'the wound is consistent with a blunt object being applied with enough force to fracture the skull'. Detectives become confident translators of these terms: 'It means she was probably hit over the head with the bit of pipe we found in the back yard.' In many cases, though, the forensic scientist's caution leaves the police investigation with no direct lines to follow, only the possibility of establishing a link to the culprit once a suspect has been found by other means.

Guidance from behavioural science, then, indicating ways of thinking about the criminal, or characteristics that may distinguish him from other possible suspects, has a rather different feel to it. The subtle nuances that are relevant to the examination of the actions that take place in a crime put even more demands on effective contact between the police and psychologists than in other areas of expert help. Each party to this dialogue has much to learn from the other. The Midlands student rapes investigation provided a good example of this.

In the early summer of 1988 a number of indecent assaults and full rapes had become known to the local police officers. These had all occurred in the same area, south of the city centre, not far from the university. It is an area of bed-sits, big Victorian houses divided into one-room apartments, mainly lived in by young men and women, many of them students. Scattered among these houses, which were built a century and a half ago for the merchants of the city who had made it rich, are multi-storey blocks of council housing creating a mixed and anonymous conglomeration of rented accommodation.

The city has over 25,000 students, a mobile population with little focus or coherence.

Each of the rapes had been followed up separately but none of the inquiries had got anywhere. This was a crime-prone part of the city and police officers and computers were already over-committed. If these other crimes, such as murder, drug-dealing and theft, were not considered more important by many police officers, then they were probably considered easier to investigate and more likely to lead to a conviction. (This would *not* be a significant criterion used when deciding to set up a *major* investigation.)

However, the city is fortunate in having an effective sexual assault referral service. It had been set up three years earlier in response to concerns that rape victims were not being helped adequately. It is partly supported by the police while being completely independent, and it is committed to the rights of rape survivors 'to a collaborative service provided by medical personnel, counsellors and investigators and a right to choose any or all of these services'. Women can approach the centre directly even if they do not wish to make a report to the police. Victims are encouraged to report to the police and are offered help and support in coping with what that might entail. From the point of view of investigators, the existence of the assault referral centre is a distinct advantage in that most sexual assaults in the area do eventually come to police attention. In the late spring of 1988 some of the staff of the centre were already convinced that a serial rapist was at large in the city. By late summer of 1988 the police knew that nine assaults had been committed by black assailants in the same area of the city. All the attacks had been indoors, the victims being young women whom the police described as 'living and sleeping alone'.

In some areas of the city virtually every house has

students living in it, and most young women living alone would be students. This density of students caused some confusion in the early days of the investigation because all the victims were found to be students. This led some police officers to assume that the offender was deliberately setting out to attack students. It is necessary to have some knowledge of how chance and probability operate to realize that even a random selection of houses in this area of the city could produce young women who are all students. Adrian Babb attacked in an area where he would find elderly women. He increased the probability of finding the type of victim he wanted by the area he went to. But he attacked in a very restricted area and the age of his victims was a very obvious common characteristic. Being a student is not so obvious and the area over which the attacks took place was much more widespread. It was therefore more likely that the offender was seeking out single women rather than especially looking for known students.

Some officers suspected that this was a series committed by one man, but there was no solid forensic evidence to link the crimes, only the type of victim, the time period, the area and the general description of the offender given by the victims. None of these circumstantial details would stand up in court, so detectives do not give them much weight. Furthermore, the resources needed to set up a special incident room were not easily available. With the end of the academic year, many of the people most able to help the police were dispersing, making an intensive inquiry very difficult. Indeed, the criminal might have moved away with the students and taken his awkward problem with him.

In October, with the return of students for the new academic year, one more similar attack took place.

Reading closely through the victims' accounts of the ten assaults, the police officers were taken with the consistency with which the offender asked the victim to take his penis and help him to penetrate her. They found it curiously distinct that he should need this assistance. This characteristic behaviour seems to have tipped the balance in convincing senior officers that one man was responsible for all the crimes. It may have played some part in the resulting major investigation being given the operational name of 'Support'. (Some officers claimed the title was chosen 'to encourage a friendly and hopefully cooperative response' from individuals 'invited' to supply samples. A film crew was later coyly told that it was in recognition of the help given by the sexual assault referral service.)

Once the police admitted that they were treating the crimes as a series committed by one man, there was outrage among the students. It became apparent that these ten crimes covered a period of eighteen months in which it seemed that police activity had been rather uncoordinated. Yet the consequences for women students were enormous. Special buses were introduced for them, rape alarms were distributed, and patterns of social activity greatly constrained. As the local paper put it: 'Students are angered both by the multiple rapist's threat to their security, constricting their lifestyles, and by the slowness of police to admit his presence.' Each rape had received media coverage when it happened. The reaction was against the police's delay in realizing that one person may have been responsible for so many assaults.

In their defence the police are quoted as saying that 'it was not until July that they were convinced by scientific tests that one individual was responsible for all ten attacks'. In fact, as the court proceedings later made clear, it was not until October that the DNA results became available linking the fourth and the ninth offence in the series. The 'scientific tests' quoted were little more than police experience and intuition, but the pressures on the police to make some morale-boosting statements were very great indeed. They therefore announced to the press that they had enlisted my help 'to evaluate every detail of the attacks and compile a profile of the wanted man's lifestyle and environment'.

At this stage the police were confident that their offender was a local man who was deliberately choosing to attack particular students. They therefore interviewed all the victims again, in great detail, trying to establish some common connections between them. Did they have newspapers delivered by the same boy or drink in the same pubs? But no common factors could be found, except the obvious ones which by now had been rather buried in the plethora of detail. Indeed, a chart summarizing the offences had been completed and covered a great length of wall in the incident room.

Detectives were also impressed that the victims were unaware of their attacker until he was beside them in bed, having already put his hand over their mouths. Police saw this as an indication that he was an expert burglar, so then they had to decide whether he was 'a seasoned criminal or a sex fiend'. They trawled all black males who had criminal records, giving priority to those who had been convicted of rape – even men who were now fifty years old, despite the description by victims of a much younger man – and also looking closely at men with convictions for other sexual offences and aggressive crimes. They eliminated people who were in prison at the time of the attacks or who had a blood group different from that found at the fourth and eighth crimes in the series. None of the DNA tests on 360 suspects examined accorded with the samples taken from these two offences.

It looked as if a more considered behavioural analysis would be helpful. By analysing over sixty solved rapes we had found that the actions of any villain could be broken down into discrete components with some confidence. Examination of which of these pieces of behaviour usually occurred in the same crime, such as using a knife *as well as* blindfolding, had also given us some idea of the shape, or 'structure' as I like to call it, of the actions. This helped to add weight to some obvious points. For example, no one in our sample of solved rapes who was insulting and extremely verbally aggressive to his victim also complimented the victim, say, on her good looks. Such, curiously inappropriate, admiration was typical of less physically vicious assaults. But other actions are less obviously distinct or tied together. Published studies based in the main on interviews with assailants long after the fact do not really allow detailed examination of the actual crimes to be made, but to sort out offence behaviour we do have to get down to the fine detail of actions in offences.

Most of what happens in a sexual assault is not penile penetration per vaginum, although this is the activity on which police interviews focus in order to establish if it is a rape or, as the law sees it, merely a sexual assault. Legal considerations also give emphasis to anything that would indicate consent or lack of it. But much, much more happens in an assault that is relevant to understanding the offence and the offender. The sexual activity itself may be very varied. Premature or very delayed ejaculation, and a variety of other forms of sexual dysfunction are common, as is fellatio. Cunnilingus is not rare either, or buggery. Any or all of these can be perpetrated on the victim in a variety of sequences and a number of times. Like the police in the Midlands, I had assumed from very early on in our research that some aspects of the criminal's sexual actions could be very readily taken as his trademark and would not only be helpful in indicating links between crimes but could also point us to characteristics of the criminal of use to detectives.

I had supposed that if some of the central aspects of the offender's sexual actions were closely examined, then that would be helpful in indicating whether the crimes had been committed by the same or different offenders. Consider the following critical points taken from the statements of the victims of the ten offences committed in the same general area of the Midlands. The victims had all given similar descriptions of the offenders. Were they all committed by the same offender? If not, how would you distinguish between the offences?

He said to the first victim: 'I'm not going to fuck you.'
To the second victim: 'Get hold of me, hold it, put it in.'
Third: 'Put this in your mouth.'
Fourth: 'You do it, you'll have to put it in.'
Fifth: 'Put it inside you' . . . 'Put it back.'
Sixth: 'I just want to feel you.'
Seventh: 'Put it in.'
Eighth: 'Put this in.'
Ninth: 'You put it in.'
Tenth: '. . . it fell out. He said, "You put it in. Put it in."'

Here the assistance required by the offender distinguishes the second, third, fourth, fifth, seventh, ninth and tenth crimes from those other crimes in which no penetration occurred. In the sixth offence the criminal was disturbed and left in a hurry. It might be reasonable to assume that the first offence was an exploration and therefore no penetration was intended. This would lead to the conclusion that this offender's sexual style required the victim to assist him with vaginal penetration. If that was so, then what might be concluded about the characteristics of a persistent rapist who consistently sought such help?

Before developing an intensive psychoanalysis of this intriguing behaviour, there are a number of cautions worth noting. For example, we need to know how common such a request is among rapists. As curious as it may seem, it may not be a distinguishing characteristic at all. Indeed, without a full survey of a large number of rapes which indicates the frequency of different actions we do not know if this seemingly curious act is typical of a whole class of rapists. Neither the publications of clinicians nor of FBI agents help us to know how common this is. Furthermore, it may be common in consenting sexual relationships. Readers will know whether such a request has had any place in their own sexual experience, but even the most thorough and intrusive scientific studies have not noted these figures.

Detailed examination of the victims' accounts also reveals some subtleties in even this most specific of requests. In the second, fifth and tenth attacks the assailant's demand for assistance is reported to have occurred as a consequence of his erectile insufficiency making penetration difficult for him. In the third the demand is to put his penis into the victim's mouth; an action that is common in the sexual assaults on which we have the details. The vagaries of statement-taking mean that it is never possible to be absolutely sure that if an action is not mentioned then it did not occur. The question is at least raised as to whether these differences in the exact context of the rapist's request carry any significance.

The request for assistance dealt with only one of the very many actions that constituted the offence. Consideration of another set of aspects, such as the mode of early control of the victim, could lead to different ways of thinking about the offences. After all, first contact with the victim, before she has a chance to react, could be taken as the offender revealing his own 'pure' behaviour unmodified by

the reactions of the other party to the transactions and so
be seen as most essentially charateristic of him.

These are the victims' reports of those very first moments of frightening contact.

First Victim: 'I don't know what woke me, I think it was
the man's presence and thinking someone
was touching me. I wasn't sure what. I was
so frightened. He put his hand over my eyes
and mouth.'

Second: 'I saw the figure of a man dressed all in black
which filled the crack in the door. I realized at
that point that he'd also seen me and then he
flung the bedroom door open. He walked into
the bedroom holding a knife at his shoulder
level.'

Third: 'I turned towards the door and saw a male
coming towards me.'

Fourth: 'I remember waking up and realizing that
there was something cold on my neck. Then I
heard a man's voice say "Don't scream. I've
got a knife and I'll use it".'

Fifth: 'I turned over on to my back from my stomach
and saw the man by my bed. He began to climb
on to my bed. I started to scream and noticed
he was holding a knife in his right hand.'

Sixth: 'I felt something touch my shoulder and I
woke up. I then saw a man crouched down on
my right side. I heard him say "I'm a burglar,
I've got a knife".'

Seventh: 'I felt a hand being placed over my mouth. Initially I thought it was somebody playing a
joke, but when the person said "Shut up" in a
menacing manner I realized it wasn't a joke.'

Eighth: 'I rolled over and saw a man with a knife

coming close to my bed.'

Ninth: 'As I was halfway to standing up I suddenly saw a man standing on the stairs. I was so shocked at seeing the man and immediately started to scream. The man began to come towards me. He said, "Shut up".'

Tenth: 'I became aware of something over my face surrounding my face all over, it was rough on my face and of a voice muttering. I must have said what's up or something. The voice said, "Shut up".'

Apparently, in every case the victim was asleep when the assailant entered her house. Is there any significance in the fact that on some occasions he was close by her side before she woke up, ready to control her, whereas in others she was already awake before he came near? What about the knife and the readiness or otherwise with which he revealed it? What about his instruction to her to 'shut up'?

This detailed scrutiny of the criminal's action serves to illustrate two central points. The first is that there is a great deal of potentially very important detail here. It is unlikely that any detective can recall all the details of exactly what happened in every case without confusion. Most police officers are therefore likely to remember details that are salient to them and build up simplified pictures in their mind of each incident for discussion and comparison. The second point is that attention to different details will lead to different views of whether the offences are the work of one man or more than one. If we rely on details of the sexual act we may conclude that it is one person. Yet if we take account of whether he wakes the victim or waits for her to awaken we may come to the conclusion that more than one assailant is involved in the series of different offences.

The complexity of deciding, purely on behavioural

information, whether there is more than one offender in a series goes even further. There are quite natural and understandable processes that would lead to changes in the offender's actions. I have already indicated differences that may be due to the victim's response. If she fights back immediately or someone comes to her assistance, or if she has taken sleeping pills, then the assailant may react differently in response. Often those police officers who do not consider the interaction between two people that is the essence of violent assaults look for consistency in a criminal's actions quite independently of what the victim does, hoping to treat actions as a form of rigid *modus operandi* or specific clue.

The setting carries broader implications too. An attacker in a large house where no one is present except the victim may feel no need to keep the victim quiet or to move her to a more secluded location where he can assault her. If he attacks outdoors, though, these might be just the considerations that are uppermost in his mind because of fear of being disturbed. The fascinating question that follows is whether criminals ever deliberately choose to attack in one location or the other, possibly because of what those locations imply for control of the victim, and the risk of being caught. If so, then the choice of location itself may reveal something about the offender and his background, as it did for the 'Tower Block Rapist', Adrian Babb.

One unexpected consistency that we found early on in our examination of serial rapists made us optimistic that there were interpretable patterns, if only we knew how to look for them. The great majority of such criminals were surprisingly consistent in the venue they would choose to carry out their assault. Only a small minority would attack indoors as well as outdoors; they tended to stick to one sort of venue or the other. Early explorations also suggested that the outdoor attackers were much less experienced as criminals, more impulsive and bizarre. The reasons for this are not clear but appear to relate to the planning and forethought that goes into breaking into a house, compared with the more overtly impulsive quality of an outdoor assault.

Natural variations in the offender's action may also be expected to occur for reasons of learning or development as they so obviously did for John Duffy. Many other examples abound. For example, one man attacked a woman who screamed and fought him off. The next time, his first action was to control the woman with a knife, then he gagged her. Here he showed a direct change because of what he had learned from his previous crime. In another example a burglar was surprised by a woman who shouted, 'Don't rape me.' The next house he broke into, rape was the main thing on his mind. Violent criminals have also been found to learn other, more subtle lessons from their victims. One, for example, was told by his first victim that she would swear on her mother's life not to report him. In a later assault he demanded that the victim should 'swear on her mother's life' not to call the police.

Changes may also take place because of internal developments in the man himself. His sex drive or ability to run away quickly are obvious examples. Less obvious ones may be the break-up of a relationship or loss of a job. All these possibilities need to be considered while still trying to find the essence of what the man is doing when he commits the crime. A combination of aspects has to be taken on board. Somehow we have to map out the criminal's actions and see where the map points us.

When we were approached about the student rapes in mid-March 1989, a major inquiry was in full swing. They had eleven people in the incident room, twenty-five outside and over twenty more on night patrols. As in so many large police inquiries, even with the advantage of large computer systems, there was a risk of being swamped by the detailed information.

The victim statements were worrying in a number of ways. The criminal's behaviour varied in the details of the violence and the amount of time he spent with the victim. Simply looking at the offences as a sequence over time suggested that he was becoming more confident and violent. Rupert and I spoke about Duffy who went on from rapes which were not especially violent to kill later victims. We felt obliged to produce a quick interim report for the investigators, voicing our concerns.

To simplify the material so that some sense could be made of it, we carried out a preliminary computer analysis of the patterns of behaviour. This was the same analysis we had carried out on the 'Railway' rapes to see if there were some central common theme. Essentially the computer draws a square plot and represents each crime as a dot in that square. The closer together the dots, the more similar is the pattern of behaviour of the crimes that those dots represent.

Researchers in Israel, less precise than British academics in their use of English, who helped to develop these analysis techniques, call the pictures generated by the computer 'maps'. They are indeed secret, behavioural maps of the criminal world of the offender created from consideration of his actions. They plot a violent geometry showing how alike are the actions in each crime.

The computer works only with what it is given. If no mention is made to it of the description of the offenders or where the attacks take place, but just their actions, then the computer will plot the crimes in its own neutral box as best it can. In effect, it is performing a very similar task to the one the detectives were carrying out for Margaret and Lynne. But the difference is that it is giving its best estimate, using without fear or favour all the behavioural

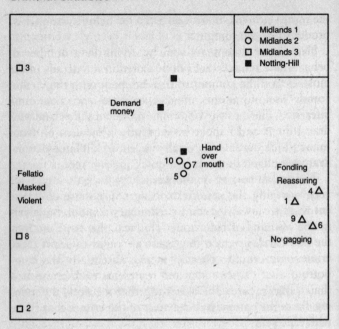

Figure i: A computer analysis of the ten Midland rapes and three Notting Hill rapes showing similarity in patterns of behaviour (actions typical of each offence are indicated. The numbers give the chronological sequence of the offences).

information that it is given. The key here is the information that the computer is given. We continued to explore the implications of feeding it details of one set of actions or another, but by the middle of 1989 we were working with ten aspects of behaviour, such as the means the offender used to control his victim, his conversation with her and his sexual activity. Our earlier studies had shown that these actions really did capture the full profile of the criminal's activities. The actions selected were critical to the results produced. With different behaviours the pattern produced by the computer could have been very different.

Here, more than anywhere else, the difference between behavioural science and Sherlock Holmes and beyond is most clear. The comparison of behavioural profiles is a comparison of patterns, not the linking of one clue to one inference. The term 'offender profiling' does appropriately draw attention to the configuration of the many points that a profile must have. One point, or clue, no matter how dramatic, does not make a profile.

The preliminary maps that the computer generated were very worrying. Trying this analysis in a number of different ways we always found that the second and third crimes in the Midlands series formed an island on their own on the left-hand side of the square plot with all the other crimes over to the right, typically spread from top to bottom. The crimes to the left were clearly more violent than those on the right. Punching the victims and threatening them with a knife were typical of those on the left, whereas in the offences on the right the assailant was more likely to reassure the victims that they would not get hurt.

This could mean at least two things: that the offender had a very varied style of behaviour, or that there was more than one offender involved. Whichever of these possibilities we selected we felt that the police needed as rapid a response as we could give them. We decided to draw up a quick preliminary report based on the bulk of offences that held together on the right of the plot, ignoring for the moment those offences that seemed to indicate very different types of behaviour. We planned to return to those after we had explored further various other sets of behaviours.

On 1 April 1989, within a couple of weeks of getting the details on the ten Midlands offences, a quick report was sent to the police, containing suggestions on directions for police investigations, emphasizing our fears of how these violent crimes could escalate to murder. The report drew attention to the number of strange components in this series of rapes and their relationships to other crimes we had examined. Duffy had gone on to murder from relatively non-vicious rapes. That was a constant refrain to our discussions. In just one case in this Midlands city the victim had been washed – the ninth. The assailant's intention had obviously been to remove any forensic evidence. But why had he not done that in other cases? Ironically, the ninth case had been linked to the fourth by DNA, despite the washing, but why had he not been as careful in the tenth case? A sample from that had already gone for testing.

The report we sent to the police was our eighth contribution to an ongoing investigation and only the second to focus entirely on a series of sexual assaults. It pointed out that the offender often appeared calm and in control during the attacks. He did not usually appear to be unduly frightened by shouts and struggles, nor did he retaliate with violence beyond that necessary to control the victims. He appeared to be at ease moving around the various premises, even when others were present, and showed no surprise at finding a young woman alone in a room. The general impression that emerged was of a person who planned his assaults, drawing upon considerable experience of breaking into houses in the area. Our initial analysis suggested that he was targeting particular types of premises in certain areas, rather than particular individuals.

His implied relationship with women appeared to be confident, yet distant. From the conversation reported he did not appear ever to try and talk them into submission, implying a typical, rather cold, relationship with women, who were seen as objects for his gratification. The examination of the sexual activities indicated a development from early exploration to going prepared to the rape.

The crimes showed the style of an experienced burglar. Indeed, previous burglaries in some of the premises could well have been carried out by the same offender. Earlier cases had indicated the possibility of such offenders carrying out relatively opportunistic burglaries and discovering that the flats they had broken into were occupied by a single woman. This then supported their fantasy life, leading to an eventual desire to make contact with such women, of which the rapes were the consequences.

The times of the crimes were noteworthy for their consistency and were unusual in relation to other series we had considered. They suggested he might be returning from a night shift or be on his way to some form of work.

The report also tried to unravel the variations in the crimes as some form of development over time. The first crime appeared exploratory and our analysis showed that he developed in both the range of sexually related activities and the preparation for those activities. In some of the later attacks he also appeared to increase his use of violent control to force compliance from his victims.

Referring to the computer analysis, we pointed out that this showed a marked change in activities between incidents 3 and 4 and a lesser change from incidents 5 to 6. We suggested that as these changes in pattern both coincided with a longer time interval between attacks, they could well indicate some change in the offender's lifestyle. The first interval in particular, from 9 December 1987 to 9 June 1988, was especially worthy of note as it was long enough to be consistent with a prison sentence.

In considering the actual location of the crimes we came to the conclusion that they were carried out broadly along a north-west–south-east axis, within reasonable walking distance of each other. There is a movement up and down this axis, earlier crimes at the bottom, then up to the top, then back down again. This is a pattern that we had observed for a few other criminals, all of whom lived in the area of their crimes. These considerations suggested a base central to the crimes within a particular area.

A number of factors pointed to the offender having a criminal history and being very aware of possible police investigative procedures. The wearing of disguises, socks and gloves not only showed that he feared later recognition, but also that he chose devices (such as socks) that he could explain to a police officer if stopped. It certainly suggested that he was aware of the possibility of being charged for 'going equipped' to commit a crime and might well have been so charged in the past.

Of particular significance was the washing of the victim in incident nine because we had no indication of him even wiping the victim in earlier or later assaults. It therefore seemed possible that the offender had had a blood or similar samples taken some time before incident nine, but that this had not led to any follow-on inquiry and he therefore thought it no longer of any importance. Given that he had raped on 8 December 1988 and washed his next victim on 19 December, the most probable assumption was that the sample had been taken from him between these dates. The possibility of a sample being taken before the attack on 8 December, however, could not be discounted.

The results from the lab, analysing the DNA from the last assault, number ten, came in late May, spurring the police to contact us. 'The DNA from number ten is not the same man as four and nine,' they said, clearly rather annoyed with us. With all our clever computer tricks, why had we not told them there were two offenders? Did this mean that the 'profile' we had written for them was useless?

They were rather nonplussed when I said that the existence of two offenders helped to answer a lot of the questions we had been asking ourselves. Take just the question of why the victim was washed in offence nine but not offence ten. The DNA showed these were two different offenders. Offence nine was therefore the last offence we had for one of the offenders. The offender who committed offence ten had probably never washed his victims. Furthermore, the publicity given to the offences could well have made the criminal aware of the risk he had taken in offence four by leaving body fluids. So the next time he attacked did he try to clean up after himself? But where does that put the man who perpetrated four and nine in relation to offences five, six, seven and eight? In offence six he was disturbed before he could ejaculate so it was difficult to form a view on his 'forensic awareness' there. But five, seven and eight were complete rapes. Were they his offences or not?

These were the range of questions that the police in the Midlands were trying to unravel while we were looking at our computer plot with new eyes, attempting to see if that pattern of ten dots could be cajoled into giving up its secrets. To help us we explored the plot further by feeding into the analysis crimes by known offenders. These solved offences acted like beacons in an anonymous landscape, providing identifiable markers that could be used to distinguish between the unsolved crimes. These markers gave even stronger distinctions between the crimes, putting two, three and eight into one group on the left of the plot, with five, seven and ten in the middle and the remainder, one, four, six and nine clearly over to the right. The known rapist's crimes were in the middle also, closest to the second group. He was a long-standing burglar who had graduated to rape, a married man with young children. The simplest conclusion, then, was that these were broadly the characteristics of the one offender, but probably not of the other.

The distinct DNA for case ten was the crucial jigsaw piece. It revealed the outline that helped us unlock the relationships between all the other offences. We were now able to consider the implications of other known features of the cases. In two offences, one and four, the assailant was noted by the victims to be wearing spectacles during the assault. But four was definitely linked to nine by DNA. There are therefore three offences, one, four and nine that appear to be produced by one offender, let us call him X.

In three cases the mode of entry was the rather clumsy, and unexpectedly distinct, one of climbing in through a back window. These were cases one, four and six. The first two here were already linked by the spectacles so it seems reasonable to tie in six to the crimes perpetrated by X, assigning to him the four cases of one, four, six and nine. They were in a distinct region on the computer map of behaviour, especially when the 'marker' cases were included. In these the offender was less vicious and further away from the known criminal. Curiously, that fitted with the disturbance during offence six frightening him away. Being less determined or experienced in criminal ways, such a man would be more likely to put himself in a situation where his presence would be noted.

Looking at the computer plot with this new perspective, it made much more sense. The points to the right of the plot were cases one, four, six and nine. The computer knew nothing about DNA, or spectacles, or the washing of the victim. All it had were the similarities in the action profiles of the offences derived from the ten actions we had given it. But it was also telling us that one, four, six and nine could readily be the work of one man. In this pattern, offence nine had indeed been the subsequent crime, after four, at which X had left seminal evidence.

The fifth, seventh and tenth offences also fell in a distinct region of the computer plot. The DNA evidence therefore linked whoever produced a sample similar to that left at offence ten to five and seven, offender Y.

We could say a lot more about these groups of offences once we had recognized them. The offences of the known rapist, when put into the analysis, were happy to stand next to the groupings of rapist Y. Was he then the same type of burglar rapist, with X a rather different character?

One further dramatic piece of evidence now emerged once we had assigned the offences to two different people. The fifth, seventh and tenth crimes, which our analysis had linked to offender Y, were in the north-western part of the Midlands city, an area covered by the ten rapes. Offender X was operating in another, distinct, equally limited area. The first, fourth, sixth and ninth attacks were in the south-eastern part of the original area of the city. Here was corroboration indeed. Two distinct areas, each about one mile square with apparently different people committing their crimes in each area. This certainly fitted with everything else we knew about offence locations in British cities. The scale of territory over which each attacker roamed was well within what we had found for others.

The second, third and eighth attacks were behaviourally very different and also sat in the geography of the crimes at the extremes of the two groupings. Offences two and eight were on the northern edge of the north-western grouping and offence 3 was on the eastern edge of the south-eastern grouping. These offences therefore remained (and remain) problematic. Do these represent a third or even third and fourth offender?

Our quick preliminary report had undoubtedly confused two offenders, although the assignment of the weight of our inferences to the offences that clustered on the right of the computer plot had meant that it was biased more to offender X than to anyone else. Our suggestions, though, as to the likely base of the offenders now needed further tuning to take account of the two different regions in which the offenders were operating.

Taking the geographical ideas together with the different patterns of behaviour revealed by the computer analysis, our confidence grew that we could disentangle our original account and generate two distinct 'profiles'. This required going back to the behavioural material with our new-found understanding.

The distinctiveness of the offenders gathered momentum as we studied the behaviour in more detail and closely examined the various computer print-outs. The details added up to produce strong outlines. The person whose crimes stood distinctly on the right of our plot sometimes wore spectacles during an offence and climbed in through the back windows of houses (apparently unaware that obtaining entry by forcing the front door was less risky at that time of night). He was very ready to tell his victim that he was not going to hurt her, indicating throughout the conversation his own concern about the victim's reaction to him. In one assault the victim had an asthma attack as he was starting to touch her. He left her without continuing the sexual assault, after saying, 'I don't want anything, I just want to feel you.' This was the man who was beside his victims before they woke up, often with a knife already pressed against them. He was never viciously aggressive, although he did hit the victim who had the asthma attack, clearly confused about what was happening, thinking she was playing a trick on him.

As this picture of offender X became ever more clear, Rupert, in the ways of police officers, gave him a label to distinguish him, calling him 'The Wimp'. This was not a wholly accurate soubriquet because the man was climbing into occupied houses at night and using the threat of a knife to force women to let him rape them. What the term did emphasize, though, was that here was a man who was confused about his relationship to his victims. He did not appear to be a seasoned burglar, although he told some victims that he was a burglar. He was a man seeking out sexual contact with women, apparently because there was no other way available to him. Many of his sexual actions were apparently exploratory.

The 'support', from which the series got its title, did appear to have a genuine need for help underlying it, and although it is difficult to tell exactly from the unelaborated words on the pages of a statement, the nature of the rapists' personal request does appear to be reflected in the exact wording that is used. To the fourth victim X said, 'You do it, you'll have to put it in.' To the sixth he said, 'I just want to feel you,' and to the ninth he said, 'You put it in.' In two cases he emphasized the victim's actions. This contrasted with the fifth, seventh and tenth in which the three different victims all quote him as saying, 'Put it in.' Here the instruction was far less personal; it was a vicious demand to facilitate the rape. Rupert labelled this assailant 'Macho Man'. The slight differences in how the instructions are written in the statements have a strange consistency to them. If this is combined with the more aggressive style of the second offender, then it is possible to hear a difference between the aggressive instruction ('Put it in') and the request for help ('You put it in').

The 'Wimp', then, had all the hallmarks of a man who did not have regular contact with women, who quite probably wandered the streets peeping into windows. Probably a lonely man and in the older range for rapists, who are typically in their mid-twenties, having come to attack through the mounting frustrations of his life. He would have little previous criminal history, if any, and live in the vicinity of the south-eastern part of the city.

Offender Y, 'Macho Man', was the man we expected to

be found living in the area of the north-west. He revealed many of the habits of experienced criminals, entering by an insecure front door, sometimes disconnecting the telephone, taking chequebooks or other property that could be sold only through the criminal underworld. Significantly, too, he was a violent man who woke his victims as he entered their room, immediately threatening them with a knife and telling them to shut up. To keep his victims quiet he forced his hand into their mouths with such violence that in one case he scratched the back of the victim's throat. He would tell them to move up and down as he was raping them, saying things like, 'You're not doing much for me.' This was a man who was used to controlling women. Just considering his approach to the victims showed his confidence in being able to bend them to his will. In the fifth, seventh and tenth crimes the victim's first awareness of the offender was when she felt him close, touching her, either with his hand over her mouth or clearly holding a knife. Indeed, in the fifth offence the victim screamed, but for both the subsequent victims of the same offender, their first experience was of a hand over their mouth. Most of the other victims in the series awoke before the man was close enough to put his hand over their faces. In one case she saw him standing on the stairs before he entered her room.

This 'macho' rapist showed his history of contact with women and exerting control over them. His behavioural pattern had been found in the computer analysis to be similar to another known rapist who had a previous conviction for burglary, as well as being married.

At the end of March, before we had disentangled the two (or more) offenders, the police had already identified a man who we will call George as a possible suspect for the ten offences. A police officer on night patrol had seen him 'acting suspiciously' in the area of the rapes. The tenth offence was uppermost in the minds of the police, suspects at this stage being asked only about that March attack. With the knowledge that they had a good sample for DNA comparison from that attack, George was asked to provide blood. He was more than ready to do so. He had a good alibi for the attack and was clearly confident that he could not be linked to it. Indeed, with hindsight we can see that even as a suspect for the ninth attack in December he would have felt safe, having made the victim wash herself. Eventually the DNA evidence cleared George from offence ten, but the evidence for the other two offences in which there was some body-fluid was still unclear by mid-May 1989.

This lack of clarity in the evidence is difficult to comprehend for people versed in the study of probabilities. The lab could only say that George's DNA could match that found in crimes four and nine with the odds at three million to one against it being merely a chance association. The legal view seems to be that there are about thirty million men in Britain, so such odds did not specifically identify George. The police needed to be able to support their already astronomic odds by further information on the suspect.

Surveillance was therefore put on George, an intensive and expensive activity. This showed he was continuing to prowl and peep in some of the areas of the offences. Furthermore, although he had no previous convictions it was found that he had been cautioned in 1986 for 'behaviour likely to cause a breach of the peace' when he was found masturbating outside the flat of two girls. By late June 1989 this was added to the identification material from the spectacles observed at offences four and nine. The strengthening of the DNA analysis to one in ten million gave the police the confidence that he had committed the first nine rapes in the series, for which he was duly charged.

In Surrey we had not been party to any of these investigative considerations, although two police officers had spent a week with us helping to re-analyse the behavioural information. (Their colleagues had been so impressed that they had survived a week in the exotic realms of a university that when they returned they were awarded a parchment and card mortarboard in honour of their new-found status.) However, this did not initially add any weight to our growing conclusions about two offenders and the crimes they had committed. Our initial reluctance to challenge the strongly held view of very experienced officers, that one man was responsible for all the offences, appeared to have led to a general doubt about the utility of our conclusions.

At the end of June 1989, George was charged with the first nine of the rapes in the 'Support' series, but the DNA had made clear that the tenth offence was committed by somebody else. It was only when a second suspect, who we will call Martin, had been identified for that last rape that the distinctions we had drawn, with the help of our computer plot, began to be taken seriously.

Martin had come to police notice in the winter of 1988 because of a chequebook that had disappeared from the house in which the fifth rape had been committed. This chequebook turned up in police inquiries associated with Martin. Linking Martin to the chequebook had been a product of painstaking police research. Fingerprints on the chequebook had been identified and led to a long chain of contacts being unravelled, Martin being about ten links removed from the person whose fingerprints had been identified. By very careful elimination they were able to focus on Martin as a possible suspect.

Detectives had always considered the possibility that the rapist had taken the chequebook and sold it on, so they were not surprised that Martin was happy to help their inquiries by giving a blood sample in relation to the samples of semen obtained from the fourth and ninth offences. They were also not surprised to find that he had good alibis for at least four of the nine assaults. His association with the cheque-book had given him some indirect connection with the rape, but at that stage there was no especially strong reason to suspect a seasoned burglar in contact with prostitutes and known to have girlfriends.

Martin, of course, was comfortable in the knowledge that he had not committed the assaults for which the blood samples were taken from him. He probably also thought that the police were so convinced that there was one man for all nine rapes that he attacked again in March; by now, though, he was very concerned that the victim should not see his face, telling her not to look and covering her head with a pillow so that he could escape without being seen. He knew he was in the police records but thought he had already been eliminated through the blood-tests that attempted to link him to the wrong cases.

In late June 1989 the laboratory established that Martin's DNA was the same as that found in the last crime of the series. But not only had the chequebook that brought Martin in as a suspect come from offence five, but our analyses had put offences five and seven into the same group as offence ten. In the process of sorting out who should be charged with what, there were a few days when both Martin and George were being charged with the same crime. The problem was how to explain to a court the behavioural links that tied the fifth, seventh and tenth crimes to Martin. Close examination of the statements from the offences showed that it was very clear that Martin had viciously controlled all three victims by forcing hands down their throats. Medical officers and forensic scientists were prepared to say that they had never come

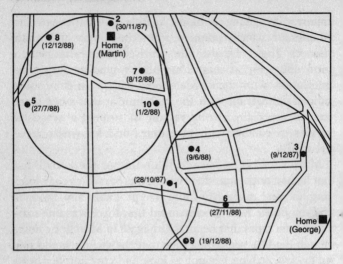

Map v: Midlands city, indicating the location and residence of the Midland rapes and rapists (numbers indicate sequence of offences).

across that form of control before. It was so unusual that they were prepared to say it linked the three cases without any doubt, tying all three to Martin because of the DNA link to offence nine.

Martin was given a sentence of seventeen years. Twenty-three years old, with an extensive criminal record, he was regarded by the police as very much part of the criminal underworld, with suspicions that he was involved in drug-dealing and in pimping. The photograph of him shows a handsome young man looking with open-mouthed confidence at the camera, a person who believed he could steal sex by force in the way he got so many other things he wanted.

George was described in newspapers, after he was sentenced to fourteen years' imprisonment, as a college failure, a twenty-seven-year-old loner living 'in the midst of bright, attractive young people living in flats and houses near his home'. He was described as never having had a girlfriend and as being a 'mother's boy', but the photograph of a puzzled, bespectacled man with a faint moustache reveals someone who never really understood the extent of the fear and anger that the shadow of his actions threw over a large community. He was trapped eventually by the police because they were investigating him for a crime he knew he had not committed. He had not considered that they would eventually realize their mistake and connect him with the same blood-test to earlier crimes. Even the care with which he had washed his last victim, an indication of the attention to forensic detail that might be expected of an ex-college student as much as an ex-con, was not enough to hide the critical evidence for his crimes.

The victims played different roles in the actions of the offenders. For George the victim was a confused substitute for the genuine relationships he desired. For Martin the victims were just other women to use.

These cases serve to demonstrate both the difficulty and the importance of distinguishing between crimes that may be linked to the same offender. When there are only the actions of the offender to work with, as Lynne and Margaret's experiments showed so clearly, it may be very difficult to decide what to give prominence to. Quite subtle aspects of what is said and done may be critical in disentangling the series, and can hold the key to understanding the make-up of each offender. The computer analysis certainly helped us to see the wood for the trees and to give guidance on the distinctions between the cases. Once recognized these could easily be defended in court without any need to refer to my complex arithmetic.

The initial concern which encouraged us to give such a

hasty response to the local police – that the observed variations in behaviour could indicate escalating violence – was partly borne out in ways that we had not expected. Martin, who was confident that the DNA would not implicate him, violently gagged some of his victims with his hand. He may have been prepared to kill if he thought it would guarantee his liberty. He certainly treated his victims as objects significant only to his sexual desires. Perhaps this is where murder and rape overlap closely: in the meaning that the victim has for the assailant.

Chapter Eight

OBJECTS OF MURDER

In rape the significance of the woman as an object for the man's gratification is obvious enough. Even though the varying aspects of this gratification may be elusive, they can probably be uncovered if we know where and how to look. But is this relevant to the even more violent crime of murder? If it is, can it help us understand the people who commit such crimes and, in so doing, lead the police to them? Is the violent killing of another person too brutal to allow us the analysis that is so helpful in the investigation of rape?

Murder in the family, where two people know each other well and have fed on each other's emotions for many years, can be understood as a passionate outburst that explodes into a violent killing. Here one person feels so strongly about another that, as awful as the crime might be, most of us can see in ourselves the seeds of similar outbursts. But the murder of total strangers: where does that kind of aggression come from? How can its different features be dissected to point us to the distinguishing facets of the killer? How do the victims play a role in the lives of their assailants whom they may never see or know?

The details of a number of violent killings helped me to see that there were important connections between the detection of rape and of murder, and that some similar principles might apply. But to learn these lessons I had to gain a richer understanding of how people treat each other as instruments for their own gratification.

Perhaps the most important lesson I learned was when I was asked to visit the scene where a young woman had been murdered in Cardiff. She had been well known to the police as a prostitute, working in what used to be called the Tiger Bay area before the docklands development got under way. The scene of her death was described to me over the telephone as 'a brothel near the docks'.

Like many people, my idea of a brothel had been drawn from fiction and the movies. Then I saw the police photographs of the viciously knifed body of Lynette White, lying on the floor of the room where she used to take her clients, her 'brothel'. The small, buff-coloured room had a dirty, torn carpet and dirty curtains. The bed, consisting of a mattress with no cover or any other form of bedding on it, more or less filled the room.

By the time I got there the room had been neutralized in the detailed way that only police scientists and scene of crime officers can do. Every drop of blood, every foreign fibre and hand-dab had been examined, and all that was left were the faded brown stains on the worn carpet where once the pool of blood had seeped through.

The police photographs of the victim provided a brutal contrast to the artful arrangement of even the most gory of cinematographic horror pictures. Police photographers never compose their shots to do anything other than record the scene and the body as clearly as they can. This usually means emphasizing the wounds and blood splashes, the bindings and the general disarray that surrounds most murders. The photographs of the murdered prostitute in Cardiff were the grisliest pictures I had ever seen; over fifty stab wounds all over the body, the neck hacked at, the wrists gouged.

Before the police asked Rupert and me to give an opinion, they had talked to every woman who worked on the street in Cardiff and knew a great deal indeed about the victim and her family. She was a young girl born in Cardiff, with little talent and few job prospects. Her mother died when she was young and her father took up with another woman. Like such women have for centuries she found her way into selling her body to men before she left school, only to be thrown out of her home by her father who felt his honour among his friends would suffer. That action condemned her to this only means of survival.

The police had closely questioned Stephen Miller, the 'boyfriend' for whom Lynette was the only source of the money with which he paid for his drugs, and whom the police alleged to be her pimp. Miller was convicted of the murder, but later freed on appeal. The police had also located a great many of her punters, regular and less regular, discovering along the way, in a matter of weeks, facts about prostitution that would take a university research team years to unravel. Police officers found they were interviewing clients of these women who were already well known to them, not as criminals but as lawyers and bank managers, garage owners and councillors.

When I was introduced by detectives to the working women in the local pub, near the place where Lynette White was murdered, I had my preconceptions further challenged. Most of the half-dozen women drinking there in their break between 'Johns' were of indeterminate middle age, overweight, lacking any overt sensuality, except for the tight jumpers and short skirts that they need to advertise their availability. Anyone who has any doubts about the authority of the feminist argument that women are treated as objects for the sexual satisfaction of men, need only spend a short time with the few-pounds-a-go, street prostitutes of Cardiff to be convinced how many men can use a woman's body as a source to satisfy their appetite, without any need for or attempt at contact between two human beings, except that which is necessary for the exchange of money.

There is a strange rhetoric that keeps alive the idea that the punters really care. Kevin Toolis, a journalist who specializes in writing stories about the seamy and bizarre, wrote at length about the life of Lynette White. He quotes, without comment, the words of her friends: 'She was really a good worker there. She had a lot of nice gentlemen friends, a lot of regulars. A lot of them tried to get her away from Miller.' Toolis describes Lynette White as 'younger and prettier than most of the other street girls. She had brown curly shoulder-length hair, blue eyes and clear complexion. Her height of 5ft 3ins accentuated her figure.'

She was liked by the other street girls and the murder had shocked them. They therefore cooperated fully with the police. This meant that by the time I visited what was left of the brothel the police could give me a very full account of Lynette White's story, highlighting its unexplained components.

The wounds were ghastly, but their very intensity and variety had to tell us something. First there were so many knife wounds, far more than were needed to kill the small woman. They also varied in depth and the parts of the body that were penetrated. Some were powerful, vicious stabs; others almost exploratory incisions. Some of these wounds were far from being the violent, almost random onslaught that might be associated with a wild frenzy: the hands were almost severed at the wrists and there appeared also to have been an attempt to cut off the head.

As in other actions, such as sexual assaults or even burglary, the details of what the offender actually does in a murder offer us an account of that offender. It is as much a communication about the sort of person committing the crime as posture and facial expression might be in indicating how well a student understands what a lecturer is saying. How could this attack be interpreted? The most obvious matter to explore was the attempt to sever the hands and head. Here were very specific actions that should reveal a distinct message. I discussed them with a clinical psychologist colleague who had little experience of criminal pathology but who was none the less well versed in the ideas of clinical interpretations of the meanings of actions to patients. His response was immediate: 'Wow! What a wonderfully symbolic act. A real attempt to turn the victim into a non-person, to remove her personality. But I wonder why he gave up before he'd completed the task? Perhaps he was overcome with the horror of what he was doing?'

Curiously, the conclusions that might be drawn from this interpretation are not that different from those that Rupert and I discussed, taking a more conventional detective perspective. The clinical view implies that the victim has some personal and emotional significance for the offender and the attack is an attempt to destroy that significance by destroying those aspects of the body that make it a particular person. The victim is therefore not just any person as far as the offender is concerned, but special to them. This implies an established contact with the victim, a familiarity, a relationship. But it is none the less a relationship that is built upon a victim as a body, a person who can be nullified by the removal of head and hands.

The perspective endorsed by Rupert, as a police investigator, was more down to earth. Recognition of the body by the police would be very difficult without the head or the fingerprints. The removal of these vital sources would therefore make it difficult to identify the victim. This would reduce the risk to the assailant, because if the police do not know who the victim is then they have less chance of establishing who her contacts were.

With each of these three arguments we end up with the same inference: the victim and the assailant had an established relationship that could be discovered by the police. No interpretation contradicts another. They all point to Lynette being seen by her murderer as little more than a body that posed a threat if it could be identified.

The most obvious suspect, then, would be a close associate of the victim, the man she gave her earnings to, for example, her pimp. Such a person would be a prime suspect anyway and had already been closely questioned by the police by the time I visited the scene, without any evidence emerging to prove he was the culprit.

Our report to the Cardiff police explored the possibility that the murderer was a client angered, say, by some remark Lynette had made. On all murders of prostitutes, detectives are daunted by the possibility that one of her many anonymous clients could have committed the crime, providing a vast field of suspects, many of whom cannot be traced. We certainly kept this option open in our report to the police, but with hindsight it is difficult to imagine the circumstances under which a casual, anonymous client would inflict the number and variety of wounds found here. If a punter murdered a prostitute in a fit of rage, he would be expected to leave as quickly as possible and not linger about trying to cut off her hands. The exception to this would be those cases in which the body is systematically, and possibly ritually, mutilated as when the breasts, for example, are carefully sliced off. Lynette's wounds had none of that almost surgical quality to them. Nor were they focused on the breasts or genital areas as such 'ritual' mutilations often are.

I do not think a study has ever been carried out into the murders of prostitutes. It is probably not regarded as a 'serious enough' problem. It is certainly not open to easy examination. My guess would be that it is within ongoing relationships that violence against prostitutes is most likely to burst out to a vicious level, not attacks from clients. It is still the case that the majority of murders happen within an established relationship, not between strangers. Paying for sex is already a form of power and control, a use of the woman as a body. Such domination would seem to me to reduce the need or desire to violate the woman further, in the great majority of cases. A different explanation, the determination to silence a potential witness, say as part of a theft, would not be expected to produce such a variety of wounds. In this case, anyway, money was found at the scene, suggesting that theft was not a significant motive.

Relationships of a more permanent kind that prostitutes have with men are often likely to be based on physical control and acts of violence. How often this violence spills over into murder is just not known. The world in which male and female prostitutes live is extremely difficult for police officers to penetrate. Many unsolved murders are of people who sell their bodies. In the depth of this ignorance it can only be assumed that the usual human emotions of rage and jealousy, despair and even indignation, that lead a person to kill someone they know, are also likely to be the prevalent causes of the murder of prostitutes.

In our early considerations of Lynette White, though, we were still open to the possibility of a client having committed the murder. An unused condom had been found on the bed, also hinting at an attack during the early stages of purchased sex. Yet the bitter logic of our argument about the relationship between the murderer and the victim was seen as very significant by the Cardiff investigators. They gave it probably stronger emphasis than we did ourselves.

Our report, while emphasizing the relationship between killer and victim, also drew attention to the mixture and amount of stabbings. Any act against another person is carried on a wave of emotion. Different kinds and degrees of emotion will be reflected in different kinds of actions. The number of stabs and their differences, the mixture of tentative cuts and vicious thrusts, the start at severing the head and hands but failure to complete, provide a mixture of messages.

The wild frenzy of the murder, but the lack of any fingerprints or similar evidence, also revealed a mixture of approaches to the act of murder. Was this then an attacker with wild mood swings during his attack, frenzy quickly followed by remorse? Or were these different 'styles', an indication that different people were involved in the murder, signifying that more than one person was responsible?

Today I would be more confident in my interpretation of the amount and mixture of these aspects of the killing than I was then. Now we have collected more examples of such brutality. Fortunately the number of examples are still rare in Britain, but so many stabbings and such a mixture have always occurred when there was more than one assailant. The frenzy of an attack, whether it is a murder or a sexual assault that does not lead to death, is also typical of crimes in which drugs or alcohol have removed the last vestiges of self-control from the attacker. As psychologists put it, drugs dis-inhibit, remove the in-hibitions that even murderers often show. The wounds may be speaking, then, of at least two assailants, perhaps more, and a strong further possibility of at least one of these people being dis-inhibited by drugs or drink.

The FBI Behavioral Science Unit account of such a murder would also add the further point that many of its qualities were 'disorganized'. The violence and mutilation as well as the unthought-through frenzy and the leaving of the body at the scene are all taken as hallmarks of this type of murderer. In terms of the central behavioural traits of the crime, its distinguishing facets, the labelling of it as 'disorganized' draws attention to aspects of the style of the killing that can tell us something of the style of life of the killer. This is not the style of killing that a professional or skilled worker who can hold down a regular job is likely to carry out. Furthermore, a hardened thief intent on murdering as part of the course of a burglary would choose a victim where there was more likelihood of monetary gain.

This is the type of murder carried out by a person who is essentially impulsive and easily loses control, who drifts from one way of surviving to another. Peter Sutcliffe and Dennis Nilsen, who abducted their victims and hid the bodies, presented an organized face to society and dealt with many aspects of their crimes in a similarly organized way. A man who chops at the wrists of a dead prostitute in the room where he has murdered her, then leaves her body in a pool of blood, is no arch villain who plans his life or has a 'mission' to kill. He is much more likely to be a small-time criminal with some previous criminal record for acts of violence or petty theft.

Perhaps even more important, the criminal who reveals confusion in his assault is also less likely to be a person who goes searching for his victim. Here is the sort of criminal who is rarely far from home when he commits a crime. Paradoxically, it is precisely the lack of intelligence applied to the crimes that produces the interpretability of the patterns of the criminal's actions. They are shaped by simple, recognizable forces, by familiarity and convenience.

Our speculations about the people who had murdered Lynette came as a surprise to the police who had been working on the case for months. This was not because of any startlingly different possibilities we had unearthed, but because our suggestions were so close to the ideas that they had already formulated. Unknown to us, the police saw our report pointing back to Miller and his associates, even though their inquiry at that stage had not been able to find any strong evidence linking these prime suspects to the murder. They even had one of Lynette's close friends undergo hypnosis to see if she could provide any more clues to the actions of Lynette around the time of the murder, but this had produced no further useful information. As a consequence, at the time of our involvement, the investigation was running out of steam and there were plans to reassign officers to other duties and wind up the inquiry.

At that stage I did not know enough about the criminal world to realize the full degradation that would have been the daily experience of Lynette. I had no awareness of the way in which the man she regarded as her boyfriend would have been using her to obtain money to buy his drugs, he himself being used and manipulated by the person who supplied him. Our descriptions of the people who murdered her were taken by the police to point to her boyfriend. Lynette's close associates were re-interviewed, including the friend who had been interviewed under hypnosis. This led them back through a maze of lies and counter-accusations until an almost incredible story took shape. During the last few days of her life Lynette was hiding from Miller, possibly trying to forge some new existence away from the sleazy brothel. Friends of Lynette's reported that Miller and others caught up with her in her first-floor room, attempting to force her to give up any money she might have made. In the ensuing fight she was killed. In court five people were alleged to have been present during her murder, some as horrified spectators urged to make token stabs so that they would be party to the crime to ensure their silence.

Three of these, including Stephen Miller, were convicted and sentenced to life imprisonment. A conviction against which they successfully appealed.

The murder of Lynette White also illustrates how much room there is for development of the simple typology of 'disorganized' or 'organized' types of murder. The whole network of aspects of an offence, the many facets of the shadow that is cast, can each be examined for what it might reveal about the killer. In this case a curious aspect of the murder was the implication that there was a close familiarity between the murderer and his victim, yet the murder scene itself had a haphazard, disorganized quality. With familiarity and contact with the victim, surely there were other opportunities for a more careful murder, with less risk of the victim being linked to the killer? The disorganization has to be looked at in the context of the shadowy world of street prostitutes, where people use each other for their own gratification.

People like Lynette who aspire for relationships that move beyond unthinking abuse are often destined to end up as victims. Seeing the context in which her life was lived, I became more aware of how all violent crime must grow out of the perception of others as instruments. The investigation of the crime must therefore also attempt to understand what sort of instrument the victim presents for the assailant, whether the crime is overtly sexual or not. A direct interpretation, in context, of the significance of the victim to the offender is probably the best starting point. The actual setting may help us to understand the people who are to be found there and their relationships to each other.

Lynette White was a source of money. Everyone used her as an object. She must have wanted some personal relationship that went beyond all this, love, to keep going, but it was too late for her. Other people did not see her that way.

Prostitutes are very vulnerable people living on the fringes of legality and therefore at great risk from the other criminals with whom they mix. They are quite obviously treated more as animate objects than as people who feel and think. The step from being a sexual object to being the subject of violence is not a very big one. There are so many ways in which a woman who earns her living from selling her body can be treated without empathy; as a thing to supply money; to be beaten into submission; and as expendable. But what of other women who become the targets of men's violence? Are there any similarities or differences in what they suffer that can help us catch the perpetrators? Can this evolving theory of the victim as object be developed to help catch those who kill women they do not know, especially if those women do not have a high-risk lifestyle?

One murder that I was asked to help detect illustrated particularly well the very different considerations that come into play for a different type of victim. Mrs Bhatti was fifty-three when she was murdered on Sunday 12 June 1988. It being her custom, on occasion, to walk early in the park, it is assumed that she got up, dressed and walked along the High Street to the small London park in Southall near where she lived. This walk would not have taken more than five minutes. She was seen approaching the park at around 5.55 a.m. The personal stereo found at the murder scene indicates that Mrs Bhatti was wearing this as she walked around the park.

From witness statements, and the general patterns observed in other settings, it seems likely that people walking in the park tend to turn to the left on entering and walk a circuit that brings them round along the path at the far side near Green Drive and then back along the central path towards Boyd Avenue.

A number of people appear to have been in the park around 6.00 a.m., although the majority of them seem to have been at the Green Drive end. None of those identified mentioned anything untoward.

The attack took place near and in the bushes that provide cover from the road in an area of the park that is probably not much used in the early hours. It is noteworthy that two separate respondents indicated that it was a set of bushes that they went to use as a urinal. It therefore is clearly recognized by people using the park as reasonably secluded and free from direct surveillance. One of these witnesses saw the body and called a passing police officer. She did not see it in the bushes until she was very close, also supporting the view that this was a surprisingly secluded location in a busy, small, urban park.

The nature of the attack itself can be gauged from the forensic evidence and photographs taken at the scene. Mrs Bhatti was beaten about the face, probably with a hand or fist, sexually assaulted orally and beaten a number of times over the head, probably with a cider bottle. She was jabbed in the face, probably with a broken bottle, and received other cuts and abrasions, especially on her wrist. We were informed by police officers that the cuts to the face and wrist were probably perimortem and that the cause of death was actually strangulation, although the blows to the head probably rendered Mrs Bhatti unconscious. There was blood splashing on the underside of the leaves; this would indicate that the blows took place in the bushes.

This all suggests that Mrs Bhatti was approached and punched to induce submission. The location of the head wounds low on the back of the head and to the right would suggest that these were inflicted when the victim was down, from the right-hand side. The location of the clothing and the other objects would suggest that the victim had been pulled into the bushes.

Mrs Bhatti's handbag was found over the fence in the grounds adjacent to the Red Lion Hotel at a distance consistent with it being thrown there. It contained part of a broken bottle. Further back in the park, beyond a fenced-off area accessible over a broken fence, Mrs Bhatti's payslip was found at about 7.45 a.m.

Another disorganized murderer, but here the victim lived far from the high-risk lifestyle of Lynette White. Mrs Pushpa Bhatti was a gentle teacher and devout Christian, a lay preacher well respected in her community and adored by her husband and three children. Unlike the investigation of Lynette White's murder, where there was a plethora of possible suspects, many closely associated with the victim, the detectives looking at Mrs Bhatti's murder had no one to consider directly and those closest to her could not have played any part whatsoever. Even distant contacts were very unlikely to harbour any grudge against this widely admired person. Two weeks after the killing the newspapers reported the police as being 'baffled'.

Details of the crime, though, speak volumes. By drawing on the emerging principles for relating offence behaviour to offence characteristics, a picture of the offender was proposed. The starting point here is not so much the implications of relationship with the victim, as it was with the killing of Lynette White, but the offender's relationship to the setting in which the killing took place. The barren room in Tiger Bay could be taken for granted as defining some of the characteristics of the lifestyle of the person who went there and killed. Such a person, at the very least, had contact with prostitution which was the only reason the room was ever entered. But Southall Park is used by the full range of people who live in the area. It was not an unusual place for a female lay preacher to be on an early Sunday morning in the summer.

Yet one of our firmest hypotheses about a criminal's actions, an hypothesis growing in strength and clarity as our studies unfold, is that knowledge and familiarity with an area is a prerequisite for many violent crimes. Like a person going shopping, a criminal will also go to locations that are convenient. Our report to the police pointed out that the particular bush used and the throwing of the handbag over the fence, and the disposal of the payslip at the back of the park, in a semi-private location, all pointed to someone who was reasonably familiar with the park. He would certainly have been wandering around it before the attack and may well have been a frequent visitor there.

This suggestion was taken further by considering the location in which the victim's bag was left and the payslip taken from it. These indicated someone escaping to Green Drive and beyond, quite possibly in a southerly direction, intent on getting over the railway line.

As is true of most of the murders we have examined, this one would be described by the FBI as being 'disorganized'. The use of a public location, where people were possibly present, the violence beyond the need to control the victim, the limited attempt to conceal the body, the disposal of bag and payslip in places where they were soon found, the bottle remains and general disarray around the body, all point to a characteristically chaotic crime.

The likelihood that the assailant lived locally also helps to elaborate the 'disorganized' quality of the offence. Some planning had gone into it. There was a pattern to it, yet it still showed an impulsivity indicating some history of impetuous violent crime. Our research would put such an offender living quite near the crime. The knowledge of the park, the nature of the offence and the route taken in leaving the scene, all point to an offender being resident within reasonable walking distance of the park.

The committing of this violent crime near to home by an impulsive person would also indicate that this was not his first crime. His other crimes were considered to be just as likely to have taken place in familiar, convenient locations, in other words in the same general area. Some form of mugging, indecent assault or rape by the offender less than a mile from this crime in the past five years seemed very probable. Our report to the police therefore emphasized that the identification of these related crimes would be of great assistance to the investigation.

From consideration of a number of such assaults, attacks outdoors seem often to involve the preselection of an area by the offender with which he is familiar, rather than the preselection or targeting of particular victims. These offenders attack where they are comfortable and in surroundings which are known to them and where they may be confident of effecting escape. The victim is then selected by the circumstances in which she becomes available to the attacker and vulnerable to the attack.

Typically the offender would have approached the victim, perhaps conversationally, before the full assault began. If that was so, then this crime was not a sudden overpowering attack. This happens very infrequently in cases we have seen. The escalation of the attack was most probably the result of the victim's reaction to an approach by which the offender's 'rage' was triggered to the extent of inflicting such savage injury.

Our report elaborated further:

This would be expected to be committed by a person who was not generally regarded as particularly intelligent, who works in an unskilled job if at all.

The crime may in part be a product of sexual problems the offender has, and be linked to an upbringing in a context of hostile discipline, with contact with a father being intermittent. Instability in the father's occupation is also likely.

General statistics would put the offender in late

teens to late 20s. The degree of violence might well indicate the middle of this range.

The type of impulsive, socially disturbed individual indicated by the above characteristics is less likely to be in a permanent relationship with a woman and may well live alone.

The report also drew on studies from the United States which indicated that sexual homicides were usually committed by people of the same ethnic origins as the victim. There were some difficulties applying this principle to the murder of Mrs Bhatti, both because the photographs we had did not enable us to judge if an assailant would have judged her to be Indian or Caucasian, and because we did not know if the results reported in the United States would translate to Southall, an area with a very great ethnic mix. We therefore made only the most tentative suggestion that the killer would be white.

We now know that, whatever the facts for North America, there is no simple relationship between the ethnicity of the victim and of the assailant. Furthermore, local experience of the police in Southall has indicated that a number of attacks on Asian women were carried out by people of Afro-Caribbean origin. These two points taken together would have made our suggestions as to the ethnicity of the murderer lean much more to a member of the local black community.

The criminal background of the offender could be indicated with much more confidence, because our own studies had shown that there were characteristics typical of these sorts of impulsive, violent, outdoor sex offenders. We therefore considered it very likely indeed that the offender had some form of criminal record, possibly for a sex-related crime or for ABH or GBH or for crimes linked to mugging. Such a criminal history meant that it would not be surprising if the offender had already been considered as part of the ongoing inquiry.

Two weeks before we submitted our report to the police in Southall, a rape took place in a cemetery less than a mile from Southall Park. The victim was a twenty-two-year-old pregnant woman who was so shocked by the assault that she aborted. The offender put a jacket over her head so that she would not be able to identify him later. The police were able to trace that assailant through description and sale of objects stolen during the assault. The attacker, Michael Ogiste, was known to the police from earlier crimes he had committed, but some senior officers did not think that he was the sort of man who could have murdered his victim. When they spoke to me about this suspect they also expressed concern that he fitted very closely the description in our report except for one feature that they thought must be crucial: he was black. We had suggested a white assailant and the officers involved were clearly not able to take account of the cautiousness with which we had made proposals on ethnic origins.

DNA tests indicated that this suspect had been responsible for the murder of Mrs Bhatti, so he went to trial. In later discussions the Southall police were quick to point out that he was already under arrest before they received our report. Perhaps worthy of note, though, is that working from reasonably overt, systematic principles, we could generate a description so accurate that when our report arrived it was immediately recognized as being a description of a man already in custody. If we had been able to report earlier, might we have been able to save a young, pregnant woman from the trauma of violent assault and consequent miscarriage?

Michael Ogiste was just turning twenty when he was arrested. He lived alone with his mother less than a mile from Southall Park, south of the railway line. He was unemployed at the time of the offence, having had un-skilled work previously. When he was eighteen he had been convicted for crimes of theft and violence, and imprisoned. In later informal conversations, local officers pointed out that when Ogiste was arrested the number of sexual assaults reported in the area dropped quite noticeably. The court declared Michael Ogiste a psychopath and he was therefore considered insane and sentenced 'for a period without limit of time'.

One of the strange coincidences in this case was that Ogiste's mother was a strictly religious person, like his victim, active in church life. It may have been that the victim was practising hymns as she walked around Southall Park on a sunny Sunday morning. A pleasant-looking woman in her early fifties, Mrs Bhatti was hardly a conventional object of sexual desire as Lynette White was, but she represented something to Ogiste. He denies the murder so there is no way, at present, of establishing what went through his mind when he attacked her. The violence of his attack, none the less, reveals that he was determined to overpower her; he did not want only to subdue her or make her submit. He stole things from her as well as sexually assaulting her. The victim meant something to the offender. As impulsive as the offence was, it still involved the choice of a location and a victim. The action and its target had significance to the offender. In order to find the culprit, we required an understanding of what that significance was.

In different ways Lynette White and Pushpa Bhatti were treated by their killers as objects who had little significance as particular people. They were targets that the assailant wanted to control and make use of. An extreme and very obvious form of this is revealed by criminals who have virtually no contact at all with their victims apart from the attack.

In one case we were asked to comment on an attack on a woman walking down a shopping street in the middle of the day. She was suddenly knifed by a man she had never seen before. The same man similarly attacked another complete stranger a few days later. In another case, a large number of attractive young women each became aware that acid had been squirted at them while they were travelling on the London underground. Again there had been no contact between the assailant and his victims other than the covert attack with the acid. Perhaps the most revealing aspect of these acid attacks was that it was squirted on their buttocks. In addition, the acid formed a squiggle not unlike the graffiti signatures that abound on our city walls. It was as if the assailant was 'making his mark' on these victims, like the numbers put on victims in German concentration camps. The pain and distress his actions caused to his victims were subordinate to his attempt to have some impact on them. Such men appear to have very little contact with women generally, to see them as distant objects. This may well reflect a general disturbance in their relationships with all people.

Knife or acid attacks on strangers are a step away from more directly murderous sprees that catch the world headlines from time to time. The consideration of one of these will serve to illustrate this frightening phenomenon.

Around midday on Wednesday 19 August 1987 Mrs Myra Rose found four-year-old Hannah Godfrey and her two-year-old brother walking hand in hand along a road in the Savernake Forest, a thick mixture of trees that spreads out over a few square miles in north Wessex about forty miles north of Stonehenge in southern England. The children had been having a picnic in the forest with their mother, Susan, on the way to visit their grandmother for her birthday. Hannah said to Mrs Rose: 'A man in black shot my mummy.' Susan Godfrey's body was found not very far away in the forest with thirteen bullet wounds, having been shot in the back at close range and left for dead where she fell.

This was the first of a number of unprovoked murders that Michael Ryan committed that day. Following his killing of Susan Godfrey, which probably happened as he attempted to rape her, Ryan returned from the forest to his home less than ten miles away. On the way he called in to a petrol station to fill his car and a petrol can. The cashier, who knew him from many previous visits, urged him to pay quickly because she was hurrying off. He responded by shooting at her with an Underwood M1 carbine. Fortunately she was able to hide behind the counter until, the gun eventually failing to fire, he drove away.

At his home in Southview, Ryan loaded his car with weapons and survival apparatus, such as maps and water bottles and a bullet-proof waistcoat. He then set fire to the house. He attempted to shoot his dog but, as he later reported, he could not bring himself to do this with his eyes open. Consequently he just wounded it. When he got into his car he could not get it to start. His reaction was to shoot at it a number of times with his Kalashnikov AK47.

He now moved along Southview, shooting with his AK47 and Beretta 9mm pistol at anyone in his path. This included his mother returning from a shopping trip. He shot her twice as she confronted him and twice again in the back where she fell. Walking from Southview to his old school about half a mile away he killed another eight people and wounded a further eight. By the time he ran out of ammunition for the AK47 and was down to the last magazine for his pistol, waiting on the top floor of the school for the police to find him, he had killed seventeen people and injured a further fifteen. His final violent act at the end of the day that led to the newspaper headlines throughout the world associating the name of the small town of Hungerford with 'massacre', was to shoot himself.

Later inquiries revealed that Michael Ryan was twenty-seven years old when he shot himself, his mother and a number of neighbours who had known him for many years. He was a quiet, introverted person whose only friend and confidante appears to have been his mother. His father had died, at the age of eighty, three years before Ryan's murdering spree. This death appears to have lifted a load off Michael's shoulders. His father had always been a big, athletically built man, an ex-army captain who dominated Michael and his mother. His mother was twenty years his father's junior and appears to have protected Michael from his father's criticisms as, increasingly, his father revealed his deep dissatisfaction with his son's lack of achievement or success.

Michael Ryan escaped from this ambience of conflict in his many lone walks, which appear to have been increasingly caught up in a disturbed mixture of fantasy and firearms. From about the age of fourteen he had air weapons and before he obtained the Kalashnikov and other assault rifles he had a collection of military memorabilia. His contacts with others grew further distant as he became more involved in his lonely military games, and he had only intermittent casual work. His game-playing spilled over into the far-fetched stories he told acquaintances of being befriended by a reclusive colonel, of learning to fly and so on. By his late twenties it seems likely that most people had ceased to have any real meaning for him. He saw them as creatures who could be controlled by his superior fire-power.

The 'massacre' in Hungerford has some spine-chilling similarities to many other tragedies in which a lone individual kills a number of people in one connected 'spree' of mayhem. These events are sometimes labelled by behavioural scientists as *mass* killings, to distinguish them from *serial* murders in which the killings happen over an extended period of time and often in a number of different locations. There are many distinct differences between these two types of multiple killings.

The mass murder is typically a tragedy in almost the classical, literary sense. A predetermined, almost inevitable, unfolding process whereby a person acts out an inner rage that most often ends in his own death. It is a form of suicide. Even when the man is caught alive he usually has been narrowly prevented from killing himself. For example Julian Knight, who killed seven people and wounded nineteen others in Melbourne in 1987, during what became known as the Hoddle Street massacre, admitted after his capture: 'I was going to shoot myself but I'd lost the bullet I'd put in my jeans pocket.'

Shakespeare realized this close association of murder with suicide in his portrayal of Hamlet, whose own death is implicit from the beginning of the play which ends with three bodies on the stage besides Hamlet's. The almost casual killing of Polonius starts the sequence of murders which makes all the others unavoidable. Macbeth, by comparison, is more obviously a serial murderer who, if he is not stopped, will go on killing until force of arms prevents him.

Dramatists, whether of the stature of Shakespeare or lesser mortals, build these individuals into powerful symbols for human experience. They expand the character to capture feelings and emotions that will move their audience to new levels of personal insight. In doing that they move away from the very limited and blinkered view that real criminals have of the world.

Considering only the initial murder of Susan Godfrey by Ryan, the body at the crime scene presents some superficial similarities to the way Lynette White's was found and that of Pushpa Bhatti, but there were important differences too.

The use of an assault rifle to kill a person as she ran away, prior to any sexual assault, shows the extent to which Susan Godfrey was an entity to be controlled or destroyed. Lynette White's significance to her killers was revealed by the location in which she was killed as much as by the nature of the stab wounds. She was seen as a resource, in their possession, by those who killed her. Pushpa Bhatti was murdered in the course of a sexual assault. She represented an opportunity for Ogiste but also a threat. All three very different women in very different settings were dealt with by their murderers as less than fully human, as mechanisms that were to be bent to their assailants' will. They fought against the role imposed on them; in dying they maintained their own humanity.

The majority of murders in Britain are quickly solved by the police, usually because the killer is well known to the victim and often because, filled with remorse, the murderer virtually gives himself up. Those cases where detection is more difficult are the ones that stretch police capabilities. These are the ones for which detailed behavioural analysis is most relevant but they are also inherently the most difficult to solve.

Detailed records of murders are nowadays often made available to me on police videos. Their unblinking look at the aftermath of murder carries a clinical, undramatic precision that contrasts with fictional television, but does show more clearly than any cops and robbers drama the problems that murder investigators face and how important it is for them to be able to read the traces, and remove the shadows, that the killer leaves.

One police video I remember especially well. Over the bright stripes of the usual colour card, the video starts with a voice intoning the place, time and date in the matter-of-fact way that appears to be unique to police officers. The colour card jerks out of view and a pleasant terraced house in warm, grey sandstone appears on the screen with a red-and-white striped plastic tape draped in front of it. The huddle of police officers beside the door, and the background noise of their official conversations over radios, indicate that this is not the film of an opening ceremony but something far more sinister.

The camera moves towards the house and the neutral eye takes us into the small entrance hall, the cameraman pausing at the door to get his bearings. The police radios are now a distant background to the breathing of the cameraman and the shuffle of his feet in the debris of the hall. Someone asks if the sound is on and gets a grunted 'Yep'.

The stairs at the end of the small hallway show clear signs that someone has started a fire there: burnt paper and smoke marks on the wall. The camera turns left into the small front room and slowly films the armchair and sofa that remain as charred skeletons. Smoke and the remains of the fire-fighting have turned the room into a derelict shell in which the memory of the solitary inhabitant lingers in the overturned wastebasket and destroyed lamp over a burnt-out television.

The camera turns full circle and proceeds carefully up narrow, twisted stairs. A small bathroom and kitchen are glimpsed off the stairs with a panning shot that draws most attention to the smoke-darkened walls and over-turned wastebaskets. Then up the twisting stairs again which at the top reveal a pile of burnt paper and even more blackened walls. Attempting to get a good shot of these decrepit remains the cameraman is stopped by a voice saying, 'Don't go back any further.' The camera then moves round to the right, passing the doorway to a bedroom, moving across the untidy bed and down to the floor. A chalk-white figure is lying there, like an undressed dummy from a shop window. But this is not a model. Its intestines are bursting through the stomach wall. It is the body of a murder victim.

The shock of this image still echoes within me, although since that first distressing sight I have been called on to study far more gruesome pictures of mutilated bodies. That was the moment when I realized how far I had strayed outside the cosy realms of university research to confront the challenge of violent crime.

The pictures on the police video have much of the peculiar mixture of the obvious and the unexpected that seem to be typical of murder. The attempt to set the house on fire, which had brought out the fire brigade, leading to the discovery of the body, seems unnecessary and adds further risk to the culprit's actions. There had even been more than one attempt to start a fire, in the living-room and under the body itself. Yet these attempts had not been very effective, although this was an old building with wooden floors. The fire had slowly smouldered for some time. Another oddity: the nightdress found, inside out, behind the front door, but no indication of any sexual activity on the remains. There was general disarray and an unkempt look to the house which had boxes of fruit pastilles everywhere and drawers full of unused tights.

As the list of abnormal features became longer, it started to dawn on the officers at the scene of the crime that some of them reflected the victim's lifestyle and could be either irrelevant to the case or the key to understanding the murderer's actions. But which was which?

The complications of what the scene reveals about the crime increase when the details of how the body was left are considered. Beyond the mutilations to the body there is the failed attempt to burn it and the patterns of blood around it. The location and direction of bloodstains and exactly how the victim died can speak volumes about what actually happened. Experts can tell from the angle and direction of a splash whether the blood came from a vein or artery and therefore where the body was when any particular wound was inflicted, thus building up a detailed account of the struggle. The haunting phrase comes back: 'Dead bodies don't splash.' The grimness of the principle that underlies all forensic investigations throws a shadow over the scene: 'All contacts leave a trace.' The run of blood next to the body, then, suggests it was moved after death. But why? To set a fire underneath it? But if you are going to burn the house down, why stop to try and burn the body?

The careful investigations by forensic experts that will eventually enable the police to know what the victim had to eat and when, how long she had been lying there before the fire was started, what accelerant was used, who made the nightdress, where the tights were bought and many, many other minutiae drawn from the physical evidence, lead back again and again to questions about the actions that produced this crime, about the person who perpetrated it and about his victim and her relationship to him. The physical analysis of the forensic material, as invaluable as it is when a case comes to court, does not tell much about the people involved and their actual behaviour that is so critical to finding the culprit.

The actions of the attacker seem to have been bizarre, but speaking to neighbours and local shopkeepers soon revealed that the victim herself was a very strange person. The police uncovered a history of intense psychiatric disturbance, an estranged husband and little close contact between the victim and anyone else. The thickening plot began to make police officers feel that they were getting out of their depth. They didn't know how such mentally disturbed people behave: how would they react to a casual intruder? Would they have close friends? The detectives felt that they were dealing with people who lived by other rules, unknown to them. This eventually led them to seek help from me.

Their questions posed a major challenge. Are these violent acts, which may be overtly or covertly sexual, beyond the pale of ordinary experience and comprehension? Is this a search for a distorted human being? If it is, what maps and guide posts can help ordinary folk to understand this other world?

Yet there is an important paradox here. If it is fathomable within conventional understanding then its study is even more important because it will help to illuminate ordinary sexuality and its association with aggression. By studying the bizarre we should gain more direct knowledge of ourselves and where the divide between good and evil can really be drawn.

It was the strangeness of the victim and the peculiarities of the crime scene that brought the police to me; especially the fact that there may have been some sexual motivation. Although the forensic and medical evidence did not indicate any sexual activity during the assault, the naked female body was enough to suggest that possibility. The likelihood of the attack being carried out by a stranger was a further reason for bringing me in. Initial investigations had ruled out the husband, who was nowhere near at the time and could have committed a much simpler crime, less open to detection. The victim had so few other close contacts, appearing to live the life of a recluse, that virtually anybody who could have got into the house would have been a stranger to her. The two things that cause many police investigators particular difficulties are sex crimes and stranger assaults. They cannot draw upon their own experience to understand these crimes. A victim who has an unfamiliar lifestyle as well magnifies their difficulties in understanding what has happened and therefore how to proceed.

Before I started to contribute to police inquiries, my contacts with criminal investigations had been so sparse that my beliefs about what happened were greatly influenced by the elegance and unremitting logic of the fictional crime stories that fill the television channels. Even the documentary films that give an account of actual investigations have to give a shape to them that will make interesting viewing, thereby obscuring the ambiguity and confusion that can characterize many complex investigations.

A television play or documentary may show a few experts looking around the site where a murder victim was found, but it is rare to emphasize that this location is the starting point for the police investigation. The actual offence is the focus of all subsequent activity. In crimes against people this includes a very careful consideration of the victim. The inquiries then move outwards to relatives, friends and neighbours until the network of contacts shows a clear enough picture for more focused action. If the victim's lifestyle is difficult to comprehend, or if it is inherently very vulnerable, like that of a prostitute or promiscuous homosexual, then this starting point is fraught with difficulties.

How have violent criminals who have attacked a number of strangers been caught, then, if the investigation of these crimes is so inherently difficult? A policeman on normal patrol duty at night saw an old van with a light not working. As a routine check he radioed for details of the owner. While he was talking on the radio his partner proceeded calmly over to the vehicle. The van's owner leaned out of the car and shot at the police officer with a sawn-off shotgun. By the time the identity of the van's owner was known, his criminal significance was already well understood by the officers on the spot.

In another actual example police patrols had been

instructed to investigate all cars in which prostitutes might be plying their trade with the explicitly stated intention of driving the trade out of town. One quiet evening two policemen approached two saloon cars in a dark alley. As they questioned the people in the first car the client jumped out of the second and attempted to run off. One officer gave chase while the second went to talk to the female left in the car. He discovered that she was dead, recently stabbed through the heart. Perhaps her client was responsible for other attacks in other places?

A woman walking home one afternoon through a graveyard was jumped on by a man who tried to rape her. She vaguely recognized him as being like someone, well known to the police, who lived nearby. The suspect was arrested and routine checking of blood-matches suggested he might have been involved in a recent murder. Further forensic evidence from the murder scene confirmed this.

These are examples from recent British investigations of which I have detailed knowledge. Some have even been featured in television documentaries in which the police spokesmen have appropriately been proud of the good police work that led to the arrest and conviction of these violent criminals. But the contribution of chance cannot be dismissed. In that regard at least, the coincidence that keeps detective fiction moving often plays a role in police investigations. The cynic would say that if the police deploy enough people over enough time and the criminal continues to offend, then the laws of probability will take over. The dice will eventually turn up double six if they are thrown often enough.

My own view is that this cynical perspective is not valid for many police investigations, which are well structured and organized, leading to conviction by the steady impact of applied logic. Invitations to me to help inquiries are also a direct attempt to increase the overall competence of criminal investigation.

Part of the need for this help lies in the fact that there is considerable room for confusion and the following of false trails in the open-ended search process with which a hunt for a murderer may start. The woman found dead by the fire brigade may have been killed by any passing burglar, by an acquaintance or relative. It might have been intentional or accidental, part of another crime or the determined objective of the assailant. All there is for the detectives is a mutilated body in a smoke-blackened house. The wounds of a murdered Caesar may speak to Mark Antony but they are often silent when the victim is an unknown man or woman attacked by a stranger.

When the police video came to an end, the images that remained were of the smallness of the house, the winding stairs, the remains of the smoke from the fire and that chalk-white body which it seemed so intrusive to pause on that the first time through I found myself averting my gaze. It was only after the TV monitor was turned off that I realized we had never seen the camera operator's feet. So, we had never been shown what was happening at key points on the ground as he moved through the building. What was thought of as the latest technological assistance to criminal investigation turned out to be little more than a useful set of images with which to capture the atmosphere of the scene. Detailed analysis, in this case at least, came from careful study of the photographs and the written material that a case creates.

Is this where my contribution lies? In telling people not to forget their feet? In slowing the action down so that there is the time to and the chance to find patterns? But in the heat of the action there is a risk in this slower approach: the culprit might move, and the common-sense view that has shaped past investigations might be destroyed. Creative people have often accepted the Greek myth that if you ever look at your muse directly it will disappear and your inventiveness with it. Perhaps that is the risk of cold science.

It is a risk. If we are to have these men of action pause for even a moment, we must deliver to them something that makes their pausing worthwhile. But until they slow down the action enough for us to study it, how can we be sure that there will be anything for us to say to them? How do we know that there will be shapes in the mirror that we can interpret? They may just be flickering shadows that do not settle long enough for us to read them. We cannot bring the criminal act into a sterile laboratory and examine it there with objective neutrality like a body undergoing a post-mortem. We must collect our samples of human actions where they are dropped. Yet all the distortions introduced as they are passed from hand to hand along the way may make them too vague to translate.

The clarity of hindsight shows that emerging principles do enable us to interpret the shadowy patterns that come from all the acts associated with murder. The actions take on an ever more meaningful shape as the number of examples grows, but the number grows slowly because each example depends upon the effort and effectiveness of a police investigation. There therefore exist many more violent crimes in which the actions of the criminal are crying out for interpretation but the validity of that interpretation will not be known until someone is convicted of the crimes.

Perhaps the most poignant example of this is the murder that occurred up the small, winding stairs. The strange mixture of fire and wounds, the bizarre lifestyle of the victim, the small town where violent crime is so rare. All these facets, when combined with what we now know of murder, pointed to a local man whom the police had interviewed. He knew the victim before the night of the attack and himself had a history of mental disturbance. But there is not enough evidence to arrest and convict him. Until a court gives a verdict, we will never know for sure if our interpretations are correct.

Part Four

————◆————

RESOLUTIONS

*They see only their own shadows,
the shadows of one another, which the
fire throws on the opposite wall of
the cave.*

PLATO, REPUBLIC VII, 514A

Chapter Nine

STORIES WE LIVE BY

Rapists and murderers leave traces of their own life stories in their criminal actions. Detectives start with the details of an assault, or the body at the scene of a murder. I have struggled to find a Rosetta stone to help police officers interpret these traces. This is a quest for a way of translating the residue of a crime into the language of actions on which police can act. Such an attempt to interpret the shadows a criminal casts is a search for a special type of theory of criminal behaviour: one that would help detectives to make sense of the life that gave rise to the crimes.

For rapists and murderers, and probably for most other criminals, the life that must be revealed is hidden. Therefore, at the heart of any theory will be some account of the secret, inner life of offenders and how it is reflected in their deeds. But we must not forget the paradox of this criminal, inner life. The existence of a hidden story implies that there is another story which is open to view; a non-criminal existence.

All the men whose capture has been discussed in earlier chapters did, at various times, live normal, unthreatening lives with other people. Duffy spent nights with a girl who was an acquaintance, sometimes sharing her bed without ever abusing that trust to force himself upon her. She knew him as a friend who was upset about the break-up with his wife.

When the police came to Colin Pitchfork's house to

arrest him he admitted to his wife that he had murdered two girls. She slapped his face as if she had discovered lipstick on his collar. He was her husband and he had cheated her. When she first discovered the truth it was difficult to separate that from the man she knew so well. Yet Pitchfork the father and husband was never very distant from Pitchfork the rapist and murderer. He had committed one of the murders while his baby slept a few yards away in the back of his car. All the time he was with his victim he was aware that he would soon need to get home so that his wife would not suspect anything.

Adrian Babb was regarded as a good son by his parents and a helpful assistant at the swimming pool where he worked. He committed some of his sexual assaults on elderly women on his way back from playing for a local football team. Indeed, one of the clues that might have been followed up by the police was the comment made by some of his victims that he had no unusual smells. One woman even said he smelled clean. He had probably had a shower after the game.

Other violent men for whom the police have searched have led some part of their lives as apparently normal and without menace. Robert Black was regarded by his neighbours as a pleasant, quiet man before he was charged with the abduction of a young girl. Peter Sutcliffe was so apparently benign that he avoided police suspicion in five different interviews with them before eventually being charged with thirteen murders. In the United States one of the most notorious of all serial killers, Ted Bundy, was recommended by a senator for law school. Albert Fish, who killed and possibly ate his child victims in New York in the mid-1930s, was seen as a kind old man who took people's children for walks. Sixty years later, Jeffrey Dahmer was convicted in Milwaukee for the murder of sixteen young men. Prior to his arrest the police had actually returned one of his victims to his custody, thinking that such a polite young man could not mean any harm. Indeed, most people arrested for a series of violent crimes reveal an earlier, or parallel, life that shows no outward indication of their inner violence. These killers and rapists all merged so well into the backdrop of urban life that it took major police inquiries to identify them.

It is important to realize that I am not drawing attention only to the secret nature of the crimes, necessary for the assailant to avoid detection and capture. It is the psychological capacities all these men show that is so astounding. They were able to exist as normal, law-abiding citizens, often for long periods. They could cope with the vicissitudes of daily life without the need to reveal anger or rage. Their violent outbursts were always only a part of their life story. Any explanation of criminal actions must therefore also explain why the majority of a criminal's behaviour is not overtly anti-social, violent or bizarre. It is in their secret lives that they unmask the evil part of their nature.

Perhaps this view of criminality is not as far removed as it may seem from daily experience. When you are alone with yourself, who are you? When you are not with other people who immediately think of you as a wife or daughter, home-owner, customer, manager, financial specialist, experienced tennis player, neighbour, Chelsea supporter, or any of the many other roles that you might take, who exactly are you? Do you have a 'true' self? Or are you just a mixture of the different selves that other people have assigned you? If you are a mixture, are there equal portions of each of these public selves in the concoction, or does your private self (who you are to you) have a dominant role, say of wife or financial expert? Is there perhaps some other hidden role in which you see yourself, of which not even those close to you are aware? Are you a courageous fighter for truth, maybe; a perceptive reader of the human condition; or possibly even a secret seeker of revenge; a late-night marauder who has power over weak women? We all have hidden as well as public selves. Sometimes our hidden selves are very different indeed from those that others know.

Those who study abnormal mental processes – clinical psychologists and psychiatrists – like to talk about the fantasies of their patients. FBI agents have adopted this vocabulary when they try to elaborate their own understanding of violent criminals. But it seems to me that the term 'fantasy' – with all its implications of unreality, illusion and lack of contact with the world everybody else sees – pushes our views of violent criminals too much into the realms of fiction. What they do may feel like a nightmare to those who experience it, but it is horrifically locked into reality. Unlike the free-floating, unshapen world of dreams and fantasies, the actions of violent men do have a discernible structure to them. It is this personal, secret truth that violent men live which cries out for explanation, not the overlay of symbolism which therapists and detectives may place on the shadows criminals cast.

EXPLANATIONS

The conventional approach to explaining the actions of criminals is to look for causes within their biological or psychological make-up. The actions themselves are seen as protuberances on a deeper malaise. Inferences are made about what really is the inner sickness of the man. A different set of theories sees the actions of criminals as a reflection of their social milieu.

All these theories cope with the hidden nature of crime by proposing a propensity for criminal actions under certain conditions. They are usually vague about which particular conditions bring the criminality to the surface, recognizing that each person's life experiences may provide specific triggers. Different theories, though, do draw attention to different aspects of the situation that may be relevant. My own view is that all of these explanations of criminality, violent or otherwise, have major flaws, but that an emerging combination of them does help us to understand violent (and possibly other) crimes in ways that are directly relevant to detectives. In order to understand this new fusion of theories we therefore need to review the earlier perspectives on which it draws.

Biological theories of criminality lead to a search for an understanding of violence in the physical make-up of the criminal, whether in properties of the brain or damage to it, hormone imbalance or faulty chromosomes. These explanations can be traced to the discoveries in chemistry and biology that built up momentum at the end of the eighteenth century. They gave rise to a fond belief, still endorsed by many today, that all aspects of human action and experience can be reduced to biochemical formulae. The view that a person was little more than a combination of physics and chemistry enthused Mary Shelley to invent that most enduring image of the evil monster in her book *Frankenstein*.

As the theory of evolution took hold in the middle of the nineteenth century, even more overt links were made between a person's actions and their physical constitution. The phrenologists were convinced that the faculties of the mind were such a direct product of the structure of the brain that they would be revealed through cranial bumps. These ideas had their parallel, in the 1870s, in the study of criminals in Italy by Cesare Lombroso. He and his many followers proposed that criminals were a throwback to more primitive species, and that there were 'congenital criminal types'. Their criminal propensities could be discerned from detailed features of their physiognomy, such as an asymmetrical cranium, long lower jaw, flattened nose and scanty beard. Together with these 'stigmata' they were also considered to have low sensitivity to pain.

Lombroso's ideas were very influential. To this day there are still proposals put forward that criminals have distinct physical characteristics that are not caused by their diet or life experiences. For example, Joel Norris in a book on serial killers, first published in 1988, lists twenty-three characteristics that he thinks are evidence of genetic disorders, and by inference indicative of a potential serial murderer. They form a list of which Lombroso would have been proud, including asymmetrical ears, abnormalities in teeth and a head circumference outside a normal range.

Norris gives no evidence for his proposals nor does he seem aware of the very careful studies of Charles Goring carried out at the turn of the century to test Lombroso's hypotheses. Working together with one of the founders of modern statistics, Karl Pearson, Goring assiduously examined more than three thousand entrants to English prisons over an eight-year period. He measured the various physical traits which Lombroso had claimed were the characteristics of criminals and compared the results with measurements made of law-abiding graduates of Cambridge and Oxford universities. Goring's conclusions were very clear indeed: 'both with regard to measurements and the presence of physical anomalies in criminals, our statistics present a startling conformity with similar statistics of the law-abiding class. Our inevitable conclusion must be that there is no such thing as a physical criminal type' (Charles Goring, *The English Convict*, 1913, p.173).

Although the view that criminals are a primitive species has faded in most quarters, the idea that human actions can be explained solely in biological and physical terms is still dominant in many explanations of criminal, as of other, behaviour. People are still often thought of as a conglomeration of mechanisms. Variations in the way their components are built are thought to lead to the differences between people. This is the 'monstrous creation' vision of people. Those who do not fit the norms of society are either badly built or their original programming has got out of control.

If a person were put together without basic human conscience –with just the mechanical components of what made him human – then he would be like Dr Frankenstein's monster, a fiend who would eventually destroy his creator. Here was the basic explanation for criminality. Evil men were put together with missing bits. They did not have 'the fear of God before their eyes', as one legal indictment had it in the last century. Innate depravity made the criminal susceptible to 'the seductions of the evil one'.

Instead of a clear physical defect, as argued by Lombroso, psychiatrists who wished to hold on to the biological basis of criminality talked of a disease that could not be seen under the microscope, but was 'mental'. Insanity was deemed to have many forms, including 'moral insanity'. People argued about whether or not a person's soul could be diseased although his mind was not. A pathology, or illness, of the psyche was thought to be the cause of anti-social behaviour. These people who did not have what were regarded as the more directly observable psychopathies, such as schizophrenia or mental subnormality, ended up in a catch-all group. The term 'psychopath' was born to cover those people who were not obviously mad or of low intelligence but who did not embrace the acceptable codes of social practice.

While it is now rare for psychiatrists to discuss diseases of the soul, terminology from those more certain days is still with us. Many still regard criminal actions as evidence of a hidden mental disease. Just as a person who has jaundice can exist normally, even though from time to time he must take to his bed, so the festering disease within a criminal will sometimes lead him to crime. From this view criminals appear normal but carry about an unseen hole, or badly decayed area, in their persona where guilt or remorse should be. The non-threatening appearance of the criminal is the human machinery working normally, but from time to time the defects in the machinery of the psyche will throw the person out of kilter, producing violent crimes.

The idea that criminals are born that way – made out of some sort of criminal material that will show its true colours given the opportunity – does not really stand up to close scrutiny. If there are these biological determinants they must be at their peak in young men from deprived sections of society, because they are the people who commit most crimes. But if they are, why do they afflict only some young men in these sub-groups and leave others unscathed? More importantly, what biological mechanisms would create the unfolding changes that are characteristic of the development of individual criminals? Why do imbalanced hormones, or minimal brain damage, cause youngsters to steal fruit and older criminals to carry out bank robberies? How do these processes give rise to the limited repertoires that are typical of individual criminals, such as 'Jack the Ripper's' targeting of prostitutes or Babb's selection of elderly women?

Even if there were convincing answers to these questions, how would they help the police? Some of Lombroso's followers did go so far as to suggest that innate characteristics were different for thieves, murderers and sex offenders. Different criminals could therefore be identified by their particular type of 'stigmata', but systematic study has shown over and over again that the declared differences do not distinguish between convicts and other groups drawn from the same socioeconomic backgrounds.

The lack of logic or evidence for the biological explanations of violent crime does not stop people from still purveying these bizarre notions. Fortunately, most police officers have not been convinced that they should record the shape of a person's ears when they carry out house-to-house inquiries. Without such specific, overt physical details it is difficult to know how the biological perspective could assist police investigations. Certainly the complexity and idiosyncrasy of the patterns of criminals' actions strain the credibility of any belief in particular, detailed genetic or biochemical characteristics that could be inferred by police investigators from a study of the crime scene and victim statements.

There is, of course, likely to be some biological basis to psychological differences between people. This could contribute to their general characteristics in such a way that under certain circumstances they might be more prone to commit a crime than a person who had less of that particular aspect of their biological make-up. But this chain of influences is so long and marginal that for most practical purposes it is irrelevant. Indeed, drawing attention to it probably does more to detract from useful considerations than to contribute to them. The important, yet subtle, difference between Martin and George in their student rapes in the Midlands could not be disentangled from any assumptions about their genetic make-up. It is difficult to see how any ideas that Duffy may have had minor brain damage could have helped to indicate where he may have lived. It was known in a section of Chicago's homosexual community that Jeffrey Dahmer had unusual sexual proclivities, but explanations of them in any biological terms would not have made the local police take the potential for serial murder within that community any more or less seriously.

A second type of explanation contrasts with the fundamentally mechanical, biological model of human beings. Biologists assign no role to the understanding that the criminal has of himself and his world. In contrast, the second approach, which I will sketch also very broadly, does focus on psychological mechanisms in the mind of the violent criminal. Some of the oldest explanations ever put forward to explain human sin are of a fundamentally psychological nature. For millennia the fall from grace has been seen as the product of the conflict of desires, eating of the forbidden fruit.

Beyond the Biblical account of human frailty, the tragedy of Oedipus is probably one of the earliest and most intense visions of this inner human conflict. In this Greek tragedy the central character is attempting to act honourably but his fundamental human weaknesses and lack of full knowledge inadvertently lead him to kill his father and marry his mother. Try as he will to live a virtuous life, the original sin, present within him at birth, ultimately leads him to his doom. Oedipus reveals a mixture of motivations. He is destroyed in the battle between different desires.

The earliest philosophers recognized the power of these inner conflicts. Plato wrote about the human being trying to control a chariot hauled by three horses, each pulling in a different direction. Many of us are aware of this fundamental conflict between what we know to be the appropriate action, what we wish to be the case and what our conscience indicates should be the case. No one is free of the experience of doing something that he knows he should not or that he later regrets. Oedipus enshrines this struggle as a battle with the fates, but Christian thinkers reinterpreted it as a vision of the internal struggle within each person between good and evil. The base desires we are born with were personified by the devil. When that devil was seen to be incarnate in other people, as in the suppression of witches or the Spanish inquisition, then the person possessed had to be killed. Subsequent religious conflicts, from the Crusades to the present day, have replaced internal, metaphorical battles by actual wars. Killing others is sanctioned because their evil desires are dominant.

More recent psychological theorizing has seen this battle between inner forces as a precarious balancing act. If the balance swings one way or the other, mental disturbance results. Many psychological theories concern themselves with the mechanisms people use to keep their experience of the world in balance. For example, it is argued that if people do something that is logically at odds with views they have expressed – such as eating meat when they are declared vegetarians – then they will reinterpret their experiences in order to maintain a coherent view of the world. The lapsed vegetarians will say they did not want to insult their host, or that it is only red meat they will not eat. It is claimed that people will reduce cognitive dissonance by attempting to act on their beliefs, or change their beliefs to fit in with their actions.

Another view of the internal psychological struggle is that people have to control their emotions in order to stay within socially acceptable bounds, but the control process can be faulty. So, it is argued, they may be 'over-controlled', their feelings eventually bursting out when they can no longer be suppressed. Or they may be 'under-controlled', reacting emotionally to many minor incidents. The balance is therefore seen as similar to the pressure valve on a water boiler. If the valve is faulty then violent behaviour may be the result.

A perspective that owes less to hydraulic analogies, but still reflects the idea of a balance of desires, is the notion that crime compensates for deficiencies in a person's experience. He may feel weak in non-criminal life, but committing crimes makes him feel strong. The inner conflict here is rather more subtle, being a self-assessment of a mismatch between achievement and potential. The criminal is thought to feel put upon by others and seeks power through his crimes. Like Oedipus, the criminal is walking a tightrope between what he knows is acceptable and what he feels is honourable. In many situations he acts acceptably; he is a good father and husband. But his fall is ordained. Eventually his actions will reflect his true desires.

These notions of inner conflict may get us closer to distinguishing between criminals when we have them before us in court or in therapy, but they present a fundamental problem when used to help investigations. The approach always hedges its bets. If everyone has the propensity for many conflicting motivations, how do we know which is being represented in a crime? A person who is fundamentally good may allow his inner badness to burst out into violence. So a violent act will lead us to look for, say, a controlled person who normally shows no signs of violence. In Freudian terms the 'compensation' resolves problematic personal relationships. It is the young man put upon by a domineering mother who goes out to attack other women in retaliation against the mother he is afraid to challenge. But the opposite of this argument is also tenable. If the violent act is produced by someone who has no conscience then we must look for a person who is well known to be violent. The hostility is not 'displaced' so it may be displayed in many non-criminal situations.

The inner conflict, compensation/displacement approach therefore always leaves a major question for any criminal investigation. If there are always opposite possibilities, which of them is relevant to any criminal situation? In a violent crime are we looking for a man known to be violent or one known not to be? The answer may lie in the details of the violence, but what that implies is that there is a certain sort of violence typical of a man known generally to be violent and another sort for the person who is not. Perhaps, then, we should be discriminating between types of violence, not making assumptions about inner conflict. Explorations of the psychological processes may take us a little way towards understanding violence but it is difficult to see how it can help to explain the repertoires that characterize criminals, or why the changes and developments in a criminal's activities should occur.

Knowing that Babb might have hated himself for what he was doing, or that Ogiste was trying to compensate for some perceived sexual inadequacy, might help us a little in any subsequent interviews with suspects. It is not really the stuff that police officers can ask about in house-to-house inquiries. How could the knowledge of Nilsen's psychopathology have speeded up his apprehension? The writer Brian Masters argued that Dennis Nilsen killed his homosexual lovers as a form of compensation for his inability to relate closely to other people. By keeping their bodies with him, it was claimed, he was finding some form of company to fill his loneliness. Whether this explanation has any validity or not, it is difficult to base any investigative strategy upon it. However, the knowledge that quiet, well-spoken, isolated, promiscuous homosexuals may on rare occasions kill and mutilate the young men they pick up could have alerted the Milwaukee police to the actions of Jeffrey Dahmer.

There is a third general approach to understanding violent crime that contrasts with the biological and psychological: the social perspective. Here the causes of crime are seen as being within the network of personal contacts that show people the criminal path. This idea was the foundation of our modern penal system. The reforming Quakers believed that if a man were separated from the villains who had led him astray, put into solitary confinement with the Bible to study, then this would correct his errant ways and reform him. The power of this social perspective was encapsulated in the term 'reformatory'. In the USA many prisons are still called 'correctional' establishments. If you believe that there are fundamental biological or psychological deficiencies that cause criminality, then you will not believe that you can 'correct' a person by locking him up. The determination of the courts to keep young offenders out of prisons, away from the company of older criminals, serves to illustrate the irony of the failure of prisons to achieve the Quakers' goals.

The social explanation of crime is very different in emphasis from the other two perspectives. Oedipus, like Frankenstein's monster, is a solitary figure. Neither of them is part of a criminal sub-culture, tutored in the ways of crime by their close associates. Those around them are mere artefacts, there to create the means whereby they can be led to self-destruction. The solitariness of these fictional characters reveals the view that similar conflicts are expected to erupt in other times and other places. Those conflicts are thought of as the essence of humanity. In these stories there is no emphasis on the possibility that they may emerge out of social transactions.

Yet, although Frankenstein's monster was the precursor of many modern fictional automata, these later translations lost a theme central to Mary Shelley's book. She presents the ugly creation of Viktor Frankenstein as developing into an evil fiend only when he is ousted by society. This has a number of consequences in the evolution of the monster. One is that he is never able to develop productive, warm relationships with other people, thereby becoming increasingly callous. The second is that the only illustrations he is given of how to behave are those of other people reacting viciously to him. One other most important consequence, central to Frankenstein's tragedy, is the monster's desire to have a female of his kind made with whom he can form a mutually supportive relationship. As we all know, Viktor refuses this request, realizing that there are some fatal flaws in the make-up of the fiend that would only be magnified if he had a sexual partner with whom to produce offspring.

Mary Shelley's novel leaves us with the question of whether the evil nature of the monster was really created by a lack of emotional shape and support, as would be expected of any child abandoned by its family at birth, made worse by the vicious way he is treated. The novel then, rather than the monster himself, provides a perceptive example of the third general class of explanations for criminal behaviour. It gives emphasis to a criminal's social group and the way he learns to act, being taught by those around him. Current assessments of criminality tend to be most sympathetic to this social perspective, seeing crime as endemic within particular families and sub-sections of society.

There is clearly some validity to the social explanation – criminals are generally drawn from a limited range of social backgrounds – but it cannot be the whole story. John Cannan killed at least one woman and violently assaulted a number of others, yet he came from a comfortable, middle-class background and the other members of his family had had no contact with the law. The same could be said of many notorious serial killers and men who rape a number of women. The society these men keep does not obviously provide them with violent criminal models to copy. The same society, whatever its illustrations of violence, does not appear to have led many of the brothers and sisters of vicious men into similar patterns of behaviour.

The inner, secret nature of violent crime, the very 'alternativeness' of the criminal stories they live, is possibly one of the strongest challenges to the social learning perspective. If the violence is a secret part of the hidden thoughts of a criminal, how can it be shaped by contact with other people? The criminal fraternity itself condemns rape and child abuse, describing such offenders as 'nonces' because what they do is of no instrumental value – a nonsense. So how does a sub-culture support it? There is also the related problem of how people learn hidden, secret patterns of behaviour. Social processes are open to view. Yet the brutal actions of Duffy, Dahmer, and thousands of other violent men, are secret creations of their own.

Even if there were a very strong validity to sociological explanations of violent crime, they do have distinct disadvantages for police investigations. They emphasize what makes people similar to each other rather than highlighting the crucial differences that lead to the identification of a suspect. For instance, an awareness that the killers of Lynette White mixed in the same milieu as she did is a useful starting point for the inquiry, but hardly goes beyond what many detectives would have immediately assumed.

The biological, psychological and sociological explanations I have sketched all take us some steps towards understanding, and investigating, violent crimes. For although each has major flaws, in combination they provide foundations on which fruitful, further perspectives can be built. But, to take these ideas a step forward the system of explanations needs to be set in motion. All the approaches I have summarized are essentially static. A criminal is seen as being assigned his behavioural pattern either at birth or when he joins a criminal group. The inner conflicts have been viewed as part of a person's psychological make-up that will emerge in a particular way under given circumstances. All these fixed views of violent actions belie the very obviously dynamic qualities that they have. They continue, and usually change, over time. We therefore need to consider further aspects of explanation. This brings us to themes which were regarded as fundamental by the founders of modern scientific psychology.

DEVELOPMENT AND CHANGE

James Sully, heralding the dawn of modern psychology, wrote one of the first major British textbooks in the field in 1892. He started the book by emphasizing that mind is a process of growth or development: 'The ultimate problem of psychology is, indeed, to explain all the higher and more complex mental states as products of development. Hence the most important class of laws for the psychologist are the laws of mental development' (James Sully, *Outlines of Psychology*, 1892, p.7).

On the other side of the Atlantic, around the same time,

William James, arguably the father of modern psychology, wrote: 'Every smallest stroke of virtue or vice leaves its never so little scar' (William James, *The Principles of Psychology*, 1890, pp.130–31). Both Sully and James illustrate a stream of psychological thought that has seen the human state as being in a continuous process of change. The mind is always in action.

This view of human nature contrasts with that held by psychologists who focus on the fixed structures of the human condition, hard-wired into all aspects of experience. From the static view, a person's intelligence, ability to detect differences in musical tones, discriminate subtle differences between colours, their right-handedness or even how impulsive or sociable they are, are all considered as a particular aspect which, if not fixed at birth, is certainly fixed by adulthood. Many of the explorations of these psychologists are of the state and structure of an individual, often focusing on the particular human capabilities that are common to all individuals. Even when such psychologists look at the differences between people they are concerned to describe the traits that people exhibit, the characteristics which are typical of them in all circumstances.

The academic debate between those who search for common, static structures within the human psyche and those who look for dynamic processes of development was reflected in the less abstract discussions I had with Rupert Heritage and Lesley Cross about the 'Railway Rapist'. We needed to identify those aspects of the rapist's actions that were consistent, typical of him. These helped us to recognize the crimes that he had committed and link together his rape series. But we also knew that he was changing his actions as the crimes progressed. The physical description of an almost diffident, apologetic offender in the early assaults also fitted the description of a much more determined and aggressive offender in subsequent rapes. We need to know how offenders develop and change as well as their stable, consistent characteristics.

In the first half of the twentieth century, the developmental concern of psychologists was dominated by three very different people: Sigmund Freud, Jean Piaget and B. F. Skinner. Although their formulations are very different they all took their lead from Charles Darwin's theory of evolution. At the turn of the century psychologists were fascinated by the general Darwinian idea, that species emerge from primitive to more sophisticated forms by transactions with their environment. Most psychologists saw evolutionary theory as having many implications for understanding human nature. Some explored the implication that the animal origins of humankind were still present in everyone's actions. Others examined whether the stages of evolution from animals to humans were mirrored in the maturation of the sophisticated human psyche. Yet others emphasized how the actions and thoughts of one person would go through an evolutionary process of increased sophistication that was shaped by life's experiences.

Sigmund Freud, born in Austria in 1856, has had the most widespread influence. Although there is much to be said for Hans Eysenck's glib aphorism, that what was true in Freud's theories was not new and what was new was not true, this has not stopped generation after generation of students, in many different disciplines, utilizing the rich metaphors of Freud and his followers to comment on everything from advertising to xenophobia.

Of particular interest to the debate between static and dynamic qualities of human processes is the fact that although Freud and his very many followers were concerned with the basic structures of the mind that were common to everybody, they none the less elaborated a developmental process through which everybody went. They argued that it was distortions in this process of development that gave rise to the variations between people, and especially to the variations in their mental states.

Sigmund Freud was aware of the writings of Conan Doyle. He liked to think of himself as a psychological detective who could discern from minor slips of the tongue, or the symbolism of dreams, a history of associations and meanings that provided clues to critical, often traumatic, episodes in the earlier lives of his patients. As Freud developed his theories he provided ever more elaborate accounts of the underlying mechanisms that were revealed by the details of his patients' behaviour. His books are full of heroic dramas in which the various components of the psyche battle over the sanity of their host.

Most of Freud's focus was on the early stages in a person's development, the first few years of life. Later followers started to put the critical episodes in human development into a life-long sequence. One of his most broad-ranging followers was Erik Erikson who sketched out eight major stages in life in which particular interpersonal crises need to be resolved in order for the individual to progress to the next stage of maturation. These stages reflected the Darwinian idea of evolution but cast the battle for survival in the struggle between a search for identity and the demands of social roles. I have always been fascinated by the sanity of Erikson's vision and believe that his characterization of the life story as a series of encounters may have a direct contribution to make towards the understanding of criminal behaviour. So this is a perspective to which we will return.

Most Freudian, psychoanalytic, explanations of the development of violent or sexually deviant tendencies do not have the breadth of vision of Erikson's life stages. Instead they are focused on early stages in life. The inability to resolve adequately early conflicts is thought to leave distorting traces in later relationships. The now 'classic' profile, even used by novelists such as P. D. James, of the serial killer who is a 'loner who lives with his mother' is a direct product of a naive Freudian way of thinking.

The argument that leads to P. D. James's profile is somewhat as follows. The extreme aggression shown towards women by the killer is, as I mentioned earlier, a displaced attempt to gain independence from his smothering mother. The roots of this are seen as an inability to resolve the conflict, that all children are supposed to experience in their early years, between loving their father and being jealous of his relationship with their mother. By over-indulgence of the mother, or the absence of the father, the young boy is unable to metamorphose his jealousy into a socially acceptable conscience and so comes to have a hatred for his mother that he can express only in attacks on other women. This rather exotic theory, which has spawned many Hollywood thrillers (perhaps most notably Rod Steiger's *No Way to Treat a Lady*) is replete with the weaknesses I mentioned earlier, but by looking at the developmental roots it is also clear that the theory has a hard time explaining why most criminals are men. Why do we get no women serial killers living with their over-indulgent, elderly fathers?

Some psychoanalysts see this early childhood conflict re-emerging in adolescence. Then it is the characteristic rebellion of teenagers against their parents. They suggest that the rebellion will be particularly violent if it is not dealt with effectively before the person's hormonal activity creates such extremes of emotional response.

While there are many flaws in psychoanalytic theorizing,

stripped of its dramatic language the Freudian perspective does have value in drawing attention to the power of family relationships in shaping a person's ways of dealing with others. Our attention is drawn to the fact that the impact of biological processes, at different stages in a child's development, will be modified by the way he or she is dealt with by people who have significance for him or her.

The extremes of destructive relationships in childhood are those in which parents or others abuse children. Freudian theory has, therefore, possibly been of even more value in alerting us to the impact of the abuse and exploitation of children on their later psychological development. The recognition of the profound effect of child abuse is rather ironically linked to Freudian theory. Sigmund Freud argued that his patients' recollections of sexual abuse by their parents were wish-fulfilling fantasies. Yet the American psychiatrist Jeffrey Masson has demonstrated in his challenging book *The Assault on Truth* (1984), that there is every likelihood that then, as now, there was considerably more incest of many kinds than was generally recognized. Freud's patients may have been describing real events, not fantasies.

Certainly, most of the violent criminals to whom I have spoken, as well as those whose biographies I have read, do show early failures of relationships within their families. Whether this is a cause or a consequence of their criminal propensities is often difficult to disentangle. There is also the problem of explaining all those cases where people do survive disruptive, destructive family life without becoming serial rapists or murderers.

From the investigative point of view, the Freudian approach to criminal development alerts us to the significance of the family history of offenders. It also draws attention to the possibility that the criminal actions in a violent assault are likely to have precursors in the earlier life of the man for whom the police are looking. But exactly where to look and what to look for are not really indicated unless we stay close to the loner who lives with an elderly female relative.

A further problem with Freudian interpretations, and all the watered-down, sub-Freudian versions that are used as infills for newspaper accounts of violent crimes, is that the central thesis of psychoanalysis is that the person does not have direct access to the experiences that cause the inner conflicts. They are driven in to the unconscious and so are knowable only through intense, extended psycho-therapy. How is the investigator to gain access to these private experiences that the criminal himself may have buried in his unconscious? One answer to this question is that the underlying psychological problems will be revealed in other, more overt, ways. But, as we shall see, it may be possible to look for direct links between cri-minal behaviour and other daily transactions of the of-fender, without the need to get caught in the confusing metaphors and distracting buried dramas of the Freudian psyche.

The greatest contrast with the Freudian perspective on personal development is the work of the learning theorists, of whom Burrhus Frederic Skinner, an American psy-chologist born in 1904, is now widely regarded as the most significant. He applied the Darwinian idea of evolving species directly to the evolution of actions and habits. He set about explaining how a person's behaviour is shaped directly by the particular experiences of the consequences of that behaviour.

Skinner's concern was to build a science that dealt only with observable behaviour, not the unconscious, inaccess-ible assumptions of psychoanalysis. Although more police-men will have heard of Freud than have ever heard of

Skinner, his approach is more obviously relevant to police investigators. After all, all they have to go on are the actions of the criminal. They have less direct access to his thoughts and fantasies and certainly less opportunity to explore his unconscious than does the therapist.

Many of Skinner's studies focused on the simple habits of animals, especially pigeons, trained to respond in particular ways to particular stimuli. He proposed that people also could be considered as active organisms, like pigeons whose activity is shaped as a result of the consequences of prior activities. Activities that prove painful do not recur and those that prove satisfying are likely to increase in frequency, according to the Skinnerian theory of reinforcement. Few psychologists doubt the general validity of Skinner's models of learning but many question their relevance to daily experiences. Certainly in recent years psychology has become more cognitive in its orientation. Concern about studying the internal processes of thought and feeling, which help to give structure to human actions and experiences, has grown. Today even the most rigorous of learning theorists attempt to describe the perceptions and conceptions that give the reinforcing stimuli their significance. The basic challenge here is to answer questions about how an individual recognizes situations as being similar, so that the satisfactions associated with those situations are linked to a common experience.

If a person is simply seeking to repeat experiences that were found to be satisfying, then that person could move between a great variety of different experiences, any one of which might produce the same levels of satisfaction. In order that behaviour should be shaped by the experience of satisfaction, those experiences have to be linked to similar or common types of situation. This is not a problem for the scientist studying a pigeon in a box. If the pigeon is given only one type of stimulus with or without a particular type of reinforcement, then this pigeon does not need to make complex discriminations. Even as the range of stimuli are increased and the pigeon has to exhibit more subtle discriminations, the bird still is discriminating in relation to one particular reinforcement. The life of a human being outside of a cage is far more complex than that. The rewards and punishments take place within an unfolding human context.

Like the Freudians before them, then, learning theorists discovered that each individual moves through a sequence of stages that shape and structure subsequent patterns of behaviour. For the Freudian these sequences are battles, conflicts that must be won, in which the individuals' inner desires have to be tempered by the external demands of civilized society. For the learning theorists, the sequences are more fluid and flexible and it is only really the consequences of the experiences for the individual that determine the eventual effect of those experiences. The manifold possibilities for arbitrariness, in terms of what a person experiences, that are implicit within the learning theory framework are tempered by the structure of society, which tends to expose people to particular experiences in a particular order.

The 'classic' examples of learning theory explanations of bizarre anti-social behaviour are those dealing with the arbitrary emergence of fetishes. Sexual excitement, for example, may have been experienced by a pubertal boy during a painful surgical operation, when he was stroked by a nurse, who was a brunette. Later sado-masochistic activities were then linked to brunettes with similar hairstyles to the nurse. While such examples were once the stock-in-trade of 'psychological thrillers' there is remarkably little detailed evidence for them. As a leading forensic psychiatrist, D. J. West, put it, with admirable academic understatement, reviewing a number of such examples: 'The link is highly speculative, but it illustrates a popular line of thought.'

A more direct application of the learning theory approach to crime is the simple, but often ignored, point that most criminals can be expected to learn from their mistakes. 'Richard', a serial rapist, told me that after the struggles he had had with his early victims he subsequently took with him a knife and material to bind them. In disentangling the offences of Martin and George, Rupert and I had to work out what the likely changes had been in their actions as a result of the reactions of their victims. We needed to see what 'mistakes' they might have made, such as leaving semen at a crime scene, and how they had learned from that mistake to take more care not to leave such evidence in the future. The effect of any involvement they may have had with the police investigation was another aspect of their 'learning'. George had become aware of police interest in blood-testing him; Martin had not had the same learning experience and consequently was less careful. Indeed, our search for an evolution in the actions of offenders during the course of their crime series was itself stimulated by notions from learning theory.

At the present time, the weakness of this approach for investigations is its lack of specificity. Which actions change through the experiences of the criminal and which remain constant? What particular experiences are likely to be salient to him? Are the same things salient for all criminals? There may be ways of answering these questions, but they will probably take us beyond the traditional learning theory focus on limited aspects of behaviour.

Although Freudian theory and Skinnerian theory are fundamentally opposed in their approach to science and to psychology, there are many strands that they have in common. Like evolutionary theory on which they are built, the most notable commonality to these two schools of psychology is that they see human life unfolding through a series of episodes. The outcome of each episode carries implications for what will happen in the next stage of growth. Distortions in these learning processes, or in the resolution of conflict situations, leave their mark on the individual, in disturbed ways of behaving, in neurosis and psychosis, in styles of interacting with others, in personality characteristics and modes of expression. Both approaches leave conscious thought processes out of the picture. For Freud and his followers, it is unconscious motivation which is of central interest. For Skinner and the learning theorists, the focus is on behaviour. To understand how a person's way of thinking may develop we have to turn to a third giant of modern psychology: Jean Piaget, the Swiss psychologist born in 1896.

In some ways Piaget's contribution has been the most dramatic and underrated. For Piaget, unlike for Freud and Skinner, experience was secondary to the unfolding of the natural processes of maturation within the individual. Provided the growing infant was able to have access to the appropriate mixture of environmental possibilities, he would develop through a series of stages from specific, concrete operations on the world through to more abstract formal dealings with representations of the world.

From Piaget's vast range of writings I want to draw out two especially relevant points. One is the notion that there is almost a mathematical inevitability to the sequence of stages in human maturation. The second point is that these developments move from the more concrete to the more abstract. The importance of these two points stems as much from the general framework they provide for considering human cognitive development, as from their particular application to the ways in which young children evolve into intellectually mature adults. It is proposed that adults may go through parallel processes of increasing cognitive sophistication whenever they move into new realms of thought, whether it be architecture or fraud.

In other words, it is the process to which Piaget draws attention that I believe can help us solve crimes, not the particular products or points of development that Piagetian theory may emphasize. This is an especially subtle point which requires a little more detail.

Piaget's studies focused on the ways in which children develop an understanding from infancy to young adulthood of basic concepts such as size, shape and number, but he did show that these basic concepts were fundamental to other more intricate issues, notably, for us, morality. Thus, one suggestion from these ideas is that criminals will have reached only a low level of moral development. In other words, criminals are hypothesized to be operating at a concrete stage of moral thought in which they evaluate crimes only in terms of the likelihood of being caught or the pleasures of the crime itself. More morally mature adults are expected to think in terms of what is socially acceptable, or, at the most mature levels, in terms of general ethical principles. Unfortunately, the research evidence does not support these elegantly simple views of criminal ethical understanding. People appear to be able to operate at different ethical levels, depending on the circumstances, and known offenders are no less able to see morality in terms of general principles than are those who have not committed crimes.

The mistake is to see a stage of moral development as a sort of static personality characteristic rather than as a phase in an unfolding process. Piaget gives us a way of understanding what unfolding criminal sophistication might mean. The young offender operating out of immediate opportunity has little cognitive sophistication. The possibilities of the moment are paramount, just as the much younger child can act only as if objects are what they appear to be. As the offender becomes more experienced it would be hypothesized that he will see his criminal actions more abstractly, and be able to form a view on their implications and consequences. I know of no systematic research testing these ideas but the biographies of violent criminals provide a great many illustrations of the process in action. Duffy's career in crime is a graphic example of a man whose initial actions are casual and unsophisticated, but who was later able to take an overview of what he was doing and plan his crimes in some detail.

To take a further illustration: the developing abstraction of what he was doing was also appallingly clear in Jeffrey Dahmer's series of murders. His first murder was a sudden, unplanned outburst, but he eventually developed a procedure for finding and drugging his victims. Eventually, this procedure became a criminal calculus for providing him with relics of his victims.

The ideas of cognitive development go beyond the learning theorists'. Not only are criminals' actions expected to show an increased effectiveness, greater 'success', 'learning from mistakes', but cognitive development would lead to plans evolving for crimes; principles and procedures being developed by the offender to make his objectives more achievable.

Another way of viewing cognitive sophistication is to refer back to the discussion in an earlier chapter of what it meant to regard FBI agents as 'experts'. It was pointed out that, in contrast to the novice, the expert had increased sensitivity to salient aspects of the situation and could draw upon implicit knowledge of known patterns of action. The criminal who becomes an expert develops analogous cognitive skills.

Putting the psychoanalytic, learning and cognitive perspectives together does indeed give a dynamic quality to our understanding of human actions and experiences. They provide a mixture of themes for growth and change within the individual. The natural unfolding of human maturation processes is modified by the particular satisfactions and pains of the situations that are experienced. Both internal and external developmental processes reflect a natural sequence of interpersonal conflicts which each person has to resolve. But these formulations are still too academic, in the sense of being too removed from the details of daily life, to provide a thorough basis for translating a rapist's or murderer's actions into directions for criminal investigations.

AGENCY

The biological, psychological and social explanations of criminal behaviour get close, but not very close, to the problems detectives have to face. The developmental processes tend to focus on the early years of childhood or to be couched in abstract terms across the life-span. The detective needs a framework that is more immediate in its relationship to particular crimes. There is a further weakness in many of the different psychological explanations of violent crime: paradoxically, they all place the actual perpetrator at some distance from the cause of his actions. His genetic make-up, or his inner conflicts, or his social group and upbringing are seen as the cause of the crime, never the person himself. This is strangely at variance with our everyday understanding and with fundamental legal assumptions. In only the most extreme cases does the law accept that a person is not responsible for his actions. These are cases where it is clear that a person is acting in ways far beyond his conscious control, or that he is unable to comprehend the moral implications of what he has done. In all other circumstances the courts follow the common-sense view that the individual standing in front of them is accountable for his deeds. Can academic explanations of crime ever be compatible with this common-sense approach? Could explanations that give the criminal a dominant role ever be of use to police investigators?

The 'common-sense' approach sees the criminal as an active agent. He is not pushed by his hormones or unconscious drives, dragged by the fates or shaped willy-nilly by those around him. Neither is the criminal on a helter-skelter ride of destruction, produced by mathematically inevitable consequences of his ways of thinking. All those processes may indeed have an influence but the main role is played by a person seeing, thinking and acting. Through his actions the criminal tells us about how he has chosen to live his life. The challenge is to reveal his destructive life story, to uncover the plot in which crime appears to play such a significant part. Furthermore, in violent crimes, as I have mentioned, we need to understand how a secret pattern of criminal actions evolves together with the more overt, less threatening, daily dealings of the perpetrators.

The assignment of a dominant role to the person in his dealings with the world relates to a distinct tradition within psychology. This is the approach to understanding people that is much more self-conscious than those I have already, briefly, reviewed; a tradition that focuses on the person's own understanding of his experiences.

The earliest and most significant writings in this tradition were the *Confessions* of St Augustine, who was born in 354 in North Africa of a Christian mother and pagan father. He emphasized that 'Truth dwells in the inner man' and showed how much could be understood about human experience from intense, self-conscious introspection. This approach was given considerable emphasis in the modern era by a number of the founding fathers of modern psychology. For example, the German psychologist Wilhelm Wundt, credited with establishing the first psychology laboratory, said that personal introspection was the most important method for studying the mind.

The earliest modern psychologists were also happy to talk about human will and the way in which our understanding of the opportunities available gave structure to our actions. So even when behaviourists held strongest sway there still continued a stream of psychological exploration that went beyond observable actions. There have always been psychologists whose primary interest was the understanding that an individual was prepared to express about his circumstances and the people with whom he interacted.

However, clinical psychologists clearly demonstrated that a person's interpretation of his life's events could be very distorted. Clinicians try to help patients whose ways of experiencing the world are clearly unsatisfactory; that is why the patients seek help. So the introspections of their patients may be regarded as biased accounts that do not accurately or productively reflect what the patient knows, wants or feels. This can be seen as an extreme development of the problem of the 'personal equation' that set scientific psychology in motion. The therapist recognizes that it is not just the judgement of the movement of a distant star that is biased, but the judgement that the judge has of himself.

George Kelly, an American psychologist, who published his major work in 1955, showed how each person's unique biases can be understood. He argued that the set of constructs that a person puts together to give sense to his life has to be the key to our understanding of that person. Does he think of people in terms of power and glory, or in terms of support and friendship? Where does any individual place himself in this matrix of concepts? In many conversations with violent men, I have been struck by the power of Kelly's insights. They often cast the world into winners and losers, men who are real men and those who are wimps. In the language of Kelly their construct systems are limited and maladaptive. For Kelly the role of therapy is to help to rebuild construct systems which will enable the person to operate more effectively.

NARRATIVE

The earlier review of psychology indicated, in a nutshell, that the person is a consequence of both states and processes. We have also seen that each person becomes an expert on their own particular history of experiences, although their expertise will always be biased and will not always be helpful. As a consequence, a person's experiences will have moderately stable components, derived from the person's capabilities and social milieu, but there will also be changing qualities as their skills and conceptualizations develop and evolve in contact with the world around them. How can each of us make sense of this dynamic stability? How do we form a view of ourselves as distinct people, aware of our biological propensities, our state of being, but also aware of the way our actions and experiences are shaped and change? How do we resolve the paradox of being one person yet of constantly changing?

Over the past few years, a number of writers from many different disciplines have answered this central paradox of existence by proposing that we construct life stories for ourselves. We invent autobiographical narratives in which the central character has some semblance of continuity. The leaders of this movement are happy to find origins in the work of Freud and especially Erikson, or of George Kelly. They emphasize the stages in human narratives and the significance of particular episodes in moving a person's personal narrative on. Narrative psychologists also see important connections with explorations in history and studies of literature. This is revealed most clearly in how seriously they take the modes of expression by which personal stories are recounted.

Many studies of narrative focus on the life stories of capable, highly verbal people: Martin Luther, Mahatma Gandhi or Erik Erikson himself. Others deal with people who are able and prepared to give detailed reports of their lives and how they are lived. The narratives with which we are concerned are expressed in violent actions and the traces left in the aftermath of those crimes. They are like shadow puppets telling us a life story in a stilted, alien language.

When considering personal narratives it is tempting to regard everyone as a polished autobiographer who has written out the plot against which he will live his life. There is also often an assumption that if a person is telling a story about themselves, then that story will be a fiction. Narratives may be confused and distorted but they can still be fruitful ways of understanding a person's life. The stories we tell ourselves and each other about ourselves do have great power in giving shape and meaning to our lives. It is the narrative *form* of these accounts, not their elegance or veracity, that it is crucial to understand. Arthur Danto, an analytic philosopher, wrote in 1965: 'Narration exemplifies one of the basic ways in which we represent the world. The language of beginnings and endings, of turning points and climaxes, is [such] that our image of our own lives must be deeply narrational.'

Talking to violent criminals about their lives reveals how they often understand their actions as episodes with 'turning points and climaxes'. One burly offender, in his early thirties, convicted of many violent assaults including rape, told me about his life entirely in terms of events when he had had contact with the police. He indicated that he had spent some time getting a trade qualification, but that was not a significant episode in the life story he presented to me. He saw himself as a child rejected by his mother on the death of his father and misunderstood thereafter in incident after incident.

A deeper understanding of how narratives inform our lives comes from attempts in the 1970s to develop computer programs that could communicate effectively with their users. Two very different psychologists, Roger Schank, concerned with computer intelligence, and Robert Abelson, a social psychologist, set about trying to outline 'how concepts are structured in the human mind', with the intention of discovering how to program computers so that they 'can understand and interact with the outside world'. They found that computers could not interact effectively unless they knew the 'script' on which the interaction was based. Many psychologists quickly recognized that it was not only computers that needed scripts to be able to know how to act. We all do.

People learn ways of acting through taking on, or being assigned, particular roles. These integrated groupings of learned habits become dominant scripts that shape people's lives until they require modification because they are no longer found to be effective. What the cognitively-oriented computer programmers discovered was that in order for their computers to have any semblance of understanding they needed to contain a set of rules of how a person would react under particular circumstances. These computer programmers even found that they needed to put certain limits on what was possible in a particular situation, otherwise the program would cover too wide a range of options to be feasible.

What a person considers possible in any given situation is the script the person has for that situation. A script is a way of achieving a particular goal, but once the script is in action the original goal may be forgotten. The person may not even realize that he is living out a script that he has developed for himself. Narratives, then, are patterns of expected actions, organized, often loosely, around personal objectives. A person may decide that he must relieve his sexual frustration and that he deserves such relief, but thinks that the only way this can be achieved is by coercing a vulnerable woman. From previous knowledge, gained perhaps in domestic encounters, he may utilize a particular form of coercion. If this is successful from his point of view, the 'rape script' will be born and the original objectives may be forgotten. His personal narrative has changed and he now sees himself playing the role of 'rapist'. In Duffy's case, as with a number of other serial rapists, the script became so dominant that, as the prosecution emphasized in court, he carried with him the props for his role in the form of a 'rape kit' consisting of tissues and matches to destroy evidence of his assault.

A narrative links the actors to their actions. It provides a coherent framework in which to see the meaning of the shadows that criminals cast. As Donald Polkinghorne put it in 1988: 'Narrative is the fundamental scheme for linking individual human actions and events into inter-related aspects of an understandable composite.' For Polkinghorne, the crucial contribution of a narrative approach is that it shows the ways in which events have significance for one another. It is out of the recognition of the connectiveness of the events that lives take on meaning. Thus narrative encapsulates both the dynamic and the episodic nature of human existence at the same time as it provides meaning.

By indicating agency and direction the narrative framework also 'Configures a sequence of events into a unified happening'. The storyline gives shape and meaning to the whole flux of human affairs. The dynamic linking of episodes into a meaningful whole out of which the individual's own agency emerges as a dominant strand, therefore brings together both the episodic significance of the Freudian framework, without necessarily accepting the particular episodes to which Freud draws attention, and the unfolding maturational perspective that is the great contribution of Piagetian theory. The fact that the events and episodes have consequences for individuals (and provide a natural basis for expecting people to change the direction of their storyline) also accords comfortably with Skinnerian doctrine.

IDENTITY

The plots we live by make one further, crucial contribution to each person's experience of the world. Our notions of our unique identity come from the parts played by our role in our autobiography. One man convicted of violent assault told me that he could not tolerate being insulted. He had waited two years to beat up a man who cheated him out of money, nursing his grievance as a matter of personal esteem, building up a plot that he would eventually act out in what he saw as an heroic climax.

We give shape to our contacts with others and our personal experiences by an implicit acceptance that the sequence of our lives has a central protagonist, our self, who lives through various episodes, reacting to the consequences by drawing upon a repertoire of possible actions. Although this all sounds desperately self-conscious, most of it happens below the levels of personal awareness. Certainly by adulthood our views of ourselves and our capabilities are firmly fashioned and usually accepted unthinkingly.

From time to time, as in all stories, there are crucial episodes that challenge our views. The tendency is to act to maintain the established character, but sometimes these critical episodes lead to a reassessment of the central plot and a reconsideration of how it is likely to unfold. The storylines are therefore usually shaped by our experience of our capacities and abilities in relation to the possibilities we perceive in the world around us. Although we invent ourselves, for most people these are not fictitious inventions. They have direct roots in our encounters with reality.

'Richard', convicted of a number of violent rapes, told me that his first assault was an attempt to force a girl he knew to have his baby. He said he grabbed her by the throat so that she allowed him to rape her with little fight, although she was profoundly distressed by the assault, shouting at him that if she was pregnant she would just flush it down the toilet. But his story was already unfolding. He remembers the feeling of power afterwards, the sense of control. Not long after that episode he went armed with a kitchen knife looking for potential victims. He cast himself in the role of rapist.

The first violent assault that Richard committed was an episode from which he learned that another exciting, secret narrative could be lived. The hidden story did not burst out fully formed. He went through a period of great confusion. He attempted suicide and unsuccessfully sought psychiatric help. He was searching for another way to live that would give him the feeling of significance and control that the first attack gave him. After he attacked the same girl a second time he knew the secret life for which he was reaching. When further attempts to get others to help him find another track failed, he started following women he did not know and viciously raping them.

Richard shows us that the evolving life story of which a person is aware is in effect their *identity*. The American psychologist Dan McAdams put this view very clearly: 'Identity . . . is a dynamic narrative configuration, taking initial shape in adolescence and continuing to evolve there-after, that binds together past, present, and future, bestow-ing upon the individual that sense of inner sameness and continuity' (Dan McAdams, *Power, Intimacy and the Life Story: Personological Enquiries into Identity*, 1988, p. 29).

Of particular note in McAdams's fascinating book is his argument that life stories take on their shape in late adolescence. Such a view is certainly consistent with the fact that most offenders commit themselves to a life of crime or avoid such a career in their late teens. If this is the time at which dominant life stories are established we would expect a frequent harking back to that era in the accounts people give of themselves. Certainly, novelists frequently turn to their adolescence to explain the roots of their inspiration.

McAdams also draws attention to another important point. Life stories may be confused or clear, or as he calls them well-formed or ill-formed. There is likely to be more tension and confusion in the ill-formed life story, of course. Ill-formed stories may break up into very separate, poss-ibly conflicting, narratives. They may also be changed dramatically by episodes in which the central character experiences relatively minor mishaps. Perhaps here is the clue to the hidden nature of the narratives that violent offenders live: their dominant narratives are confused and sensitive to episodes that most people would ignore; their plots can be set off course by experiences that their friends and relatives might never notice. This may give violent criminals the experience of living a number of separate lives. Their narrative does not have any coherence, so it is experienced as many stories not just one.

The multiplicity of life stories is the starting point for therapy for Miller Mair, a British clinical psychologist. He emphasizes the fact that a person may live a number of different storylines at any point in time, different narratives emerging for different purposes in different situations. As a psychotherapist, Mair regards this as an important issue, using the therapeutic setting as a way of bringing to the surface many different plots that a person may be living.

Mair and other clinical psychologists see their role as the repairing of damaged stories, or as enabling people to examine different plots that might be relevant to the same events. In the most extreme circumstances they encourage people to recognize quite different events as salient in order to build different histories for themselves, and as a consequence more comfortable and psychologically acceptable futures. But such reconstruction would probably be extremely difficult for most violent offenders. The different tectonic plates of their lives are often so distinct that it would take a major life-threatening upheaval to bring them back together.

For many of us the narratives we live are openly, often proudly, expressed. In our work the career path we follow is likely to be a public story of successes and failures with key episodes and central roles as well as many walk-on parts. In the family the roles of father and mother, son and daughter will have unfolding themes that also have a recognized progression to them. But besides these, and the other stories we live by, are the hidden narratives; the people we see ourselves as being. They will draw upon the experiences and developments in all the other, usually more public, storylines but they will also have their own covert dynamic. For most people these inner narratives are either consistent with the other stories they live or they are well hidden, drawn upon perhaps for reverie. For the violent men who rape and kill, the inner narratives erupt into action.

Many violent men are aware of the different lives they live, recognizing in themselves the extreme fictional expression of this state in the story of *Dr Jekyll and Mr Hyde*. In one recent case on which I advised, the police arrested a man who lived an apparently happy family life with his wife and two children. After careful, almost gentle, questioning the man said: 'Look I want to tell you the whole story. I really got two lives.' He then went on eventually to admit raping eleven women. Colin Pitchfork provides a different, but equally graphic example. As he was being driven to the police station, having admitted his murders to his wife, he said to the police officers escorting him: 'There's two parts to me, a good and a bad side.' Then, referring to family and friends who knew only the 'good side' of this ex-scout leader, he said: 'I must let some people know what's happened before they read it all in the papers.'

More recently Andrei Chikatilo, a schoolteacher in Rostov, convicted of killing fifty-three children and young women over a period of twelve years, said: 'I gave myself to my work, my studies, my family, my children, my grandchildren, and there was nothing else in my life, but when I found myself in a different setting, I became a different person, uncontrollable, as if some evil force controlled me against my will and I could not resist.' Yet the Soviet psychiatrist who interviewed Chikatilo said: 'He feels no remorse for his victims, only pity for himself.'

CULTURE

Where do these life stories come from? One answer to this question is to say that stories and their associated scripts are all around us. Oedipus, Hamlet, Frankenstein, Jekyll and Hyde, James Bond, Clint Eastwood's man with no name, Rambo and many other well-recognized fictional protagonists all encapsulate strong personal histories on which we draw. In other words, the stories that we use in constructing our inner narratives are drawn from the culture and society in which we live. The exploits that one person extols to another, the achievements that family, friends and work colleagues admire or deride, the escapades that newspapers choose to report and follow to their conclusions, fictional stories from nursery tales to Hollywood movies with soap operas in between, all provide a rich repertoire of possible roles and ways to act them out.

Each person has access to different subsets of this repertoire and pays note to different parts of it. The salient characteristics of the actors in our scripts are also identified by the issues that are of concern around us. One consequence of this differentiation is that different plots are dominant for different groups. For example, the typical representation of women as victims rather than protagonists is reflected in the fact that it is relatively rare for women to write themselves into actively violent scenarios (except as victims).

At a larger scale it would appear that cultures, and subcultures, have dominant themes in their common narrative. Indeed, variations between cultures are variations in the stories that they prefer. The world-view held by a culture is a view of what happens to their heroes and their victims. There can be no coincidence that Japan has a high incidence of suicide and also enshrines within its classic dramas of *Kabuki* and *Bunraku* the resolution of the hero's central conflict by him committing *seppuku*. The differences in the way violence is handled on the screen, its causes and consequences, between the few films made in Britain and those made in the USA appear to reflect the differences in the degree and nature of violence in those countries. In many films from Hollywood the violent killing of another person is an achievement, an indication of strength of character. For British films it is more likely to be an awkward necessity or a sign of incompetence.

For violent offenders there must therefore be some significance in the stories they study. It is a chilling fact that Duffy spent many hours watching videos before he first killed. Dahmer watched *Exorcist II* over and over again during his last period of systematic killing. In recent court cases in which vicious crimes have been committed by children not yet in their teens, these children have been found to have spent large proportions of their waking hours watching violent films. There is no suggestion that the films caused these horrific crimes, but it is plausible that a person, confused about his own life story, could watch simple tales of violent heroism to seek out scripts that would give his life more sense.

Of course, the stories that are told in a culture both reflect that culture and facilitate the continued production of personal narratives, so that a cycle of mutual support is maintained. In societies where dominant non-destructive narratives break down, as is currently happening in the former Yugoslavia, then inhuman violence is legitimized and emerges as the theme of the stories many people think they should live. There is nothing new to this. Throughout history people have denied the recognition of full humanity to others with whom they come into contact. Centuries of religious wars against 'unbelievers' and 'infidels', the enslavement of other races and Hitler's 'final solution' are all examples of how other groups are seen as less than human and therefore objects to be used, exploited or killed. The role of the vanquished is well defined in the plots which we teach our children. No amount of abstract political debate in former Yugoslavia can produce new scripts for the plots that the various ethnic groups have written for themselves. Just as no therapies have ever changed the inner narratives of violent criminals.

In order to decipher a criminal's actions we need to know what narrative he is drawing upon. It would help to know if there is a very large range of such narratives available, or if there are just a few key plots which each person modifies for his own purposes. Narrative psychologists are divided on this matter. Some believe that there is a limit to the variety of possible structures for all life stories. Polkinghorne, in particular, emphasizes that there are relatively few convincing ways of telling a story. Kevin Murray has even gone so far as to suggest that all life stories can be seen as one of four classic types – comedy, romance, tragedy and satire – equating them respectively with *M.A.S.H.*, *Star Wars*, *The Elephant Man* and Monty Python's *Life of Brian*. These benign examples may have some relevance to Murray and his students, but it seems unlikely that any of them captures the experiences relevant to violent rapists and murderers.

The proposal that people take their life stories off the video shelf does, of course, contradict the active, autobiographical quality that is so attractive in the narrative approach. The cafeteria view of life stories pulls the framework back into the realms of static characteristics. Instead of having distinguishing ear-lobes, criminals can be recognized by the particular heroes they endorse. Life is not that simple. Narratives are moving targets that change their shape in response to changing circumstances.

The questions still remain. Are there different types of

plot? Is there a finite limit to the plots available? How are the plots constructed? Although we have no firm, general answers to these questions it is clear that the storylines that unfold for violent criminals are a limited subset of all possible life stories. Comedy and satire are certainly not for them and it seems unlikely that the optimistic objectives of romance fall within their realms of thought. Killers and rapists live broken, destructive lives. We must understand how their distorted, disjointed, debilitating life stories are written.

It is helpful to remember that most violent men write their own tragedies against the backdrop of acceptable civilized behaviour in which they are able to participate. In this regard they are akin to people who are required to live secretly destructive lives in the service of the state; spies, saboteurs and torturers. These officially sanctioned criminals have to build up new narratives through a learning process that moves in acceptable steps from the old storyline to the new.

The training of official torturers provides a clear example of this process. Most people who carry out torture as part of their designated duties do not start as sadistic individuals. Indeed, such people may be excluded from recruitment because of the difficulty of controlling them. Recruits are encouraged along the long path to inflict pain and degradation on others in small steps. They are persuaded to regard their victims as sub-human by the accounts they are given and actions they witness. They are shown that they can gain esteem from their superiors by preying on those in their power. The torturer's own narrative takes shape in this climate in a way that allows him to feel that his personal drama will have a successful conclusion. A new subset of ways of dealing with other people becomes the dominant mode of actions for the recruit as he takes on the role of torturer.

Violent crime is not a broadening of experience but a narrowing of it. The offender's shadow belies the bleakness of his life; the two-dimensional existence in which the abuse of others becomes paramount. We will understand what causes these sombre shadows by recognizing the limited narratives that offenders live.

Chapter Ten

LIMITED NARRATIVES

CONSISTENT PATTERNS

The limits on the lives of criminals are apparent from the implicit order in their behaviour. Crime is not haphazardly distributed through time and space. Criminals are not a random sample of the population at large. Even the farthest reaches of human evil have a pattern. Whatever the mayhem violent assaults produce, they have themes and recurring constituents, dominant characteristics and identifiable structures. Although a violent criminal's shadows flicker and change, they are identifiably his. Like a predator that has only a few ways of catching its prey, a criminal has a repertoire of actions. The serial rapists and murderers we have considered have shown us that this portfolio of behaviours can often be surprisingly restricted. The area in which the crimes are committed, the type of victim that is targeted, the mode of approach taken to overpower the victim, and many other aspects of an assault are typically quite consistent for any one offender.

The range of crimes that a criminal commits may be considerable. Certainly, young offenders are usually not specialists in the types of crimes they commit. Most of the rapists we have studied do have previous convictions for theft or dishonesty, but when they carry out their violent assaults they do it in a distinctive way. We have found, for example, that a rapist who commits a number of assaults indoors is unlikely to carry out an assault outdoors. Fewer than 10 per cent of those that we have studied have attacked both indoors and outdoors. The individuals considered on earlier pages also provide plenty of illustrations of the limitations of offenders' actions. Babb assaulted only elderly women in a limited area. Nilsen, Dahmer, Sutcliffe, and even 'Jack the Ripper', were constrained in the types of victims they picked upon. All Dahmer's victims, except the first, were black men of a similar age. Duffy bound and mutilated his victims in very similar ways. It was the similarities in these actions that helped the police to link his murders and to link the murders to the rapes. Even the growing area of his offences was characteristic of Duffy, just as both Sutcliffe's and 'Jack the Ripper's' avoidance of an area in which they had recently attacked was typical of them.

Often a criminal's recurring motif will be apparently arbitrary and idiosyncratic. One rapist whose attacks were spread over a number of years always asked his victims if they were clean. Another made his victims solemnly swear that they would not report him. Yet another often told his victims that he had already served a prison sentence for rape (which was not true).

The consistent patterns that can be recognized go beyond the usual notion of *modus operandi*. MO probably plays a less important role in actual investigations than it does in many detective stories. Attempts to produce computerized 'M.O. indexes' at great expense (such as the system used by the British police, or the FBI VICAP system), have also been found to be qualified failures. This is because the computers list very particular actions or descriptions but have no capacity for that most human of capabilities, the recognition of patterns. It is not the simple addition of disparate constituents – such as the colour of a car, the wearing of a mask and the selection of a blonde victim – that make up a pattern, although it might make up an MO. A pattern has shape and meaning, it adds up to something more than the sum of its parts. It has themes, telling us a story.

This process of identifying intersecting themes, or facets of crimes that each carry a significance, is also different from the interpretation of a unique clue that carries a specific meaning. Any action may have multiple implications, and various combinations of particular actions can change those implications. For example, the targeting of elderly victims in a city where there are many other potential targets for sexual assaults would carry very different implications from similar attacks in a retirement community. The meaning of a particular action in a crime will come from the thematic pattern of which it is a part.

The themes that typify individual offenders emerge from a backdrop of characteristics common to subsets of crimes and criminals. For example, crime is not at all evenly spread throughout all ages. The vast majority of crime is committed by people in their mid-teens, but the crimes that teenagers commit tend to be rather opportunistic. If they continue with their criminal life, the nature of their crimes is likely to evolve as they develop a more sophisticated understanding of the possibilities.

The average ages at which different types of crime are committed are of considerable interest. They help us to understand the broad swathe of unfolding life patterns within which each offender weaves his distinctive web. Unfortunately, very full details of the typical ages associated with different crimes are remarkably difficult to come by. (Most statistics are collected in order to reveal general trends and to predict future prison populations.) From my own research and the few published studies, however, some trends may be postulated.

It appears, for instance, that people who commit a number of rapes on strangers tend to be in their late teens or early twenties. The average age of men who murder strangers is a little higher than that of serial rapists, twenty-three or twenty-four, although their age ranges overlap. The average age is also different for different styles of murder: a man who carries out a gangland slaying will probably be in his late twenties, whereas the person who kills an elderly woman during a burglary is likely to be five or ten years younger.

When other types of crime are considered, broad differences are also apparent. The average age of writers of threat letters and those involved in more complex blackmail and extortion is typically at least ten years higher than the average age of murderers. People who assault children are likely to be either older or younger than is typical for those who kill.

Taken as a whole, these age trends indicate an increasing degradation of others through direct contact, up until the early twenties; then a more distant, planned and controlled type of crime in subsequent years. The typical young teenage crime is, therefore, a sudden violent outburst or unpremeditated theft. By the late teens a vicious attack, or prepared burglary, on selected targets is more prevalent. An older man, determined to kill, or to abduct young children, is likely to think more about how he can get away with the crime with minimum risk to himself. This is illustrated by our findings that children who are molested by strangers are likely to be violently assaulted only by younger offenders. Men in their thirties and forties who sexually molest young children usually use a cautious approach that arouses least suspicion, such as offering to help fix a bicycle, or to provide some imported chewing-gum, as Chikatilo did.

Some individuals may go through stages indicated by the changes in average age. But, even if they come to their crimes by some other route, the impact of their own stage in life will be reflected in how they commit their crimes. This suggests to me that the themes on which a criminal draws vary as he grows older and the challenges he recognizes change. We do not have enough information at present to elaborate the details of these developments, but we can take from the general trends the need to identify themes across all violent crimes and not to focus solely on variations within one type of crime.

A further dominant characteristic of criminals may also help to clarify the limited themes that underlie their narratives. The great majority of crime is committed by men. Virtually all violent crime is committed by men. Criminal narratives must therefore be drawn from those that our society provides for men. Stories of nurturance and sharing are therefore very unlikely to be the basis of an offender's life story.

CENTRAL THEMES

Central to the stories of violence are themes about personal relationships. Out of a self-perception of loneliness and the distorted search for intimacy, there grow feelings of impotence and isolation, embedded in anger towards others who are seen as crucial in defining the criminal's identity, typically women. In their different ways, violent men attempt to use their victims to achieve their own particular ends. This brings them into vicious contact with other people, usually women.

This search for control is reflected in the ultimate actions of rape and murder. The static, recurring components of their narratives therefore portray particular facets of the type of power they wish to have over their victims. There will also be facets that reflect distortions in the forms of intimacy for which they are searching.

It was Dan McAdams who emphasized that power and intimacy were the dominant facets of all life stories, but he focused on effective, productive life stories. The lives we are considering are the very opposite. It is the breakdown in the fruitful search for acceptable power and appropriate intimacy that characterizes the inner narratives of violent men. These men are the antithesis of the processes that keep society in some sort of stable balance; supportive relationships between people and the empathetic use of influence and control. Perhaps this is another part of the general fascination with violent crime. It reveals how readily the processes that keep society in balance can be turned inside out to produce mayhem and destruction.

There are also dynamic components to unfolding criminal storylines. The changes loosely associated with age will be part of those dynamics, but particular experiences cannot be ignored; most notably, as we shall see, the experience of the crimes themselves.

The themes of intimacy, power and criminal development can be drawn out of the whole pattern of activities in a crime. Aspects of each of them may point to different features of the criminal relevant to his capture. This approach is also rather different from the identification of *types* of offence and offender. Management consultants, and those with a medical bent, find value in thinking of people like different diseases, assigning each to a particular pigeon-hole. The same has been done with rapists and murderers; missionary killers, disorganized murderers, assertive or pseudo-unselfish rapists, have all been classified, providing neat accounts which, unfortunately, never quite fit the actual facts. Even the simple dichotomy of organized and disorganized killers, which is central to the FBI explanation of profiles, requires a large catch-all, mixed category. The overlapping facets I have mentioned generate a much richer matrix of possibilities than the more limited typologies, as will become clear.

Violent attacks on people are generated by personal narratives that assign everyone but the narrator a subsidiary role. Some of us never get far beyond the childish view that others are objects to be used to satisfy our own appetites. We may rise above that egocentricity, recognizing the personal experience that others have, but our vision may be so distorted that we none the less see people as vessels for our own desires. By contrast there are many people who become supremely good at empathizing – that is, feeling and understanding – the experiences of others.

What I am suggesting here is that violent personal narratives are those in which there is an inability to create private dramas in which others share centre-stage. Giving an equal role to others is the major aspect of empathy because it accepts that they have life stories too. Being sidetracked off the road to real empathy can lead at its extreme to rape and murder.

Thus, different types of violent crime are a product of the variations in the way in which the breakdowns in empathy and distortions in feelings for others take place. For the detective an important question is the coherence between the roles an offender assigns to his victims and the roles he assigns to other people in his life.

To build on these ideas for detective work it is necessary to grapple with the difficulty created by the fact that criminals are not alien monsters. Their crimes are a product of the inner, secret narratives they are living, not the public face they present to their wives and workmates. Watching someone walk down the street it is not possible to decide whether they have a superb talent for mathematics or a special disregard for other people. Most human beings are so clearly within the same range of capabilities, the characteristics of the human species constrained within the socially accepted patterns of self-presentation, that significant variations are not discernible during normal contact. Perhaps a further reason for our fascination with violent criminals is precisely this desire to uncover the mystery of their hidden depths.

Yet these inner experiences are created from contact with others. They are the internalization of external events. They reflect the consequences of previous actions. There is therefore likely to be some sign of what those earlier experiences have been.

LIMITED NARRATIVES

What sorts of hidden stories do criminals live? I propose that violent criminals live narratives that share one common constituent. Wherever, or however, it occurs, the theme that links violent attacks on other people is the treating of the victims as less than human; they become objects of anger or desire, vehicles to satisfy the perpetrator, possessions that are jealously guarded, targets for him to act upon. This is a reflection of what I have called a lack of empathy for other people; an inability to assign them to an active role in their own or anyone else's life story. From this view there is little fundamental difference between murder, rape, violent non-sexual assaults or child molesting – all are onslaughts on other people. They may differ in the target or consequences of their actions, but the central theme is the same.

There are many subtle variations played on this theme, each variation being characteristic of the person who produces it. The range of variations is immense: from the most extreme edges of the abyss of grotesque crimes, like those that are the daily concern of the FBI at Quantico, to the fringes of normal, often accepted conduct, in what are chillingly called 'date rapes'. All can be fruitfully looked at as reflecting man's inhumanity to man (although usually it is to woman), in the direct sense of the criminal treating his victims as less than human. For the detective it is not the moral implication of this inhumanity that is important, but what the particular forms that it takes reveal.

In essence, the police need to ask: what is the role that the victim plays in the life of the offender? My central hypothesis is that this will be revealed, at least in part, through consistent themes that run through his criminal actions, such as the vulnerability of his chosen victim, the risks in his method of approaching her, and the security of the location he selects for the assault.

THE SEARCH FOR IDENTITY

What shapes the particular themes on which violent offenders draw? What leads them to sift out from the many narratives available in a culture those particular ones that lead to crime? To answer these questions it is helpful to recognize that none of us is born human. Our humanity is shaped throughout our lives from our contact with other human beings. As we grow we learn who we are and what we are. Our physical capabilities unfold within a form that is shaped, urged or constrained by all our experiences, direct and indirect. The type of person we become is neither God-given at birth, nor inevitable from our upbringing.

First dimly, then with increasing clarity, the young child develops an idea of the sort of person he is and his place in the world. This is an imaginative creation shaped by direct experience. It is an evolving personal history that acts as a script to guide future actions. We are each the central character of our own drama. Whether we see ourselves as heroes, victims, villains, losers or superstars depends on how we see our personal story unfolding. Our early years give us a view of our own worth and whether our personal narratives are romances or tragedies, comedies or melodramas. Not only do we learn to be human but we learn what sort of human being we are.

The parts in our life dramas are not assigned to us at birth, although there may be a limit to those that we can most readily fill. In the first few months of life babies experience themselves as objects, requiring other objects to satisfy their desires. Slowly the child's acceptance of himself as a person grows through episodes of support or frustration that lead to the realization that there are other people whose experiences may be like his. But this process is never complete. There is always a search to understand the unique experiences of other people.

In our early years these inner narratives that guide our actions are under constant modification. Initially our clay is moulded by others whose shape is more rigid than our own. In leaving an impression of themselves they also leave an imprint of what it means to be human and of the significance of other people to our sense of ourselves and the stories we live by.

Like the people in Plato's cave, we can only see the shadows of ourselves and other people cast on the wall. We all develop an understanding of what the shadows mean by inventing stories to describe the actions we think the shadows illustrate. Our experience is central to these narratives, but the meaning and significance of that experience derives from how we are treated by other people; the parts we are told that we play in their dramas.

In part, our views of ourselves, and the views that others have of us, are defined in terms of what we possess and what we have achieved. In cultures that enshrine material wellbeing as the paramount attainment of the society, the role of possessions is dominant. This is crucial to understanding violent assault because in the early stages of human development no distinction is made between people and objects. The child has to invent the idea that others have minds; and experience time, space, delight and anger in ways that are analogous to his own experience.

Aristotle favourably quotes Plato as saying that it is important to be brought up to find pleasure and pain in the right things, arguing that it is from this appropriate search for reward that moral virtue grows. Where a person finds pleasure or pain will be influenced to some extent by the capabilities and sensitivities with which a person is born. How much it is influenced is a matter of intense debate among psychologists. Some sex offenders, without doubt, have an abnormal sexual appetite, yet others do not. But whether a man with intense sex drive ends up as an isolated person who turns to serial rape or as a football star, who is regarded as having admirable sexual prowess, is a complex product of how he sees himself, the group he is part of and the mixture of personal propensities that he has. All of these combine in the story he writes for himself.

It seems very likely that violent offenders' narratives are distorted from their earliest years in a number of ways. They may simply not have models of empathy from which to learn because the people around them never illustrate the relevant processes. Or they may be told conflicting things about themselves; a mother who dotes on them and for whom they can do no wrong and a father who demeans them, treating them as failures, are not uncommon in the background of violent men. But there are many other ways in which the growing boy can be unsure about his identity and unclear as to which of the available life stories is appropriate for him. He will turn to the possibilities offered by the narratives around him which often include violence, aggression and the exploitation of others.

A number of men who end up as violent criminals go through a period where their lives make sense. 'Richard' had a skilled trade as a plumber. Colin Pitchfork was a baker. Adrian Babb worked as an attendant in a swimming bath. John Duffy was employed as a carpenter. All these men appeared to have lived 'normal', non-criminal lives before changes occurred that awakened their dormant stories and led them towards rape and murder. At present we know very little about the backgrounds of those rare criminals who seem to come from caring, supportive families and become involved in violent crime for the first time after their mid-teens. My hypothesis is that there will be both distinct aspects to their family experience that sowed the seeds for later violence, and critical episodes that allowed those seeds to thrive.

Many acts of violence seem to erupt at a time when the perpetrator is searching for identity and personal meaning. This possibly is one reason why so much crime is committed by teenagers. Adolescence is often the time when people explore the most appropriate life story for themselves and the boundaries of social acceptability are tested. In terms of future crime, these years are therefore crucial in determining which inner narrative will become dominant.

By the mid-teens most people will have formed a view of their own identity that includes a description of their intellect, power and ability to cope with various demands. It will also include self-perceptions of their characteristic ways of relating to other people and the significance of others in their lives. Part of this self-identity will undoubtedly include notions of the bounds of what is socially acceptable and the extent to which the person will attempt to operate within those bounds.

If the view a person has of himself is shaped before he is free of his family, it is no surprise to find that later violence has parallels in the actions of the person within the family.

Sadistic criminals were very often cruel as children and, for example, tortured animals. Just as the infant prodigy in music or mathematics usually grows up in a family where music and mathematics are encouraged and enjoyed, later to reflect this in the behaviour the adult reveals to the world, in the same way there is a consistency in the earlier activities of criminals who attack people, clearly demonstrating through the viciousness of their actions the lack of any real awareness of or feeling for the consequences of their actions. Such men have usually grown up in a household where people were treated as objects, where feelings for others were less important than acting for oneself. Certain groups or classes in any society may be more prone to create families that have these weaknesses, but it is not the class membership that creates the propensity to crime. The conditions can be found in all social groups.

The criminological and psychiatric literature is replete with accounts of the distressed and deprived childhoods of criminals. Various forms of abuse and lack of support are commonplace. But what is it that they have missed in their upbringing that can help us locate them when they turn to crime? What has been absent from their early lives has been the opportunity of learning empathy. The technical term used by some social scientists is learning 'to take the role of the other'; to step inside somebody else's shoes and experience a particular situation as they would. In the language of story-telling, this is an inability to script dramas in which all the players have similar relevance. As 'Richard' told me of one of his more violent attacks, 'She was crying as I penetrated her, but none of it was registering.' He explained that he got home through back alleys very quickly, but 'when I got in it was just like it never happened'.

In the home life of all children who develop as rapists or murderers I would hypothesize there will be a social discourse that lacks real empathy. Often, of course, this is because there is no home life. The child brought up in an institution, where those who care for the children do it as a job, almost inevitably learns that he is a commodity to be dealt with. As many as half of the children brought up in institutions find their way into homelessness and crime. But many families create an institutional mood of their own. This may be through overt physical or sexual abuse or by more subtle indications to the child that it is appropriate for one individual to treat another as an object.

The cycle of destruction and abuse may stretch back for generations. People appear to be almost as able to inherit a predisposition to sudden anger as they are to inherit blue eyes, but this inheritance may not need to be transmitted through the genetic make-up. It can just as readily be communicated through the way parents and children treat each other.

For reasons that I do not think are fully understood, such a background appears to be more likely to give rise to violent crime when it is suffered by boys than by girls. Perhaps girls learn to survive in these circumstances by writing stories that cast them as exploited victims, whereas boys draw upon the popular stereotypes of men as the users of other people. If you are shown from an early age that you are less than fully human, this not only leads you to think of other people as instruments, but also to think of yourself in a similar way. The two roles of vengeful monster and of instrument who suffers from other people may be adopted by those whose upbringing lacks empathy. In our culture it appears that women are more likely to accept that they will be used and men are more likely to seek reprisals.

The process of learning to be human is one of building a world in which contact with other people is satisfying and productive. The isolation and separation from other people which a generation of novelists wrote about ignored the fact that most people do not feel alienated. Close personal contacts provide a feeling of self-worth and connection to others. The term 'love' has become so trite and overused because it captures the search for personal significance, through contact with others, that is central to being fully human. Because we feel what others feel, most of us also feel part of a social group. For the violent criminal, various weaknesses, which everyone experiences (such as upsurges of anger, awareness of injustice, desire for revenge and lustful urges), are not tempered by any sympathy for the suffering caused by his actions. These weaknesses take many forms, their differences reflected in different types of crime and criminal.

This is not to dismiss the variations between people which are present at birth. Just as there are variations in physical characteristics and the potential for some illnesses, there are variations in general, abstract intelligence, in the broad levels of stimulation people find most pleasant, and probably in such matters as extremes of emotional response, which may or may not be related to expressed sexual drive. But the distribution of these variations in the population is a continuous one. Subtle gradations distinguish people from each other. It is through transactions with others that the clay is moulded.

The immediate family is only one part of the contact that shapes human experience and behaviour. Studies of child abuse show that it is often friends and close relatives who are the perpetrators, rather than the immediate family. We make as much impression by exposing our children to particular possibilities outside the home as in what we provide directly for them within it.

The extent to which an 'ordinary' family can generate a mood that leads to violent crime is a vexed and very open question. One brother may become a policeman and another a villain with little in their circumstances to choose between them. Physical make-up and the particularities of individual situations cannot be ignored. Studies do report higher than average histories of head injury in some samples of violent criminals, but then there is a more intensive searching for such injuries in that population. One child may already be independent when a family crisis occurs that scars his brother for life, although there are only a few years between them. Another may be too young to be aware of the trauma. These are the complexities that will always keep alive the debate about the causes of violent crime. Many overlapping currents in a shifting sea of forces give shape to our actions. Dominant trends may be identifiable but the wave never washes on the beach at exactly the same spot.

SEXUAL NARRATIVES

For violent criminals, sexual appetites seem to have acquired a particular significance in defining the person they believe they are. They are a dominant characteristic of the protagonist in his personal narrative. They are not unique in this; our culture appears to give great significance to aspects of gender and sexuality as ways of defining people. For many of us the roles that we ascribe to other people are overlaid with sexual significance.

How is it that the acts of sex are so important in defining who people are and their social worth? Why is it that a violent physical attack on a wife by her husband may not even lead to a criminal charge, while forced sexual intercourse by a stranger that was not especially vicious can lead to many years of imprisonment? How have the sexual act and the potential for the sexual act come to dominate so much of our imagery, literature, conversation and conciousness? Why is private sexuality so important that people who in all other ways are seen as capable human beings, are redefined because their mutual choice of sexual partners is seen as abnormal?

One rapist asked by the police if he had any special sexual problems replied that he masturbated a lot more than was appropriate for a man of his age. The Judaic proscription on Onan, not to cast his seed on the ground, still reverberates through most modern societies. 'Wanker!' is still an insult. Stimulation of the erogenous zones is regarded by most people as a fundamentally social activity. It is this social nature of the sexual act that gives it such significance and power. It is seen as telling us a story about how we exist in the world, about what our roles are. Once divorced from the social relationship, sex takes on a separate, tantalizing existence.

Newspaper and magazine editors have found that sex sells their products, to women as well as to men. Stories about the love lives of celebrities excite enormous interest, while politicians and others in public life increase in significance when their activities as sexual partners are openly discussed.

Pornography takes this one step further. It treats other people as objects of desire to be used to satisfy personal lusts. It turns women and men into willing playmates in make-believe stories. For those men and women who have been able to develop some empathy for others this may stimulate their enjoyment of their partner, but if that ability to take the role of the other is weak or absent then pornography will feed the deformed imagination. Unfortunately, the debates around this topic are distorted with old religious and ideological confusions. Clearly, pornographic materials are arousing; and, by revealing possibilities, to some extent can reduce inhibitions. That is why they are purchased. Most societies have found that any disinhibiting agent, whether it be alcohol or other substances, is open to abuse by people who are especially vulnerable to its effects. Controls are therefore usually placed on the availability of these drugs. If their effects are found to be too threatening to aspects of society that it is wished to maintain, they are banned.

The people who live stories that take them to the extreme reaches of violent assault and murder are limited people. Consequently they draw from a limited set of narratives around which to live their lives. These narratives will often be confused. The offender will sometimes think of himself as hero and sometimes as victim, but the repetition of his crimes shows that the themes that shape his life have not changed. In order to find these men we have to understand the different, interweaving stories that they enact. We need to be able to identify each different drama that brings the shadow-play to life.

THE STRUCTURE OF RAPE

If we are to read the character of a criminal from his violent actions we will have to disentangle the various themes that distinguish one rapist or murderer from another. Any act can have many layers of meaning. The human horror of violent actions may confuse us, but as I learned from the cold precision of the FBI Behavioral Science Unit and my own studies of behaviour in major disasters, it is essential to peel away the different layers of significance that encrust even the most extreme inhumanities.

For any violent attack there will be hundreds of aspects of the offence that can be considered. Each of those can carry implications about many different features of the offender. The scientific quest is to identify the structure underlying all these possibilities so that a manageable framework can be created. We are asking what story the killer's actions are telling, trying to deduce the hidden themes that move him on and into violence which, if revealed, could lead the police to him.

A theme is a coherent set of actions. For example, there will be some actions, such as violent coercion of the victim, that are common to all sexual assaults. But the sub-themes will be revealed in the actions that are not common to all rapes, for instance exactly how the victim is approached, or the nature of the conversation that takes place during the assault. In order to distinguish these themes, then, we need to establish which actions go together across rapes. The co-occurrence of actions could help us to disentangle the themes that distinguish one set of assaults from another.

There are many problems in building theories of criminal actions solely on the cases brought to me by the police when they are looking for help. These cases are typically ones that present particular investigative problems. Moreover, many of the details will be ambiguous or missing until the cases are solved. Therefore, once it became clear that psychology could contribute directly to criminal investigations, Rupert and I started to amass details of solved crimes that would be open to systematic analysis. Because of our early interest in sexual assaults our studies started with the examination of rapes of strangers. Since that time other colleagues have joined us in studying a much wider range of crimes, including murder, sexual abuse of children, fraud and extortion. The studies of rape have made most progress. The results of those studies indicate some intriguing distinctions that may well be relevant to other crimes. I will therefore briefly present an indication of our studies of rape.

The aim of the studies was to find out which actions

tend to happen in the same assaults. The actions that form
a coherent pattern will reveal the dominant themes of
assaults, the objectives of the assailant and, consequently,
the story he is living when he carries out the attack.

There are potentially hundreds of actions that can
happen in a sexual assault. The first stage in the research,
therefore, was to define very carefully every possible
action. So, for example, somebody who talks his way into
a flat by indicating that he needs help or has lost his way
and then assaults his victim was defined as using a 'confidence trick' approach. 'Confidence trick' then became a
datum point for comparison with all the other actions in
the crimes. A large number of assaults were then examined. In the following illustration there were 105 separate attacks drawn from all over England.

For each assault a decision was made as to whether or
not a particular action had occurred. This produced a table
of assaults against actions, similar to the much smaller
table produced to help discriminate between the ten rapes
of students in the Midlands. To help that inquiry we
needed to carry out an analysis that would focus on the
differences between those crimes. Here our objectives were
more general, some would say more fundamental. We
wanted to identify the themes that distinguished all the
sexual assaults from which our sample was drawn, to find
the underlying narratives of rape.

A powerful computing procedure allowed us to represent each action – for example, whether a weapon was
used, or whether binding or gags were used, the type of
sexual activity and so on – as if it were a point on some
abstract map of criminal behaviour. Those actions that
frequently happen in the same crime, taking all 105 cases
into account, are close to each other on this map. Those
that seldom co-occur will be far apart. What we found was
that somebody who wears a mask to hide his identity

during the committal of an assault is very unlikely, as would be expected, to make the confidence trick approach. Therefore, the point on the map indicating the wearing of a disguise is well away from the point representing a confidence trick approach.

In the present example we have thirty-one actions, so there are thirty-one points on the map. If actions in sexual assault were opportunistic and random, with no apparent themes to them, then there would be no discernible structure to this map and we would not be able to interpret it. Yet what we have discovered in a number of studies of sexual assaults, as for other crimes, is that these maps do reveal underlying themes. Actions with narrative significance are found together on the map.

At the centre of the map we find the actions that are characteristic of rape in general: a surprise attack, the removal of the victims' clothing and vaginal penetration. Moving out from this central area are actions with lowering frequencies so that on the very edge are those behaviours that occur in only a small percentage of rapes. The really exciting discovery is the major themes that distinguish between the actions that occur in about a third of all cases.

One region of the map relates to how prepared and organized the offender is, whether he brought material with him, such as bindings and a weapon to be able to control the victim readily at the crime scene. A second region has within it actions that are overtly aggressive, including attempts to demean and insult the victim. This sits next to the region covering all the different sexual activities that can take place, showing that a variety of sexual acts is a distinct theme for rape, although it is close to aggression. A third region of the map covers bizarre attempts to develop a relationship with the victim, a sort of pseudo-'intimacy'. In this assault the offender implies

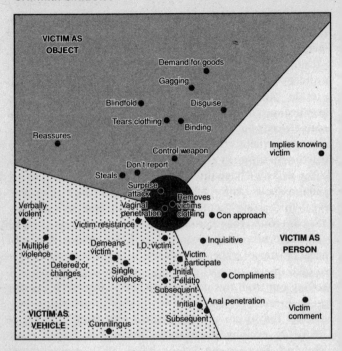

Figure ii: A computer analysis of thirty-one actions of rapists, showing their similarity of co-occurrence and the central themes characteristic of each set of behaviours (based on 105 cases).

that he knows the victim and may even compliment her and ask her about herself and for comment on his actions.

These three groupings of variables seem to me to reflect three different themes, or indeed underlying narratives, in the activities of the offender. One is the man who sees himself very much as the organized criminal. He might be classified as a person whose storyline is one of effective control to get what he wants. The second is the aggressive offender who is reflecting his anger and his determination to exert his will on the victim by violent means. The third is the offender who tells himself that he is developing some type of relationship with the victim and mistakenly sees an unfolding level of intimacy being produced by the sexual assault. Thus, the grouping of different activities carries implications for their central themes in the personal narratives of the offenders.

The advanced statistical procedure therefore gives us a way of bringing to the surface the themes that exist in a variety of sexual assaults and of relating these back to the general discussion on personal narratives that I have summarized above. The themes are not entirely unexpected. They group around the role of the victim for the offender and how he controls her to achieve his objectives. Of particular note is that the varieties of sexual activity are not distributed around the map; they appear to constitute a narrative in their own right. For some offenders the opportunity to indulge in a number of sexual acts with a coerced female is their distinguishing feature, although it comes close to violent demeaning of the victim in many cases. In other words, rape is not always about perverted sexual indulgence, although sometimes it is; it is about controlling a victim to achieve a variety of different objectives. Besides the distorted sexual relationship there may be the curious attempt to break through the offender's profound isolation by implying some sort of relationship with the victim. In the life stories of these men, women play very different roles from the object of sexual gratification in the former group. Yet another role for the victim emerges from those actions that are typified by binding and gagging a woman before raping her. She is a dangerous object that must be trussed and coerced, whom the offender will neither attempt to demean nor cajole.

The inner narratives that violent men write for themselves cast their victims in less than human roles. The horror of the shadows of their actions lies in their lack of empathy and sympathetic human contact. We need to learn to identify the distinguishing features of these evil narratives in order to recognize the men who write them.

━━━━━━━━━━━━━━●

Chapter Eleven

NARRATIVES OF EVIL

Currently the core of detection, in fact as in fiction, is deduction; the careful examination of all the clues *within* the case to establish their internal logic. Common sense and general knowledge is then drawn upon to make inferences about the perpetrator. This process of detection is neither scientific nor psychological. Science goes beyond common sense by being inductive. Facts established *outside* of any particular event are distilled, and the trends among them examined, to reveal general principles that can be applied to subsequent events. When the general principles amount to theories that predict and explain human actions the science is psychology.

A first step in building a psychology for criminal investigations was the realization that different forms of brutality and degradation, violence and coercion, could tell us about the differences in the life experiences of the men who commit these crimes. Central to this theory is the view that the crucial distinctions between the dramas that violent men write for themselves are the variations in the roles that they give their victims.

Whether a rapist or murderer treats his victim as, for example, a purely sexual object, or as someone to be insulted and demeaned, is a function of his distorted search for intimacy. The particular forms of these distortions are the key to understanding the rest of his violent behaviour. Variations in the emphases of the vicious interpersonal contact are therefore the first major themes to consider when interpreting any violent crime. They show what is the objective of the assailant's attack.

A second set of themes of an assault are revealed in how the offender acts to control his victims. The degree of power or aggression that he shows reflects his deformed approach to the control of other people. Variations on this theme run the gamut from Dahmer's acts of murder and mutilation to the verbal coercion and fraudulent coaxing of many child molesters.

The destructive mixture of a callous search for intimacy and an unsympathetic desire for control is at the heart of the hidden narratives that shape violent assaults. It is the tangled variations in the form that these facets take which provides a general framework for considering crimes as different as Ryan's spree killings in Hungerford and Martin's series of rapes in the Midlands. Each of the broadly different roles to which the victim is assigned may be manipulated by the offender exhibiting different levels of power. The facets of intimacy and control combine to produce the unique brew that characterizes any particular attack.

Even if we consider only three levels of lack of intimacy and three levels of violent domination, the multiplication gives us nine different potential mixes. This complexity is magnified further when the stage in criminal development is considered. Intimacy and power are two major components of a criminal's life story that describe him at a particular point in time. Earlier these were referred to as the 'static' components; they will be revealed through the examination of any one of his crimes. Comparison between crimes will indicate a 'dynamic' aspect to his actions, the moving target that characterizes every life. The unfolding evolution of an offender's use of power and search for intimacy therefore provides the third set of principles to help us interpret a criminal's shadows.

To make this potentially complicated framework – of intimacy, power and development – as comprehensible as possible, I shall organize the detailed description round one central premise: that it is the depths of distorted intimacy that are the fundamental ingredients of violent criminality. For simplicity, I shall restrict the consideration of the role of the victim to one of three levels: object, vehicle or person.

The first and most callous level was clearly illustrated by Babb when he said that he liked women's bodies. This statement tells us that his victims were little more than animate objects to him. He knew there were certain things necessary to keep them from great discomfort but he had no empathy for their reactions to him. In the assault the victims were not expected to play any active part at all. In these narratives the offender makes no attempt to see the world from the point of view of the person who suffers his actions.

The second level recognizes that the victim has some human significance. These rapists and murderers assign their victim a more active and sometimes even more brutal role in the violent drama. When Martin aggressively insisted on his rape victim 'putting it in', or John Cannan, who was convicted of rape and the murder of Shirley Banks in 1989, beat all his victims beyond the need to subjugate them, they were both forcing their victims to carry some of the meanings the men had derived from their contact with other women. The victims were not just objects but vehicles that had to be felt to bear a load by the offender.

A third recognizable level of the role given to the victim is the one closest to normal relationships in which the woman is a person who has thoughts and feelings. The actual person is important in the formulation and meaning of the crime to the criminal. The brutal beating and dismemberment of Lynette White is a chilling illustration of the attempt to obliterate a person.

The victim as object, vehicle or person has implications for the reactions of the offender and should not be confused with the nature of the violence itself. The violence is a product of the form of control the offender is exerting; our second, distinct facet of the crime. It is this facet which shows us how similar narratives, in terms of the relationship to the victim, can be seen in crimes as different as serial murder or 'date rape'. The victim is assigned similar roles, but the forms of control are very different.

It follows that for each of the victim roles — object, vehicle, person — it will be possible to identify different levels of control. At the extremes of control the victim is to be possessed and reduced to total subjugation, but the significance of the victim who suffers this intense, often frenzied, attack can vary considerably from one offence to the other. But whatever the meaning of the victim to the offender, mutilation of the body or extensive acts of savage brutality will take place when an assailant is transfixed by the need to exert his dominance to the point of obliterating his prey.

In the chilling calculus of violence, murder without frenzy and mutilation is not the most extreme form of assault. It provides a second level for our facet of power and control. Murder can take many different forms and be committed for many different reasons. The framework here proposes that the difference will reflect the varying functions that the victim has for the killer.

As we have noted, attacks on women rarely lack some sexual connotation. Murder of a woman unknown to the killer usually includes overt sexual acts. Furthermore, men I have spoken to who have admitted a series of rapes have often also admitted that they would have killed subsequent victims if they had not been caught. Rape has the same roots as murder. The difference between rape and murder lies in the form and degree of control the offender exerts over his victim.

The third level of control can therefore be identified when the assailant uses the woman who falls into his hands as a source of satisfaction for his lust. The desire for power over a woman is reflected in an act that is seen by the rapist as the ultimate demonstration of his own sexuality. By forcing his manliness upon her he feels that he is in control.

With a few central concepts a rich range of possible offences and offenders can be sketched out. It is too early in the life of these speculations to be sure, but I find it encouraging to see how readily the violent crimes that I and others have examined illustrate the profiles that are suggested by various levels of each of the two facets of intimacy and power. The following, more detailed examples, help to enrich the skeleton I have outlined.

VICTIMS AS OBJECTS

The vicious serial murderer is often portrayed as a brilliantly evil man with superhuman powers of evasion, coldly prepared to wreak havoc and destruction. Robot-like, he feels nothing for his victims and is therefore able to torture, kill and mutilate without a shred of remorse. The exterminating daleks of television science fiction or the more complex killing robots and mass murderers invented by Hollywood are all of this genre. They all can trace their descent to Mary Shelley's monster created by Dr Viktor Frankenstein.

A close reading of that original monster story shows that what marks the nameless fiend out from other people, and contrasts so totally with the reactions of his creator, is the absence of any remorse. It is only at the end of the novel, with the death of his creator, that the monster shows any sincere feelings for what he has perpetrated, but even then it is because this has finally sealed the loneliness of the monster's existence. Only Viktor Frankenstein had the skill to build him a female partner, so even this final loss is felt in entirely egocentric terms.

As we have seen, the psychological and sociological assumptions that Mary Shelley makes are subtle and complex, but they are not all convincing. Nevertheless, when considering real-life murderers and rapists who carry out a series of assaults against strangers, a kernel of truth can be taken from *Frankenstein*: the lack of any feeling for the victims, or what I have called the victim as *object*. The other attributes of cunning and unremitting desire to inflict pain and fear are not obviously present in those men, at least not when they start on their destructive adventures.

This lack of personal feeling or contact that dictates their inner narrative is often reflected in the fact that these men make contact with their victims in nondescript public places, on the streets, in supermarkets and parks, unless accident brings a victim to the killer's door. Perhaps this is because the life and sense of a victim is less apparent when they are removed from places, products and people that are significant to them. Sexuality and many different and often bizarre sexual acts also dominate the personal narratives of these men. Their victims are little more than objects to be explored and played with. In extreme cases these acts have almost the strange innocence that will lead a child to take a toy apart, not realizing how destructive that action is.

Because the real lives of their women victims are so irrelevant to these men, the women tend to be vulnerable victims of opportunity. Such men do not stalk and target a specific person; any woman who is available and fits into the broad range of features of interest to the assailant may become a victim if the situation allows it.

In cases of the most extreme control, where the desire to have power over the victim is especially intense, we find offenders who perpetrate the most bizarre crimes: excessive mutilations, alive and dead; the keeping of body parts as mementoes; cannibalism and other practices that treat other human beings as inanimate. A startling example of this type of violent offender was Ed Gein, a farmer from Wisconsin, who was convicted for murder in 1957. He was found to have relics from at least fifteen bodies as gruesome 'ornaments' around his house. He started his ghoulish activities by digging up bodies to examine them, wearing their skins about him, going on to kill in order to obtain other body parts.

Albert Fish, convicted of murder in New York state in 1934, was another serial killer who mutilated and ate his victims, most of them young children. He illustrates also how such men often regard their own bodies as little more than objects to be controlled. He frequently flagellated himself, burned himself and inserted needles and other metal objects into his pubic regions.

Gein and Fish are at the very extremes of sanity. The stories they and other similar criminals live would probably not be open to any coherent account. The offender has a virtual lack of contact with most of normal human reality, and an inability to distinguish thoughts from secret voices, or fantasy from reality. Such a state will colour all the criminal's actions and make normal existence extremely difficult for him. He lives a grotesque, magical existence that keeps him in a twilight world that has different rules to the one most of us know outside our nightmares.

The term *psychotic* is often used to describe this group, dragging in with it psychiatric classification schemes and references to schizophrenia and paranoia. That is not my intention. Indeed, the courts in many countries have often found such extreme criminals to be fit to plead and sane enough to be convicted, and in some cases executed. It is also important to recognize that people who are mentally ill are only rarely violent. The axe-wielding madman is very rare indeed. Most mental patients are far more dangerous to themselves than to anybody else.

These offenders are one example of a group that has no real understanding that other people do indeed feel as they do. The racist or fascist who defines people of other colours or creeds as less than human also exposes the difficulty he has in feeling the experience of others, but these very disturbed criminals take that process one stage further, not really aware of the existence of others, except perhaps in lucid moments.

Such an all-embracing inability by a criminal to feel the victim's reactions must put him on the outer edges even of criminal society. Personal relationships of any normal kind will be difficult for him. Other people are devices whose inner workings mean little to him. But he does not have to be obviously out of touch with reality in the sense that the term *psychosis* is usually used. He may be of very low intellectual ability. One man who had murdered a number of old men and women, evading police detection for some time, sat in the court during his trial masturbating, apparently oblivious to his surroundings.

Such rare offenders are unlikely to write their autobiographies or volunteer to be interviewed by the FBI. Indeed, FBI agents who have tried to interview such men found that there was little they could glean from them, other than the extraordinary nature of their thought processes. The ones who do give an account of their deeds are the more intelligent ones who have some hold on reality, and some desire to keep manipulating their image of themselves through the actions they perform.

In the framework of the FBI, these men exhibit the classical picture of disorganization in their crimes and in their lifestyles, possibly moving in and out of institutions or living solitary, dishevelled existences punctuated by the excesses of their crimes. In terms of detection, these men will often be known in the local community as relatively harmless eccentrics. From time to time, they may annoy people with whom they have contact because of their erratic ways. Their bizarre behaviour usually develops so secretly and slowly that their deeds come to notice quite accidentally.

As might be expected, their background and upbringing is typically disturbed and unhappy, spent in institutions with frequent changes of parental figures, in poverty and degradation. This does not mean, though, that they cannot find periods of stability and sanity. Albert Fish was known in his earlier years as a shy married man who doted on his six children. Like all personal narratives, significant episodes can have great importance. Fish's killings started after his wife had left him. However, it is unusual for these men to still be living with a partner at the time that their offences take place.

The driven, distorted focus of their narratives is so limiting that it is unlikely that these men will travel far to commit their crimes. They may not even try very hard to evade capture, escaping more by luck and the incompetence of the local police than by careful planning. They are still often aware, though, of the criminality of their actions and may spread their net wide to reduce the risk of being stopped in what they are doing.

Once captured, like many of those who do not really appreciate the devastation they cause, they are frequently prepared to give as full an account of their deeds as they can. They happily speak of the voices and mission that spurred them on, keen to reveal the hidden narrative they have been living for so long; their need for human blood to fight the poisons around them; their instructions from God to rid the earth of evil. But these storylines have only an internal logic. They omit reference to the parallel, more realistic stories that also enabled them to continue their killings unstopped: the reasons for hiding the bodies, the care to make contact with their victims without any overt threat, the change of venue of the murders once people had been alerted. It is the overt logic of the crimes, not the inner narratives, which leads courts to find these murderers fit to plead – sane and guilty.

When the facet of possession and control of the victim is not quite as extreme as in the cases I have just considered, yet the victim is still little more than an object for abuse, a slightly different style of murder emerges. Here the victims are more likely to be selected for very special qualities that they have. The sexual contact will be more dominant than the mutilation and dismemberment. Murder will follow as a consequence of the violent actions, not necessarily as a determined objective of the assault.

These men have not found their way so far along the road of distorted perceptions. There is therefore unlikely to be any sign of bizarre mental thoughts or psychosis in their actions. Their obsessions are their victims and how they can obtain them. Dennis Nilsen, keeping bodies under his floor, and Jeffrey Dahmer with a fridge full of body parts are typical of this group of serial killers.

The obsession with special types of bodies, such as young men or girls, and the desire to control them for his own special purposes can lead these men far afield. Their central sanity is typically distorted only around this focal obsession so that they can plan and think about their crimes carefully. They will try to create some lair in which to keep their prey without disturbance. Although they may present themselves to the world as inoffensive, their hidden preoccupations will tend to keep them separate from others. 'A quiet young man,' the neighbours will say, 'we didn't see very much of him.' He will probably hold down a non-demanding job that allows him the freedom to develop his hidden narrative, and does not require him to have much contact with people in general. He is probably not even aware of his own loneliness, so dominated is he by his secret pursuits.

When a rapist kills his victims in order to reduce the risk of detection, he is indicating an even more callous and egocentric view of his crimes than those offenders who allow their victims to survive. Killing the victim treats her as an object that the offender now considers as merely a risk. Such a viewpoint is likely to come later in criminal experience, when the assailant has already learnt to treat his victims as less than human. It is far along the road of evil. Later in the chapter we will consider this journey further.

Babb may be regarded as being at the low end of the facet of control over the victim, while still treating his victims as objects. Unlike the 'vampires' and 'cannibals', violence had no dominant role in his crimes other than to keep the victim under control, but related psychological processes can still be perceived in his actions. The less violent nature of his crimes was reflected in the less peculiar lifestyle that he, like other offenders in this sub-group, lived. These are men who are likely to be more in touch with those around them, although they are still essentially alone. They have not honed their obsessions and allowed them totally to dominate their lives.

These men will trawl in areas that they know will provide likely prey. Typically they will commute to these areas until the pressure of public concern, or police presence, forces them to move further afield. They will say little to their victims, but may come to the offence scene with weapons and binding, prepared to overpower them with minimal struggle.

These offenders often puzzle those who arrest them, answering questions about their crimes in neutral, almost disinterested terms as if they do not really understand what all the fuss is about. At a psychological level they do not understand. The victims have no more significance to these rapists than does the quarry to a hunter.

I have argued that, in some ways, all violent men treat their victims as objects. In this sense they are all evil. But in order to develop our science, subtle discriminations are necessary. Those men whose actions reveal no concern at all for the reactions or feelings of their victims, who at the extreme of control treat the actual physical body of the people they have killed as a thing to be used, have been placed in this first group for whom their prey are nothing more than animate objects. In the following groups the inhumanity of the depravity is less extreme. To my mind this makes the offences possibly more understandable but no less abhorrent.

VICTIMS AS VEHICLES

When the murderer is concerned with what sort of people his victims are, and what they represent to him in his personal life, the processes of violence are very different. The consequences to the people he beats and slaughters may well be very similar, but if we are to distinguish between the dreadful shadows these men cast over so many lives, then the crucial differences in the way they commit their crimes have to be recognized. Here the victim must carry the load of the offender's desires. She is a vehicle for him to use.

Anger with himself and the fates that have led him to his

desolate situation is the central theme of such men's stories. They cast themselves in the role of tragic hero, living out in their assaults the sense of power and freedom that they feel is absent in the other stories they are forced to live. If our first set of themes reflects the offender's view of himself as a sort of nameless monster, this group would see themselves as more akin to dramatic heroes such as Oedipus. The fates have combined against them to deny them their rightful place, and so by seizing the moment they briefly steal back the initiative, recognizing the inevitable doom that lies ahead.

The most extreme examples are the spree killers who drive into fast-food restaurants and kill all they can reach there, or who sit on a rooftop and shoot passers-by. It is difficult to see suicide as an expressive act, as a desire to tell a particular story and make an impact on the world around you, but when Michael Ryan went out with his assault rifle to perform the Hungerford massacre he was declaring his inner turmoil. He was a formidable example of a man who had to destroy the people around him to exert his identity and, in so doing, kill himself. There is a biblical parallel in the story of Samson who could destroy the Philistines only by killing himself. I have also noticed this 'Samson Syndrome' in people who find that they cannot survive in an organization. They feel that if they cannot cope within the organization then it should not continue to exist either. They therefore try to destroy the organization before they leave it.

At a less extreme level of control, when the path to self-destruction is not so all-embracing, and the man is possibly more aware of a destructive mission, his crimes will take on a more controlled, serial form. Some of these men may even believe that they are grasping a mission which they will eventually want to tell. Many will wish to see their biographies written. They are the serial killers who will sit and talk at length to FBI agents. Because they are so willing to give an account of themselves they are often thought of as typical of serial killers, but this very willingness to express their views is what distinguishes them from other violent criminals.

Their ability to express themselves and to make contact with women is at the heart of their crimes and typifies the ways in which their crimes are committed. These are offenders whose native intelligence and life opportunities have enabled them to learn how to present a sociable face to the world. They may be labelled *psychopath* or *sociopath*; both are curious terms that imply a medical, pathogenic origin yet in fact describe someone for whom no obvious organic or psychotic diagnosis can be made. The seemingly informed technical term is therefore more an admission of ignorance than an effective description. It is also confusing that the smooth manipulator of others is as likely to be called a psychopath as the man who carries out forced abductions and violent assaults with no attempt to 'con' his victims.

The technical terminology is an attempt to characterize those people whose actions are clearly and consistently criminal, often violently so, but who seem able to reveal an inner world of thoughts and feelings that are not as bizarre as their actions. These are the criminals who come nearest to exhibiting pure evil. They know what the story of human relationships ought to be, but this always appears to be a part they play, not a role with which they are at one. They can recognize what empathy may mean but they never feel it.

The play at empathy cannot be stage-managed without at least some glimmering of how others see the world. Therefore, such people are a stage removed from the sadistic and psychotic alienation of our first group. These sane but remorseless criminals have never fully developed the capacity to see the world as others do. This leads them to feel no blame or guilt for the consequences of their actions. Their lives are littered with people who thought that it was possible to share their feelings, only to find themselves used and abused. As rapists these criminals may use subterfuge to gain access to their victims, asking for help, then take advantage of their quarry's vulnerability to carry out their assault.

Their ability to make contact with others will often mean that their initial approach will be apparently open and non-threatening. But because their victims signify something for them they will select or target women of a particular appearance. These victims may therefore be conventionally attractive, or be seen by the killer as typical of women of a particular class or style. He will have much more apparently social contact with his victims than our first group, but this will be an interaction in which the victim has to be harnessed to the offender's will. It is not sufficient for them just to be used; they must be exploited.

Key episodes in the criminal's life story are crucial. The break-up of a relationship or the death of a loved one will fuel the inner despair that drives these men. In one recent case, following my work with the police they arrested a man, who I will call Allan, for a series of violent rapes. They thought that a murder in the same area could also have been Allan's work, but they were not completely confident that he had done it and had little forensic evidence. Allan admitted the rapes but denied the murder.

When police officers asked me about the possibilities I requested details of the life crises Allan had gone through around the time of his crimes, a chronology they had not at that time considered. It emerged that the rapes had started around the time of the break-up of his marriage, but that a month or so before the murder, the woman who had brought him up and who had always supported him had died, suddenly and quite young. I told the police that the coincidence was too great to ignore and they should keep a careful watch on Allan and keep in contact with his associates. Not long after, an acquaintance of the suspect reported to the police that Allan had confessed to the murder when in a very morose state. The reported confession contained many details that had never been made public and would be known only to the killer and those police investigators who had found the body.

These killers may apparently have much in common with those who treat their victims as objects, but there are a number of important differences. They will tend to have backgrounds that are more stable and conventional. There will be obvious episodes in their lives that trigger the emergence of their violent inner narratives. The locations they choose as central to their drama will be far from arbitrary and go beyond opportunism. These locations will carry some meaning, a special significance for the offender.

These men are extremely dangerous in any assault because there is no basic compassion on which they can draw to limit the horror of their crimes. The mildest reaction from their victims can lead to murder. Even those whose manipulation of others implies some degree of access, some possibility of sharing their victims' feelings, may still be so distant from any genuine empathy that they take what appears to them to be the logical way of avoiding detection and kill their victims.

John Cannan had been a moderately successful car salesman. He was a 'lady's man' who had an affable, easy way of talking to people he met for the first time, polished by his education in an expensive private school. His family background, unlike those of most serial murderers, was unremarkable. Certainly his mother and father, brother and sister had no history of criminality or abuse. Yet he is now serving life imprisonment for the murder of Shirley

Banks, a newly-wed with whom he had had no previous contact. She disappeared from Bristol in October 1987. Her body was found in Somerset a year later. He also admitted to a number of violent assaults and rapes and was suspected of a number of other murders.

Close examination of Cannan's unfolding life story shows an exploitative use of women. They were possessions or creatures to comfort him, never partners. He built up a private world, near alcoholic at times, developing an account of his activities that, increasingly, lacked any reality. From time to time he was brought up against his own failures and this was followed by violent outbursts against those near to him. By his late twenties the pattern of superficially normal behaviour had become the minor theme in his life. The major theme was using his charm to make contact with women, then raping and sometimes killing them.

Cannan is thus a clear example of the offender for whom his victims are vehicles to carry his own emotions; they have no personal significance. As one of the women friends whom he attacked said: 'He only ever really loved himself.' His anger with himself burst out in his sexual assaults, which he may even have believed started as viable relationships. There is still the search for control over others, but it is constrained by the desire to demonstrate some sort of personal contact with his unwilling victim.

In the categories of the FBI, these men will tend to be organized in their offences, travelling far and wide to make contact with suitable victims. The victims themselves are, for the offender, a reflection of significant women in their lives. Central to their personal mission are usually attempts to rebuild broken relationships that existed before violence dominated their personal narratives.

The confusion of the use of the term 'psychopath' is illustrated by the fact that these men are just as likely to be so labelled as the very different killers of our first category, who treat their victims as objects. They are seen as 'psychopathic' because they appear to break all bounds of human morality. People like Cannan are put in the same category for the very different reason that they seem able to operate as normal human beings, may even be regarded as socially skilled, but they use and exploit their victims without any apparent remorse.

These offenders have taken longer to move along their personal path to reach this state of violence, with many broken relationships along the way. It is therefore not uncommon to find that they are rather older than many that we have been considering. Also, their previous relationships often have produced children.

'Richard' was not quite as far along the line of determined control as Cannan. For him the excitement came from the power and freedom he felt in the adventure of stalking women and raping them. He had never had a really long-standing relationship that he was trying to rediscover; his path of violence had opened up earlier than that. His search for victims was therefore clearly one of marauding, moving ever further out into territories where he would be less at risk from alert citizens or policemen. The targets of his assaults were selected, though. He was a black man brought up in the streets of Liverpool. Almost accidentally he attended a school where most children were white, and where white people tended to be just that bit better off. When he grew older his family and friends forbade him any contact with the white women whom he considered superior. As his life story collapsed, he found a special excitement overpowering attractive white women and raping them. He admitted that he had thought of himself as 'white with a black skin' for a long time. Somehow in his assaults he could live out this very different identity.

When the focus of his attack represents some particular sort of opportunity for the assailant, rather than just a body to use, there is an exploitative quality to the relationship between victim and offender which many women who survive find especially distressing. This is reflected in studies we have carried out of the traumatic effects of rape. Where there is some pre-existing relationship between the man and woman the victim is likely to exhibit more obvious psychological trauma. Indeed, the ferocity of the assault will tend to be greater for pre-existing relationships. I would suggest that if the rapist believes that there is some form of existing relationship, whether his belief is valid or not, then the victim is forced to carry some of his anger, to be a vehicle for his desire to impose his will. When the target of an assault is an actual person, rather than someone who symbolizes certain types of people, then the stage is set for much of the violent crime that makes up official statistics.

VICTIMS AS PERSONS

Those violent offenders who do recognize the existence of their victims as particular people get close to what many people would regard as normal behaviour. Like the great majority of criminals, they see in others distorted representations of their own experiences. They try to understand the experience of their victims and often believe they have done so, although this is inevitably a parody of real empathy. The inner narrative of these men puts them as heroes in dramatic adventures. Here you find the rapist who has shattered a woman's life in a violent assault telling her to be more careful next time because somebody nasty could have attacked her. This is also typical of the rapist who so misunderstood the reactions of his victim that he agreed to meet her the next day, not appreciating that she would have the police waiting for him.

Those violent criminals who come close to normal social interactions are those who expect to use others, for whom the control of others or the threat of violence is seen as a natural part of daily transactions between people. Here you have George pushing his hand fiercely into his victim's mouth to control her. Men who carry out such assaults are drawn from a sub-culture in which sex can be stolen like any other possession. Some may be driven by anger, jealousy, desire for revenge over wrongs they think women have inflicted on them or a confused combination of these, but they all are impervious to the fear, shame, anger and guilt that they inflict on their victims.

Pub brawls and other forms of violence that police officers refer to as 'public order' crimes fit into this category, as do the 'domestic' killings that are the majority of murders. Often in these cases, it is an accident of circumstance who ends up as the victim and who the murderer. A relationship between two people that has been tense for some time boils over into violence. Where guns or other weapons are readily available and are regarded as legitimate means for exerting influence over others, these outbreaks can end in death.

We have all felt annoyance or even anger with someone close to us; anger that would not be felt if they were anybody else. Who they are is pivotal to our reactions. This everyday reaction can erupt into criminal violence if the criminal is part of a social group in which vicious or violent actions are commonplace and possibly even accepted. Paradoxically, then, when it is important to the assailant that the victim is a particular person, not just a body or a representative of a type of person, then there is a reasonable chance that the attacker has a long and chequered criminal history behind him. Such men often attack indoors, near where they live, spilling over into this violence from other criminal activity, such as theft or burglary. Their actions though can run the full gamut from brutal murder to confused sexual assault.

Another range of types of murder, where the particular victim is important to the killer, are those all too common attacks on elderly people living alone, often frail women. These murders are often part of burglary or fraud, rarely with any apparent sexual connotations. They are typically committed by adolescent boys who live less than a few hundred yards from the crime scene. Usually these boys know the victim and may even be a distant relative. They have decided that the person can easily provide them with some gain. A particular person has been forced to provide for the killer. It is therefore less likely that the assailant will kill in this way again.

Rapists who seek out victims they can talk to, in the confused belief that there is some personal relationship in the assault, are only one step removed from the exploitative, murdering adolescents. The victim may be followed for some considerable time, her house broken into before the assault and during the assault the rapist may ask personal details of the victim such as her name and information about her boyfriend. These offenders tell themselves stories about their attractiveness to women, sometimes even having the confused belief that once they have sexually penetrated them their relationship is assured. Rape can become a way of life for these men, their preferred form of sex.

They start their assaults close to home in almost a recreational fashion, quite often with friends. The rapes may even start as attacks on women they know, the partner of a friend, a girl met at a party. Such men will be known by their associates as two-faced, given to grabbing what they want without much concern for others. They may even have wives or regular girlfriends. The women who marry these men, though, are likely to be younger than their husband, subservient to him, and probably collude in the life of petty crime they know their partners live.

It is tempting to broaden this group to cover a great range of crimes founded in such destructive human emotions as jealousy, greed and indignation. But that would take me far beyond the crimes for which it is obvious that psychological theories and methods could help police investigations. Where there is a known relationship between the criminal and his victim it is much more likely that established, competent police procedures will lead to the apprehension of the assailant. For cases in which there is no obvious link between offender and victim the characteristics of the attacks of this group are important in two key ways. One is in drawing attention to the possibility that the offender feels the victim has particular significance. The second is that many violent offenders who are known for their attacks on strangers (as vehicles or objects) have started their criminal careers with crimes against people they know. Understanding 'the victim as person' may therefore be very helpful in understanding the genesis of most personal narratives of violence.

CRIMINAL CAREERS

How do criminal narratives develop? How does a person continue to treat other people in so callous a way and move on from minor crimes to major ones? After all, criminals are human beings. Although it is tempting to dismiss the perpetrators of violent crime as 'monsters' or 'perverts', as people who are not within the normal realms of human experience, the simple fact is that, one way or another, criminals survive in our towns and cities, making some friends, holding down jobs, at least for a while, drinking in pubs, speaking the local language. Even the most depraved serial murderer is not an alien being driven by processes totally beyond normal experience. If he were it is highly probable that the police and others would have become aware of him long before his crimes became a series. In 1888, a London newspaper commenting on the character of 'Jack the Ripper' pointed out that 'we may infer that the assassin must appeal to his victims in some way that disarms suspicion. In other words, he cannot suggest by his appearance that he is the bloodthirsty miscreant'.

Such a comment raises the curious question of what a 'bloodthirsty miscreant' should look like. Certainly in the last hundred years the photographs of serial murderers that have covered the front pages of newspapers have usually shown young men of surprisingly benign appearance. Most people would pass John Duffy in the street unawares. The fictional characters who insanely devastate towns with chainsaws, who become transformed overnight, or at phases of the moon, into freakish fiends, the Dr Jekylls and Mr Hydes, are representations of how we feel about violent, unprovoked assaults. These invented stories may even relate to how some violent men try to excuse their own actions, but real-life perpetrators draw upon narratives that we all share. They have much more about them that is normal, everyday, than is not.

It may appear a challenge to common sense to suggest that the vile and extreme behaviour of vicious criminals shares anything with the average person's. The mistake here is to assume that the actions we see carried out by a man in his mid-twenties were potentially apparent in his actions when a young boy. Some of the seeds may be recognizable, but just as training and experience can turn one child into a brilliant gymnast it can turn another into a hardened criminal. It is experience as well as training. Learning to cope with your own fears, seeing the power you can have over others, getting accustomed to thinking of yourself as a man who uses other people's bodies, all these prepare and shape a person so that he eventually does go far beyond the realms of ordinary human actions. Focusing on the end result of these processes of personal development emphasizes how different these criminals are from other human beings.

Although criminals are limited people they fall within the range of human experience. They may be extreme examples of the human condition but they are not outside it. The themes to their lives are ones with which all of us have had contact. But for the men who rape and kill these themes develop and evolve far beyond the normal range. These personal evolutions of behaviour have much in common with the normal processes of human development. It is the distortions of maturing processes, recognizable in ourselves in a milder form, that are at the heart of all criminal activity.

To see more of these distorted maturation processes it is worth remembering that all the men I have written about have committed more than one crime. Typically there are a large number of crimes in their series before they are eventually caught. This means that the direct experience of earlier crimes will influence subsequent offence behaviour.

The most extreme example of this development was Albert DeSalvo, who was eventually given a life sentence in 1967, being known to have killed at least thirteen women. His criminal career had started by the time he was twelve years old, when he had been arrested for larceny and breaking and entering. By his early teens, which he spent in a school for delinquent boys, it was clear that he had an enormous sex drive and by the age of twenty-three he was charged with his first sex offence.

In his mid-twenties DeSalvo was well established as an unusual confidence trickster. He talked his way into apartments on the pretext of representing a modelling agency searching for models. He was nicknamed 'the measuring man' for the procedure of touching women, whom he claimed willingly allowed him to record their physical details. After subsequent imprisonment for burglary his measuring activities became more violent, tying up his victims and raping them. The green trousers he wore during these attacks earned him the sobriquet of 'green man'.

The initial stages in which he had related to women as people, well enough to some of them to believe that he did represent a modelling agency, had given way to treating them as vehicles for his sexual proclivities. In the final stages of his violent career he started killing his victims and desecrating their corpses. This was when he became known as the 'Boston Strangler'. The women were now objects to him through which he could insult the police investigators and society as a whole.

John Duffy also illustrates a parallel process of criminal development. Now at last we can get closer to answering the question that Lesley Cross kept asking me during that inquiry. 'Why had a man who had escaped with rape so often gone on to murder?' I now believe that part of the answer lies in the fact that the experience of raping so often without capture had prepared him for even more violent crimes. His inner narrative was leading along a path that required more than sexual possession of his victims.

In the earliest rapes thought to have been committed by Duffy, he was the reluctant partner to a more determined and aggressive attacker. He showed real concern for his victim and anxiety at being caught. He was treating his victim as a person, although less than fully aware of the impact his assault had on her. By the time he was attacking on his own he had already raped his estranged wife. His victims were becoming more distant vehicles for him. Yet all these early offences took place near where he lived in Kilburn. As I would now predict from his lack of extensive criminal background, he always attacked unknown women outdoors. Unfortunately we do not have details of what his victims looked like, but some that I saw did look similar to his estranged wife.

When Duffy started to attack on his own he still showed the attempts at intimacy and concern for his victims that I have characterized as typical of the third category of rapist. For example, with one of his earliest victims Duffy said: 'If you do everything I say I won't hurt you.' The victim also reported: 'He fondled my breasts and said, "put your arms around me and kiss me".' With one victim, whom he had blindfolded and left, he later returned to give her directions home. But as the location of his offences moved further and further away from his home, his need for control combined with his growing perception of his victims as objects to be manipulated, resulting in the carefully created ligature that strangled a young girl in a bluebell wood.

Chapter Twelve

DECIPHERING CRIMINAL SHADOWS

When Vince McFadden asked me to help his inquiry, very few police officers, and virtually no one outside the police force, had much idea of what 'profiling' was. As I write this six years later, every time there is a major inquiry journalists ask the investigators, 'Have you commissioned a profile?' In order to demonstrate that they are doing everything necessary, senior officers will often imply that they have, even though they may think that the crime will be solved without this still unusual move.

The popular belief in 'profiling', or at least the journalistic belief, has outstripped current practice. Just as the robots and thinking machines used in industry bear no resemblance to science fiction inventions, so the contribution of behavioural science to criminal investigations still has a long way to go before it is the stock-in-trade of the detective. Fortunately, therefore, there is still time for public and legal debate on what the implications of 'profiling' might be for the law, civil liberties and the practice and training of police officers.

The use of behavioural science by law-enforcement agencies may not be to the general advantage of society. Would it lead, perhaps, to an ever-more tightly controlling police state? A country in which the police really do have diagrams of what is inside people's heads, policing thoughts and intentions? Would this mean that more innocent poeple will be set-up by detectives, who will be confident of their judgements and convinced of the suspects' guilt because of the detectives' belief in their own psychological sophistication? I think the answers to these crucial questions lie in whether it is possible to improve the general competence and professionalism of police forces, in which psychological theories and methods will play an important part, or if 'profiling' will become absorbed as just another glib set of notions, poorly understood but readily used without challenge or validation in the way that some police officers have used other psychological ideas in the past. There is a long history of potentially valuable contributions from psychology being misused by police officers because they did not understand them and did not know how to ensure that they were being used appropriately: for example, hypnotic interviewing, 'lie detectors', 'truth drugs' and, more recently, the interpretation of a suspect's 'body language'.

The many instances of police incompetence, often bordering on corruption, that have featured in newspapers over recent years are rather like cases of tradesmen botching a job because they had no professional framework to fall back on when it became too complicated for them. These must be distinguished from fraudulent and consciously dishonest police work. All groups have their rogues and the police service is possibly more prone to attracting such people than other areas of public service, but that is very different from a style of work that may, on occasion, condone shoddiness. A professional framework for police work is now being built from many sources, one of them being scientific psychology. It is very likely that once firm principles for detective work have been established within the behavioural sciences, then the number of innocent people brought to court will be reduced, because it will contribute towards the increase in the competence of detectives.

For example, it is still the case that national trawls are made for potential suspects for many crimes, with no difference in emphasis given to a man known to live hundreds of miles away compared with a local man. Yet we now have some principles that could help detectives to consider whether the actions in a crime might indicate a local man, making wider searches unnecessary. These are principles, not procedures. The craft basis of police work tends to convert any thoughtful examination of crimes into a standard set of routines that will be carried out unthinkingly. This is the approach immortalized in the classic film *Casablanca*: 'Round up the usual suspects . . .' To go beyond traditional practice a different approach to policing is necessary and this will require different types of people to those commonly recruited by police forces around the world today.

If detectives can stop being tradesmen and start becoming professionals with a firm understanding of the natural and social sciences, then they will be able to use scientific theories and methods much more effectively. Why should the decision about which person to present to court as a criminal be reached so differently from the decision about how to diagnose and treat a disease from which a person is suffering? A doctor is not expected to operate on hunch and intuition, to learn his trade merely from hearing about how others have treated patients in the past, to have no firmly established principles to operate upon, only procedures to follow. He is not expected to turn his hand to solving complex problems in very different areas of his discipline without any specialist support. Why should a detective be expected to do all these? After all, the detective's decisions can have life-and-death consequences as well.

Many detectives have little formal training beyond what occupational psychologists call 'sitting next to Nelly'; that is, learning through a form of apprenticeship from experienced practitioners. Such learning runs the risk of perpetuating traditions which may be ineffective and will probably be unchallenged. So is there no part of their training and development that provides them with some insights into criminal behaviour, that goes beyond limited personal experience, that would indicate general principles or more formal ways of thinking and talking about crime? Do they not get some understanding of the narratives criminals live by from somewhere other than the streets and the incident room?

Police officers do have formulations of criminal life stories which are often very detailed and sophisticated. They look at the motivations and intentions of villains as well as their lifestyles and preferred settings for action. I was puzzled over where these narratives come from within the training of police officers. They do not come out of the literature in criminology and other social sciences, because that is not studied. Nor do they usually come out of very detailed knowledge of the lives and actions of many criminals. There will be a mixture of experience of various criminals available to any team of police officers, but this will depend entirely on the particular mixture of crimes they happen to have investigated. Yet the narrative lines that detectives are happy to discuss do indicate a background that is rather more studied than would be expected if their only experience was anecdote and hearsay.

It dawned on me that police officers do learn a form of psychological theory that goes beyond 'Nelly' in the formal training they get in the law of the land. It is in legal accounts of how crimes are committed that policemen are provided with models of the criminal and his behaviour.

The story of the crime is given a shape by how it is presented to the court.

Central to the legal case is the intention of the suspect to commit the crime. Someone who goes into a house determined to kill is seen as more culpable than someone who kills accidentally during the course of a burglary. The law recognizes gradations of intention: going to a scene with a murderous weapon indicates more preparedness to kill than hitting out in self-defence. But the story that the court tries to establish assumes some single, central purpose, or motive, and attempts to see how that unfolds in the commission of the crime. The court is trying to establish whether or not a criminal is a badly-programmed Frankenstein's monster with desires and intentions that are uncivilized and uncontrolled. If the offender appears to be driven to satisfy unacceptable desires then he must be locked away where he can do no harm.

Many police officers accept this form of the criminal's story and seek to identify the central motive that they see guiding his actions. If it is a person who is out for financial gain, but who kills to avoid capture, then that dominant motive will be relied upon to look for someone with a history of theft. A man who rapes is seen as motivated by enormous sexual appetite and therefore is expected to have committed previous sexually-related crimes. This focus on motive sometimes turns into an obsession with 'Why did he do it?' Crimes are seen to unfold with all the force and structure of a classic tragedy. Untrammelled evil desires drive the central character on to his inevitable destruction, taking innocent victims with him.

Our examination of the details of a criminal's actions has challenged legal notions of direct cause and effect; motive and mission. A rapist brings to his crime habits and attitudes that he has nurtured over many years. A murder may have been committed in the offender's mind many times before the victim was struck. The legal distinction between premeditation and impulse will therefore usually be difficult to defend in the light of the life history of the offender. Discrete motives, encapsulated in legal definitions of crimes, as burglary, rape or murder, are obscured by the feelings of adventure, revenge, anger or justification that give life to a person's own narrative.

Legal accounts of crimes have a simple shape to them. A defendant had an objective and sought to achieve it by unacceptable means. This viewpoint on crimes may be appropriate for the resolution of blame and the fixing of sentences, but it is often unhelpful as a basis for police investigations. The criminal may be easier to apprehend if his actions in one particular offence are seen as the outcome of that offender's own, evolving story. So that, for instance, instead of looking for a man who has shown his uncontrolled sexual desire by assaulting a woman, detectives can search for a man who has found excitement in burglaries and now is building upon the feeling of superiority those crimes gave him to stalk and rape women. The contribution of psychology to criminal investigations, then, is to help replace the legal perspective on the narrative of crimes with the inner narrative that shapes the criminal's own actions. Criminals write their own stories; psychology may help us to read them.

How can detectives read a criminal's inner narrative? Is this anything more than an academic gloss on current practice? If we look directly at the story that emerges from the actions in a crime we will see that this scholarly interest does take us to the heart of a criminal's actions. But the narrative perspective has a practical value as well. The whole idea of a storyline provides a convenient framework for directing a detective's attention.

To begin with, a story is always unfolding. The actions in any particular crimes are the culmination of many other activities and the interplay between many lives. The investigator therefore needs to try and understand what has led up to the particular scene and events that he is currently examining.

The role of the main characters, especially the offender himself and the part the victim is assigned, will be the foundation on which the story will make sense. The implications of the setting for the violent actions and the meaning it assigns to the characters will also help clarify what it is that the offender is trying to achieve. The actions themselves will reveal the relationships that the rapist or murderer is assuming. At the heart of these relationships are indications of the particular types of possession and control that are characteristic of the offender's ways of dealing with people. All these aspects will show developments within and across crimes that can also help the investigator pinpoint the culprit in social and geographical time and space.

To use the psychological perspective I have outlined for detection, it has to be recognized that among the range of choices open to investigators there are two basic questions to which they have to find answers. Who is the culprit? Where is he? The issue of the evidence needed to defend a case in court is really a consequence of obtaining answers to these fundamental questions. The irony of the narrative approach is that its contribution is to show that there is something to be learned from fiction. That it is possible to set up a detective process that seeks to unfold the criminal's story, parallel to the process of collecting evidence, not driven solely by the need to establish what can be presented as fact in court.

The psychological detective must attempt to unfathom the narrative that the criminal is living. A narrative that takes the offender ever deeper into the criminal world while still providing him with the fiction of a normal, acceptable life. These two different themes of offender and citizen provide a counterpoint in a criminal's life, each reflected in how his crimes are committed but each telling us about different aspects of his existence.

The criminal story is an unfolding one of skill and competence linked to the emotions; of knowledge and confidence which come from being in control of situations which non-criminals would find daunting. For example, my job as a head of department made it sometimes necessary for me to go into the office of one of my staff when they are not there, letting myself in with the master key in order, say, to pick up a report. I carry with me the guilt that most of us have about trespassing into other people's private domains. An experienced burglar would have difficulty in understanding this guilt. He would be concerned about being caught, but he is likely to have moved far beyond any feelings of inappropriateness at being inside somebody else's personal realm. Some will feel power and excitement from being privy to another's confidential world. Many otherwise ineffective offenders secretly follow people at night, gathering a strong feeling of control and domination over their targets from this hidden action and using it to build images of their targets as victims.

The feelings associated with intrusion reflect stages in the hardening of a criminal's sensibilities. They are the internal counterpart to growing criminal experience. The way a criminal commits a crime portrays his experience as a criminal, loosely connected to his degree of criminal sophistication. If a very well-informed criminal were deliberately to choose to commit a naive crime, he would reveal his inner talent and sophistication. The real challenge of the psychological investigator is to read the cryptic signs in which criminals inadvertently leave information about themselves.

The way in which the criminal's story unfolds will also tell us about the personal world he inhabits. Does his growing experience become associated, for example, with increasing violence and mutilation, as did both 'Jack the Ripper's' and Ted Bundy's series of murders? If it does, then we are shown a criminal whose violent control over others is central to his inner narrative. He will be seeking out criminal opportunities to live out that story and may well have committed earlier crimes as precursors or had relationships with other people that would reveal similar themes.

Another way in which a criminal's story evolves is by the degree of care he takes in avoiding capture. The person who sees himself as a professional prides himself on not taking what he regards as unacceptable risks. There is, therefore, much to be learned from the nature of the risks that are taken when committing a crime. Developing this idea, Detective Constable Rupert Heritage revealed his academic aspirations early when he coined the term 'forensic awareness'. The term describes the care that the criminal has taken to ensure that he is not caught. It embraces not just avoidance of leaving fingerprints, but all the other more subtle clues that modern forensic science can make available, such as bodily stains, fibres, facial identity. This sophistication will show how serious a criminal he is and the likelihood of his having been directly involved in a previous police investigation. His experience of prison may be revealed too. Many people regard prisons as educational establishments in which budding criminals improve their skills and understanding of police practices.

The extensiveness of the criminal history of an offender is revealed by the degree of experience he shows in his crime. This can be used to indicate how likely it is that the perpetrator is already somewhere in the police record system. The amount and kind of risk that the offender takes can be added to this formula to clarify his criminal antecedents and to indicate the types of crime for which he may have been responsible in the past. The criminal antecedents can help lead police to a suspect on their records. Given that about a third of the adult male population in Britain has some sort of criminal record, there is a potentially vast data-base on which to draw if only the police knew how to search it and had the skills and resources to do so.

Even if the police can locate suspects from their records, there is still the problem of selecting from the many possibilities. This is where the likely characteristics of the person are important, as well as the particular types of crimes for which they may have been convicted. In sexual assaults, for example, police in the past have often assumed that the offender is most likely to have a history relating to sexual crimes, indecent exposure, voyeurism or more violent sex-related crimes. This may be the case for the deviant individual who may attack impulsively in settings offering a potentially high risk of detection. A man who, one morning, attacked a woman visiting the University of Surrey to attend a conference, pulling her into bushes near the main footpath, was found to have only recently been let out of prison for virtually identical crimes. His actions showed little in the way of planning and very little attempt at concealment.

However, many rapists, possibly the majority, do not have any obvious history of sex crimes. The delinquent, anti-social offender may be almost indistinguishable from other criminals with whom he shares a common culture. Maclean, who broke into houses of single women in Notting Hill, waiting to rape them, had a lapse of four years in his rapes while he served a prison sentence for burglary. His skills at breaking into houses and the time he confidently spent there waiting for his victims were clues as clear as footprints in the snow, pointing to his experience as a burglar.

If it is not possible to indicate criminal history or if the behaviour patterns suggest that the offender may not be in police records – caused by, for example, his carelessness in leaving fingerprints or other clues to his identity – it is of direct value to an investigation and of considerable personal assistance to an investigator to obtain guidance to the offender's distinguishing characteristics. The nature of the relationships within the offences – their shape or structure – is the key to this. For example, Babb was a remarkably consistent assailant. His victims, time of day, type of locations, all added up to a signature that no other rapist I have come across could ever have forged. It was no surprise to discover that he was a conscientious, regular worker, relied upon by his employers. He brought the same dependability to attacking elderly ladies. The consistent nature of his actions also gave me confidence in believing that his patterns of behaviour had direct meaning. They could be interpreted as indications of his life-style. Taking his victims to the tops of tower blocks revealed his own shaping by the world of tower blocks, lifts and roof play spaces. To him the concrete monuments were secret gardens in which he could live out his inner narrative with remarkably little fear of being caught.

The more erratic and eventually more violent actions of Duffy showed different characteristics from the start. His very inconsistency meant that his behaviour needed more subtle interpretation. His skilled job could be gleaned from the planning and intelligence revealed in some of his assaults, but their varied and erratic nature suggested that he would not be a very reliable worker. For Duffy, the vicious ligatures that he used to strangle his victims revealed more about him than his signature at the end of a letter. They showed a control over his anger which only a person who could pass acceptably in day-to-day contact with others would be able to achieve. They reflected the outbursts his wife later reported; his cajoling her to allow him to visit, then threatening her with a knife. The preparation for the murder in the woodland also shows his inner world linked to murder. His fascination with such a possibility was intriguingly revealed through his befriending of a patient with fantasies of murder when Duffy was in a psychiatric hospital claiming amnesia.

Unusual aspects of a crime can add up to indicate the type of alien individual that others may recognize. By contrast, the preparedness of the assailant to talk to his victims reveals how comfortable he is holding a casual conversation and therefore whether he is likely to do that in normal circumstances. Broadly, being able to place the offender along the range from the bizarre psychotic to the misanthropic criminal enables investigators to locate them within their likely social context, with all its concomitants. Indeed, one of the imaginative pieces of lateral thinking that FBI profilers regularly use is to elaborate on the characteristics of an offender from just such a slender base. Knowing, for example, that an offender is likely to be severely mentally disturbed, it can be readily surmised that he may have spent some time in a mental hospital and developed some of the characteristics of institutionalization, not looking after his appearance, being out of work, living in impoverished circumstances.

When not committing crimes, offenders develop life stories not very different from those around them. These contain habits of thinking that carry over into how and where they carry out their crimes; their familiarity and knowledge of the areas where they live, their day-to-day relationships with other people. But, most importantly, they carry into their crimes ways of dealing with other people. For example, the search for intimacy with a victim, perhaps revealed through a paradoxical attempt to take care of her, contrasts with the violent encounter where sexual activity is the overriding objective of the assault: women play a very different role in the life of the former case to the role they play in the life of the latter. Does he cast her as victim or culprit, as object for venting his feelings or subject of his personal drama? That is what he reveals in every aspect of his criminal actions.

The elusive complications of all this have still to be unravelled. Often it feels as if we have discovered that scratches on a stone are an ancient language, but lack the means to translate them. The person who shot a husband and wife on the Welsh coastal path told us a great deal about himself from his actions around the time of the crime. He carefully built a hide from branches to keep the bodies from even the most detailed search, so that policemen harnessed by ropes and assisted by dogs had to look for the source of the smell of decomposing bodies. The killer, or someone who had contact with him, stayed in the locality for a few days using a cheque card stolen from the victims. Yet this resolute behaviour was applied to what appeared to be a casual contact with two strangers, having curious sexual overtones. These and many other aspects of the murder tell us so much about the offender, if only we knew how to read the message that he left for us. But extensive police inquiries over two years have still failed to identify a likely suspect. In other cases, to which I have also contributed, a very likely suspect has emerged, often fitting well the 'profile' I have drawn, but there is not enough evidence to charge the man. So we remain ignorant of whether or not our theories were valid.

Having a description of an offender only goes part-way towards helping to apprehend him. This description needs to be fleshed out with details of where the offender is likely to be found.

When a crime is identified it is often difficult for a criminal to hide the location in which the crime was committed. Only in those extreme circumstances in which the place where the victim is contacted is unknown and the location for disposal of evidence, especially of a corpse, is unknown, do investigators have no possibility of locating the criminal's whereabouts, at least at the time of the crime. Yet even these negative facts (holes in the shadows) tell us something about the person and the story he is living. Usually, though, locating where the offender might be is the cornerstone of any detective work. If time can be added to place, then this specification of the criminal provides the foundations from which discovery of the criminal's identity may proceed.

The possibility of gauging the likely residential location of serial criminals may be the strongest evidence of how fundamentally limited they are. A large percentage live within a few minutes' walk of their crimes. It may eventually prove possible to account for those that do not live so close by reference to the availability of targets for them and their access to transport. Their unfolding story may also prove valuable by indicating how far they have travelled to commit a crime. Combinations of aspects of their narrative appear to be of significance: those for whom the victim is a relatively arbitrary object are less likely to travel far than those who are looking for a special vessel for their desires. Both groups will broaden their area of search as they become more engrossed in their life of violence. Our studies are also hinting at differences between black and white assailants and those who attack indoors and outdoors. Distinctive sub-groups appear to have characteristic uses of the city as venues for crime. One of the most successful components of the reports we have given to police forces has been an indication of where the assailant might live.

The psychological examination of crimes implies careful attention to many details that might not otherwise be considered. The consideration of patterns of behaviour rather than individual clues is another hallmark of this approach. For such an approach to be valuable, reliable and valid information is needed about the crime scene and the criminal's actions. Detectives need to pool their information and understanding so that the whole gory picture can be clearly seen. This means that the interviewing of victims and witnesses as well as suspects needs to be more intense and thorough than is now often the case. New demands are also placed on how police officers keep each other informed of the progress of their inquiries.

Many of the other demands on police officers brought about by changes in the law may also be eased by drawing upon behavioural science. To make effective use of the limited time available during an interview, police officers have to be much more prepared than was the case in the past. Anything that might be relevant about the suspect could benefit this planning. Any system or approach to interviewing that took account of the new circumstances could be helpful. Having a variety of sources of information that could help strengthen the belief that the person being interviewed was indeed the culprit is important for morale as well as directly indicating the important questions to ask and other possible lines of inquiry.

If detectives do develop psychological understanding

and associated procedures this will have implications for how they organize their material for the courts. The replacing of current types of criminal stories with the psychologically rich narratives that can come from profiling may enable police officers to give more convincing briefing to the prosecution counsel. The consequences for how cases are conducted and other aspects of the legal process could therefore be far-reaching.

All of this adds up to a new area of applied psychology. It covers different facets of criminal behaviour, developments of police interviewing procedures to facilitate the examination of this behaviour, changes in the group dynamics of police inquiry teams, and the psychological theories and computing procedures associated with all these aspects of investigations. Taken together, they cover a breadth and depth of psychological expertise that has a coherence and focus appropriate to a sub-discipline that has its own identifiable existence. *Investigative Psychology* seems an apposite name for this field.

What of the competence of criminals? By publishing ways of apprehending them am I arming criminals with the means of deception? Very open accounts of the approaches to an investigation, published at the time of the investigation, could have that effect; although this is more likely in the realms of detective fiction than of detective fact. One reason even a direct account may not have an influence is precisely because we are dealing with people who are locked in their own worlds, unlikely to be able to act on such information if it became available. Those who *are* able to act on such information will set out to glean it from wherever they can. Lack of readily published information is unlikely to be a barrier. Indeed, the sophistication that may be revealed by acting on such material may itself tell us something about the perpetrator.

One of the most sophisticated threats for money that

was carried out in Britain in recent years, the threat by Rodney Whitchelo to contaminate food if the manufacturer did not pay him £100,000 per year over a period of five years, was very nearly successful. He is said to have hatched the plot for his crimes after studying a similar earlier case on a training course when he was a police officer at Hendon. Ted Bundy, executed for multiple murders, was studying confidential FBI documents in his cell shortly before he was electrocuted. He had obtained these by charming them out of visiting investigators. By contrast, the price to be paid by keeping research ideas secret is that those ideas are not open to public challenge. Secret science is bad science.

A further reason why I am not worried about publication of this work is that at the root of these offences is a lack of personal insight. It is my hope that the offenders, and indeed their victims, will come to understand more about the offences. Contact I have already had with offenders who wish to change their behaviour indicates that some of them feel that the investigative psychology perspective helps them to understand the conditions they create for themselves that perpetuate their cycles of crime. It is to be hoped that victims too will be helped to cope more readily with the psychological consequences of the crimes they have suffered by understanding more of what it is that criminals do.

Looking back on what criminals have taught me, I am beginning to think that investigative psychology is not so very different from my earlier academic concerns as I once thought. A person's shadow can be read because people have a coherent, interpretable form. Try as hard as we will none of us can act in a random way. No one can maintain an enigmatic, will-o'-the-wisp persona for very long. My earlier studies of the experience of places and of how people coped when faced with a life-threatening emergency had already made clear that people impose meaning on even the most fleeting or ambiguous of experiences. We all create significance in our lives through the actions we perform. For others to discover that significance they need to understand our acts and the meanings they have for us.

Violent assaults on other people reveal the personal narratives that both reflect and structure a criminal's life, the signatures from which their personality and way of living can be interpreted. As I have shown, some of these signatures are very graphic, others are more subtle. If properly understood they give us access to many other aspects of the person to whom they are linked.

The storylines of violent criminals are so different from those of other people in society because of distortions in their themes of intimacy and appropriate use of power. The distorted relationships they have with other people may consequently be of value in providing a contrast that emphasizes what is at the core of civil human society. The ability to relate with empathy to other people and to maintain personal esteem without the need to exert coercive control over others are the antithesis of rape and murder. The extent to which we cast ourselves in roles that recognize the valid existence of others is an index of the distance we each keep from becoming violent criminals. The ways in which we deal with other people indicate something of the inner narratives we are living, just as what a victim suffers reveals the inner narrative of the assailant.

By carefully following the actions of criminals, we are attempting to uncover the stories they tell themselves. By staying close to the details of what they do, we are attempting to get into their shoes, not their minds. The same is true of the people we live and work with; the way they walk or laugh is not random, accidental or arbitrary.

It can tell us something about them, provided we have the science and the patience to decipher it. Although a shadow can be disguised, it can never be shaken off.

AFTERWORD

Since the publication of the hardback edition of *Criminal Shadows*, many of the senior police officers mentioned in earlier pages, Vince McFadden, John Hurst, Thelma Wagstaff, have now retired. The generation that is replacing them no longer sees offender profiling as some exotic idea that has been imported from the USA. Journalists still get excited about the notion that psychologists are helping police investigations, but even they tend now to use psychological profiles as a standard way of filling out a story on a major case rather than news in its own right. In one recent investigation, that held the national newspapers in thrall for weeks, it was reported that 'police and psychologists' were looking for the offender. This was reported in a matter of fact way, without comment, as if everyone would accept that psychologists have a natural role within a team of detectives.

In all the cases that have grabbed the headlines since *Criminal Shadows* was first published, such as Colin Ireland's killing of gay men, the murder of Jamie Bulger or the bodies found buried in Cromwell Road, Gloucester, the contributions of psychologists, using procedures that derive from those I have described, have been widely acclaimed as of value to the police. All this is a far cry from the situation when I started writing this book.

Yet, despite my satisfaction in this progress, this rapid uptake is fraught with dangers. There are still very few people in the police force who are able to evaluate profiling or discern the quality of the information they are given. The myth is emerging of the quasi-magical 'profiler', whose opinions are derived from his (rarely her) personal experience, not from any systematic, scientific study. For some police officers, 'profilers' have merely taken over the role of the psychics that were occasionally consulted before. The great advantage of the profiler to these investigators, though, is that he can be proudly declared as a new 'tool' for police investigations, rather than secretly consulted.

This wish to link their investigation publicly with scientific analysis is of course eminently sensible. I recently attended a meeting in Moscow with Russian police researchers. Sitting opposite my counterparts across a long, narrow table, but frustratingly distant because of the language barrier, I learnt through a translator of their fascinating studies of what they called unconventional approaches to police investigations. They included within these studies an examination of people who had what was translated as 'extraordinary abilities'. In general these were people that we would call 'psychics', men and women who provide accounts of unknown offenders on the basis of some poorly defined intuition. This intuition may be expressed as a vision or dream, but the opinion about the location of a body, the character of an offender or anything else that can help an inquiry is given without any explanation or defence. The psychic just *knows*.

Many people who now produce profiles for the police fall into the same categories as psychics and are used by investigating officers for similar reasons. Some of these profilers may be able to help on some occasions, but, without any understanding of how they produce their profiles, the results of their help will always be wildly unpredictable. An even more important long-term consideration is that we have to know how a profile was produced in order to have a basis for improving its accuracy.

Profiles that are the intuitive creation of an individual with little scientific backing are just flotsam on a sea of crime. The scientific psychologist's role is to build sturdy ships that will help detectives sail through what can almost literally amount to a sea of information. But there is no point expecting profilers to operate like 'hit-and-run' robbers, quickly turning up at an inquiry and giving an unsupported opinion without time to study closely all the facts the investigators have amassed. We need to develop the science of Investigative Psychology.

Fortunately many police officers and psychologists are prepared to put the effort into studying and developing this new branch of science. They have already taken many of the ideas from the present volume and tested them exhaustively, developing powerful new theories and procedures out of this model. Many conference presentations and academic publications have flowed from their work over the past months. The narrative theory that I outlined has proved especially fruitful and already appears to have applications to areas of crime not mentioned in this book, such as robbery and arson.

Out of this work a network of police officers and research psychologists is growing around the world that is using the approach to offender profiling introduced in this book. Their successes have been quietly acknowledged among police officers, but have not attracted the same public interest as the 'hit-and-run experts'. Curiously, the media seems less impressed that an employee of the police, whether officer or civilian, should use new scientific procedures to help solve crimes than that a lone individual, acting outside the police can give 'extraordinary' help. Conan Doyle clearly has a lot to answer for.

Fictional accounts, such as the successful television series

'Cracker' therefore continue to mislead the public into believing that 'profiling' depends on the special gifts of a (probably disturbed) individual, rather than the point I have tried to express as strongly as possible in this book, that the process of making inferences about a person from the way he commits a crime is a natural development of scientific psychology and therefore open to anyone with the appropriate knowledge and training.

The benefits of using psychology to improve the effectiveness of detective work is only one side of the story. The suspects' answers to detectives' questions also illuminate some dark corners of criminal psychology and therefore have value beyond simply apprehending the perpetrator. They will have implications for aspects of the judicial procedure as well as for treatment. Indeed, one police officer who had studied with me has already been asked in cross-examination what qualifications he had to propose that the accused had committed all the rapes with which he was charged. I would have liked to have been there to see the barrister's face when the police officer replied with a detailed account of his own academic study of rapists' behaviour.

Clinicians are already researching treatment programmes that are responsive to the variations between offenders drawing from the close examination of their behavioural profile. For example, an offender who recognizes some of the human, personal qualities of his victim really needs a different sort of treatment from an offender who uses his victims totally as objects. Crime prevention procedures can also doubtless be improved by drawing upon the psychological theories of profiling.

Again, though, a little knowledge in this area can, potentially, be very dangerous. Juries presented with profiles, whether for the defence or the prosecution, will find it difficult to evaluate them. Opinions masquerading as scientific fact could be given too much credence by an ill-informed judicial system. My view is that the courts would be better off relying on traditional forms of evidence. Similarly, a drift towards an investigative role by clinicians, focusing on the details of the crime rather than the nature of the person who carried out the offence, would be foolish.

The only way to reduce the danger of the profiler's work being misinterpreted or misappropriated is to give as much emphasis to long-term scientific studies as to the immediate resolution of pressing criminal investigations. These longer-term studies need to address the central question, towards which profiling can offer an invaluable and quantifiable answer: 'how do criminals differ from each other?' The criminology literature is remarkably quiet about variations between criminals, usually preferring to treat them all as one particular kind of person. Typically the variations that are mentioned relate to stages in their development as criminals. Yet the whole process of profiling is based upon the assumption that there will be some features that distinguish one criminal from another across his criminal career. What does it do for the theories of crime to propose that there will be many different styles of criminality? Are the causes of crime different for different types of offender? Are they likely to respond to punishment in different ways?

One of the meanings of 'shadow' in the title of this book is that hidden, secret part of us that we keep under control in order to act in a civilized way. The shadow that we all have has criminal features. For a variety of reasons some people reveal their criminal shadows more overtly by committing offences. Therefore by understanding more fully the shadows revealed by criminals we will all gain deeper insights into our own being.

ACKNOWLEDGEMENTS

Rupert Heritage is present on most of the pages of this book, which would never have existed without his full co-operation. I hope it is a suitable tribute to his wit and friendship. More recently two other police officers, Rick Holden and Stuart Kirby, have taken up studies with me. Many of the things they have taught me have found their way into the present volume. I am very grateful to them for their insights and goodwill.

A number of senior police officers have supported and helped the work covered in this book and contributed to its subsequent development. Out of many, I owe very special gratitude to John Grieve, Vince McFadden and Thelma Wagstaff. They all openly welcomed me into the world of criminal investigations. I also greatly appreciate the support which John Hurst and John Stevens have continued to give me and my colleagues.

With some temerity I approached police officers who had been involved in the various cases that I describe in the book, asking them to look over the chapters I had written. Without exception they responded quickly and with courtesy, giving me detailed comments on the veracity of what I had written as they saw it. So, although they cannot be held responsible for my account of the investigations, I am grateful for their careful assistance. My contacts with the police have, however, taught me a certain discretion. I therefore think that it is probably best not to mention their names. However, there is no secret that the following police forces have been of tremendous help both while I was writing this book and also in helping my colleagues and me in the study of criminal behaviour: Greater Manchester, Metropolitan, South Wales, Surrey and West Midlands. Other police forces and police officers also continue to contribute to the Investigative Psychology research and teaching at the University of Surrey. I hope they will all see this book as at least a small, constructive repayment of the debt I owe them.

My secretary at the University of Surrey has specifically asked not to be named in this book. I am happy to acknowledge her help which is never anonymous.

Over a number of years Rupert and I have been privileged to keep in contact with the Behavioral Science Unit at Quantico. Robert (Roy) Hazelwood, Bob Ressler, and Janet Warren have been especially kind, and generous, but John Douglas, Roland Reboussin and Ann Burgess have also shared with us their thoughts, experiences and reports. The friendly guidance and warm encouragement from them and their colleagues have been a continual source of inspiration. Their pioneering work and productive insights are the foundation of this book.

At the University of Surrey I have been particularly fortunate in the backing I have received from my colleagues. The Vice Chancellor, Anthony Kelly, has gone out of his way to facilitate my research and the writing of this book. Indeed it was from him that I appreciated the significance of Plato's shadows to the theme of my book. He gave me the greatest gift of all when he allowed me to take a sabbatical in which to write. Glynis Breakwell readily shouldered my administrative responsibilities to become Head of the Psychology Department, in which role she has continued to assist my writing and thinking, providing many valuable comments on the manuscript as it unfurled. The sub-librarian for psychology, Mark

Ashworth, has given me assistance far beyond the call of duty.

A number of undergraduates at the University of Surrey have worked with me during the writing of this book, giving help and advice in many ways. They include Adam Gregory (who helped prepare the illustrations for this book), Helen Hughes, Paul Larkin, Ellen Tzang and Graeme Vaughan. Many postgraduates have also contributed to my thinking, and added to the excitement of working in this area. They include Anne Davies, Jennifer Kilcoyne, Chris Missen and Jenny Ward. David Jordan deserves a special mention for making available to me his invaluable undergraduate dissertation on Michael Ryan.

Other friends have also eased the birth-pangs of this book. Elliott Leyton has been unstinting with his guidance and reassurance, allowing me to benefit from his enormous experience of writing and of killers. Eric Clarke and Les Blair both took time to show me where it was productive to focus. Celia Kitzinger and Amita Sinha have each given me a unique perspective of great value. Lorraine Nanke got me into crime and has continued to give me the benefits of her advice. Patrick Fleming, the television documentary director who put me in a helicopter over Birmingham, very kindly made his production notes available to me. His encouragement throughout the writing of this book is much appreciated. Thanks are also due to Margaret Wilson and Lynne Martin for details of their work on detectives' decision making.

I don't know who A. P. Watt was or is, but the agency that takes his or her name has provided me with the most delightful support team that an author could ever want. Imogen Parker nursed the book into being and saw it through various crises, Derek Johns charmingly continued her work while Nick Marston dealt wonderfully with the media spin-off.

Acknowledgements

At HarperCollins Mike Fishwick's enthusiasm for this book has been a much appreciated stimulus. Janet Law has honed the excesses of my writing with a firm but gentle touch.

My children have all made the work on this book more bearable. Hana reminded me not to become insensitive to the horror of the material with which I have had to deal. She has also done an excellent job in helping me to put together the source notes and bibliography and in preparing the index. Daniel, Lily and my wife Sandra helped to ensure that I did not lose touch with the delights of day-to-day reality as I got absorbed by this writing project.

Without Sandra's love and support, as well as the benefits of her profound understanding of human nature, I could never have written this book. This book is dedicated to her with deep love and appreciation for everything she has shared with me.

REFERENCES AND NOTES

Throughout this book 'he' is used to describe criminals and the victims are usually assumed to be women. This is because all the offenders I have considered in this book have been men and the great majority of their victims have been female. I know that men are often victims of sex crimes as well as other crimes and that there are an increasing number of violent female offenders. However, the important matters raised by the existence of male victims and female offenders are not dealt with in the present volume.

In the following notes books listed in the Select Bibliography are indicated by author and date. However, because I drew upon the books in the Select Bibliography throughout the writing of *Criminal Shadows*, I have indicated only very direct citations in the following notes.

The opening quote from G. S. Howard is from 'Culture Tales: a Narrative Approach to Thinking, Cross-Cultural Psychology and Psychotherapy', *American Psychologist*, March 1991, Vol. 46 No. 3, pp. 187–97. On page 196 Howard says that it is a paraphrase of Shakespeare, but Professor Howard has informed me that he cannot remember which quote it paraphrases.

ONE: A BETTER NET

See Kind (1987) and Swanson et al. (1992) for details of the information available at crime scenes and from witnesses.

The idea that it is possible to identify criminals from their looks is most vividly explored in the works of Lombroso, discussed in Chapter Nine. Giovanni Morelli, the Victorian art connoisseur, who used details such as ears to identify fake paintings, possibly laid the foundations for the search for anomalies of a more psychological kind. See James Hall's article in the *Guardian* 5 July 1992, 'An ear for authenticity', p. 36.

The term 'serial murderer' can be traced to J. Brophy, *The Meaning of Murder* (London: Corgi, 1966), p. 172: 'Jack the Ripper, still unidentified and still the most famous of all serial murderers', pre-dating the FBI use of the term 'serial killer' in the mid-1970s (Ressler and Shachtman, 1992, p. 35).

The historical development of our understanding of the psychology of insanity and its relationship to the development of medicine is summarized in Hearnshaw (1989).

Police Review, 22 January 1993, pp. 16–18 captures the interest by police officers in the application of psychology to detective work.

An account of the emergence of 'The M'Naghten Rules' is given in Wilson and Herrnstein (1985), pp. 502–6.

The significance of forgetting a name was explored by Sigmund Freud in one of his earliest books, *The Psychopathology of Everyday Life*, first published in 1904.

An obituary of Dr Thomas Bond is given in the Westminster Hospital Reports for 1901, available in Cambridge University Library.

Haward, L. R. C. (1981), *Forensic Psychology*. London: Batsford. Gives a number of accounts of psychological contributions to military and police investigations.

Langer, W. (1972), *The Mind of Adolf Hitler*. New York: New American Library.

Watson, P. (1980), *War on the Mind*. London: Penguin. Describes a number of psychological contributions to military/political strategy.

Rendell, R. (1991), *Devices and Desires*. London: Penguin.

Tullet, T. (1986), *Clues to Murder: Famous Forensic Murder Cases of Professor J. M. Cameron*. London: Grafton Books.

The development of the FBI profiling activities is best gleaned from Ressler (1992) and Hazelwood and Burgess (1987). Colin Wilson and Donald Seaman also provide accounts of a number of cases in their 1990 book *The Serial Killers: A Study of the Psychology of Violence* (London: W. H. Allen). The role of Brussel is also discussed in Leyton (1986).

Rumbelow, D. (1988), *The Complete Jack the Ripper*. London: Penguin.

Cross, R. (1981), *The Yorkshire Ripper*. London: Granada.

Wambaugh (1989) gives a very full account of the investigation leading to the arrest of Colin Pitchfork.

Canter, D. (ed.) (1990), *Fires and Human Behaviour*. London: David Fulton.

Police and Criminal Evidence Act (1984). London: HMSO.

Shepard, M. (1985), *Sherlock Holmes and the Case of Dr Freud*. London: Tavistock Publications.

TWO: FIRST PRINCIPLES

Although the 'hand-to-mouth' funding of research is still typical as indicated in this chapter, I am happy to acknowledge the support given by the Home Office, the US Army Basic Research Institute, DEC plc and the University of Surrey, for studies conducted subsequent to those reported in this book.

Accounts of the investigations leading to the arrest and conviction of John Duffy were given in most national newspapers on and 16 January 1988, including: the *Daily Telegraph*, *Daily Me* and the *Guardian*. The *Surrey Advertiser* gave a particularly full account.

The computer-based statistical analysis mentioned in this chapter is the same as that described in Chapters Seven and Ten technical details of which are given in Canter (1985). A brief summary of how the statistical analysis works is given in the notes to Chapter Seven.

The various psychological approaches to human development are briefly reviewed in Chapter Nine.

Psychological considerations of eye-witness testimony are given in Raskin (1989) and Stephenson (1992).

One study to illustrate the wide-ranging criminal experience rapists is Scully (1990).

The learning of sexual behaviour is discussed in Masters, W. H. and Johnson, V. E. (1966), *Human Sexual Response*. Boston: Little Brown.

The tourniquet quotation is taken from *Encyclopaedia Britannica* (1964), article on First Aid, Vol. 9, p. 313.

Locard, E. (1931–39), *Traité de criminalistique* (7 vols). Lyc Joannès Desvigne et ses Fils.

The statistical procedures described in this and subsequent chapters are a subset of the family of multi-variate analysis procedures known as non-metric multi-dimensional scaling (Canter, 1985). The following description gives an indication of how these procedures work.

The computer deals with each crime as a row and all the types of behaviours that occur as columns. The first crime is the first row, below it is a row for the second crime and so on. Forcing their way down through these rows is a tuned platoon of actions, each action a column on its own. For the Midlands rapes, the first column indicated (a) whether the criminal in each offence row had gained entry to the house by a window. The second was (b) whether he had brought a weapon to the scene with him, and so on. The other eight behaviours were: whether or not (c) the victim was blindfolded, (d) the offender was masked, (e) the offender attempted to reassure the victim she would not be hurt, (f) the offender was viciously violent, (g) gagging was with a hand or cloth, (h) cunnilingus occurred, (i) fellatio occurred, (j) fondling occurred. These ten actions, (a) to (j), were found to be effective in pinning down the actions for the range of crimes in the Midlands. The rows and columns are known as a 'data matrix'.

Armed with this matrix of rows and columns it was possible to indicate at the intersection of these two phalanxes whether the particular action had occurred in the particular offence. The computers we used prefer a 1 if the action did not occur and a 2 if it did. Filling in the numbers from a close reading of the statements by the victims is a quite precise creation of a 'profile', in a technical mathematical sense, of the offender as revealed through his actions. Each row of 1s and 2s looks much like any other string of numbers that might be used to feed the inexhaustible appetite of a modern computer.

Each row of 1s and 2s provides a very precise profile of the actions that happened in one offence. It is a real *profile* in the direct sense of specifying the outline of the offender's actions.

The computer can bring this flat fabric into a lurching semblance of life, forcing the numbers to reveal some of their secrets. Or, like raw recruits who have been through basic training, the platoon of 1s and 2s can be paraded through various manoeuvres until their underlying similarities and differences can be seen.

The task was to establish, first, if there were subsets of crimes that shared characteristics to the extent that we could reasonably assume that the same person was responsible. We could then build a better understanding of the perpetrators from the common characteristics of each subset; examining changes within them over time, and groupings in particular parts of the city, as well as particular reactions to certain victims. These patterns can also be compared with the patterns of known criminals. It seems reasonable to assume that the personal profile of known criminals would be parallel to those of the unknown assailants who had a similar behavioural profile. A simple example would be that if two attackers both snapped instructions at their victims in what might be thought of as a military style and we knew one had had a military training, then a reasonable starting point would be to assume that the unknown attacker had a military background as well. Of course, the more examples of behaviour we could compare the more confidence we would have in our assumptions. But how are we to compare these patterns of behaviour?

Like rows of soldiers, we had a platoon of numbers standing in lines one behind the other. The comparison of one row with another is the computer's way of comparing one crime pattern with another. Similarities between each row had to be assigned a value. We had to measure the correlation between the crimes. This is done by mathematical comparison of the string of 1s and 2s. The highest correlation between two crimes would be produced if the profile of 1s and 2s were the same for each row; the lowest if they were opposite (1,2,1,1, for example, being challenged by 2,1,2,2). All the values between indicate the other degrees of similarity. The calculations are unbiased and objective in not giving special weight to any particular action that might apparently seem especially awful.

Such calculations are meat and drink for the modern electronic computer. Reducing it to its simplest, it is straightforward to work out the total number of times the figures in each row are the same as each other. This total is an index of just how close, in broad, direct terms, is the similarity between the pattern of behaviours for each crime. Statistically we have done something quite bold here. Two strings of *qualities* have been compared and an overall *quantity* has been derived to indicate their similarity.

This enables us to move from the world of descriptions, where like can only be compared with like, to the much more manageable world of arithmetic in which measures of similarity, correlations, can be manipulated to reveal underlying trends.

In order to make sense of the similarities and differences of the ten crimes we were concerned with in the Midlands, it was necessary to consider all the possible correlations between the crimes. There are ten crimes of interest. Elementary mathematics reveals that if every crime is compared with every other one we would end up with forty-five comparisons. This would seem to add to the complexity of what we are studying rather than simplifying it.

Fortunately, statistically-minded psychologists have developed many procedures for reducing the complexity inherent in multiple comparisons and revealing the central trends behind all the correlations. The approach used in the present book (described in detail in Canter, 1985) is based on having each row of numbers, each crime, represented as a point in space. This is one of those abstract spaces in which mathematicians like to live. It floats, unfixed, defined entirely by what is going on within it. But the easiest way to think of it is as a blank, empty square. Inside this square there are points. Each of these points represents a crime; in the Midlands case ten points for ten crimes.

The statistical cunning comes from the process of assigning points to locations in this space. This process can be thought of as fastening each point to every other one with a piece of string. The length of the string represents how unlike the two crimes are. The shorter the string the higher the correlation between the crimes. The computer attempts to pull all these strings tight so that the closer together any two points representing two crimes, the more similar are the actions in those two crimes. The points in the square will therefore be spread out in clusters, not unlike constellations of stars in the night sky. These groupings help us to see, in one summary picture, what is going on across a number of crimes at once, but they did not tell us definitively which crimes were distinct from which others. They gave us a basis on which to build the case for such distinctions.

There is one important technical problem in all this drawing of maps from correlations. Only in circumstances where the mathematics were exceptional would all the strings become taut on a flat sheet of paper. On a limiting two-dimensional surface it would be only under very special conditions that the relationships could be mapped within those constraints. They would always end up with an approximation. Some of the pieces of string would be slack and some would be stretched, possibly beyond breaking point. The computer gives the best approximation to a map that it can.

In the Midlands investigation we already had information available on a known London rapist. We therefore took the details of three of his offences (simply adding a further three rows to the data matrix) and repeated the analysis for all thirteen crimes. We found that the 'marker' crimes from London did help to clarify some of the ambiguities that were present when the Midlands cases were the only ones that the computer analysed, by spreading out the Midlands rapes into more distinct groups.

EIGHT: OBJECTS OF MURDER

Toolis, K. (1991), 'The Game of Love and Death', *Weekend Guardian*, 11–12 May, pp. 4–6.

The feminist view of rape is discussed in Scully (1990).

Jordan D. (1988), *A Psychology of Mass Murder*, BSc Thesis, Portsmouth Polytechnic (unpublished), provided me with considerable detail on the life and death of Michael Ryan.

The high prevalence of existing relationships between murderer and victim is clear from Home Office reports, e.g. *Criminal Statistics: England and Wales* 1990. London: HMSO (Cmnd 1935), p. 81.

NINE: STORIES WE LIVE BY

The terms 'plot', 'story', 'narrative', 'theme', 'plan', 'goal' and a number of others, can be distinguished in important ways for further elaboration of the issues in this chapter, but that would take the discussion into academic niceties that are inappropriate for the present book.

Wilson and Herrnstein (1985); Bartol, C. R. (1991), *Criminal Behavior: a Psychosocial Approach*. Englewood Cliffs: Prentice

Hall; Hollin, C. R. (1989), *Psychology and Crime: an Introduction to Criminological Psychology*. London: Routledge.

Sutherland (1978) is the general reference, but the quotations are taken from the third edition published in 1939.

Lombroso, C. (1911/1968), *Crime: Its Causes and Remedies*. Montclair: Patterson Smith.

Norris, J. (1988), *Serial Killers: the Growing Menace*. London: Arrow.

Goring, C. (1913), *The English Convict: a Statistical Study*. London: Darling and Son.

Readers wishing to get a more detailed introduction to current psychology, as well as overviews of the works of Freud, Piaget and Skinner, should consult Atkinson, R. L., Atkinson, R. C., Smith, E. E. and Bem, D. L. (1993), *Introduction to Psychology*. London: Harcourt Brace Jovanovich. A review of Darwin's influence on the development of psychology is given in Hearnshaw (1989) and particularly on studies of individual differences by Wiggins, J. S. , Renner, R. K., Clove, G. L. and Rose, R. J. (1971), *The Psychology of Personality*. London: Addison-Wesley.

Stephenson (1992) reviews the studies of criminality, self-esteem and moral reasoning. Wilson and Herrnstein (1985) review the ages of criminals.

Masters, B. (1993), *The Shrine of Jeffrey Dahmer*. London: Hodder and Stoughton.

Erikson, E. H. (1963), *Childhood and Society*. New York: W. W. Norton.

Masson, J. (1984), *The Assault on Truth: Freud's Suppression of the Seduction Theory*. London: Faber.

West (1987).

Kelly, G. A. (1955), *The Psychology of Personal Constructs*. New York: W. W. Norton.

Polkinghorne, D. E. (1988), *Narrative Knowing and the Human Sciences*. Albany: State University of New York Press.

McAdams (1988).

Danto, A. (1965), *Analytic Philosophy of History*. Cambridge: Cambridge University Press.

Schank, R. and Abelson, R. (1977), *Scripts, Plans, Goals and Understanding: an Inquiry into Human Knowledge Structures*. Hillsdale: Lawrence Erlbaum.

Mair, M. (1988), 'Psychology as Storytelling', *International Journal of Personal Construct Psychology*, Vol. 1, pp. 125–37.

Murray, K. (1985), 'Life as Fiction', *Journal for the Theory of Social Behaviour*, Vol. 15, No. 2, pp. 173–88.

The studies of child sexual abuse are being carried out by Stuart Kirby and are, as yet, unpublished.

The consideration in this chapter of the backgrounds and motivations of violent men, especially sex offenders, draws on the general psychological and psychiatric literature, see e.g. Groth (1979), West (1987).

TEN: LIMITED NARRATIVES

One of the earliest comments on offenders' inner narratives was Bolitho, W. (1926), *Murder for Profit*. New York: Garden City, who wrote: 'They very commonly construct for themselves a life-romance, a personal myth in which they are the maltreated hero, which secret is the key of their battle against despair.'

Reviews of the early experiences of violent criminals and the significance of the 'role of the other' are given by Athens, L. H. (1980), *Violent Criminal Acts and Actors: a Symbolic Interactionist Study*. London: Routledge and Kegan Paul; and Athens, L. H. (1989), *The Creation of Dangerous and Violent Criminals*. London: Routledge.

The list of behaviours drawn up for the analyses presented in this chapter do owe a lot to the detailed discussions of crimes provided by Hazelwood and Burgess (1987), Ressler et al. (1988) and Leyton (1986).

The analysis of actions in rape is taken from the data collected and content analysed by Rupert Heritage, the first tranche of which was published in Canter, D. and Heritage, R. (1990), 'A Multi-variate Model of Sexual Offence Behaviour', *Journal of Forensic Psychiatry*, Vol. 1, No. 2, pp. 185–212. The full account of this research is given in Heritage, R. (1992), *Facets of Sexual Assault: First Steps in Investigative Classifications*, MPhil thesis, University of Surrey (unpublished).

The statistical procedure illustrated in this chapter has many similarities to that described in Chapter Seven. Except that this analysis (known as Smallest Space Analysis I, or SSAI) represents the behaviours, derived from the columns of the data matrix, as points in the spatial plot, whereas the procedure described in Chapter Seven (known as Multi-Dimensional Scalogram Analysis I, or MSAI) represents the rows of the data matrix as points in the spatial plot.

Studies of varieties of murderer, drawn on in this and other chapters, are being carried out by Rick Holden and are, as yet, unpublished.

ELEVEN: NARRATIVES OF EVIL

A special issue of *Criminal Behaviour and Mental Health*, 1992, Vol. 2, No. 2, is devoted to 'Psychopathic Disorder'.

Helen Hughes' (unpublished) 1992 undergraduate dissertation at the University of Surrey explored the correlations between the amount of violence in rape and the pre-existing relationship between offender and victim.

Laurie, R. (1993), *Hunting the Devil: the Search for the Russian Ripper*. London: Grafton.

Hickey (1991) provides details of the criminal life of DeSalvo, the self-confessed 'Boston Strangler'.

SELECT BIBLIOGRAPHY

Canter, D. (ed.) (1985), *Facet Theory: Approaches to Social Research*. New York: Springer-Verlag.

Groth, A. N. (1979), *Men Who Rape: the Psychology of the Offender*. New York: Plenum.

Harris, T. (1989), *The Silence of the Lambs*. London: Heinemann.

Hazelwood, R. R. and Burgess, A. (eds) (1987), *Practical Aspects of Rape Investigation: a Multidisciplinary Approach*. Amsterdam: Elsevier.

Hearnshaw, L. S. (1989), *The Shaping of Modern Psychology*. London: Routledge.

Hickey, E. W. (1991), *Serial Murderers and Their Victims*. California: Brooks/Cole.

Katz, J. (1988), *The Seductions of Crime: Moral and Sensual Attractions in Doing Evil*. New York: Basic Books.

Kind, S. S. (1987), *The Scientific Investigation of Crime*. London: Forensic Science Services Ltd.

Leyton, E. (1986), *Hunting Humans: The Rise of the Modern Multiple Murderer*. Toronto: Seal Books.

McAdams, D. P. (1988), *Power, Intimacy, and the Life Story: Personological Inquiries into Identity*. New York: Guilford Press.

Perkins, D. N. (1981), *The Mind's Best Work*. London: Harvard University Press.

Raskin, D. C. (ed.) (1989), *Psychological Methods in Criminal Investigation and Evidence*. New York: Springer Publishing.

Ressler, R. K., and Shachtman, T. (1992). *Whoever Fights Monsters*. London: Simon and Schuster.

Ressler, R. K., Burgess, A. W. and Douglas, J. E. (1988), *Sexual Homicide: Patterns and Motives*. Massachusetts: Lexington Books.

Scully, D. (1990), *Understanding Sexual Violence: a Study of Convicted Rapists*. Boston: Unwin Hyman.

Stephenson, G. M. (1992), *The Psychology of Criminal Justice*. Oxford: Blackwell.

Sutherland, E. H. (1978), *Principles of Criminology* (10th edn). New York: Harper and Row.

Swanson, C. R., Chamelin, N. C. and Territo, L. (1992), *Criminal Investigation* (5th edn). New York: McGraw-Hill.

Wambaugh, J. (1989), *The Blooding*. London: Bantam.

West, D. J. (1987), *Sexual Crimes and Confrontations: a Study of Victims and Offenders*. Aldershot: Gower.

Wilson, J. Q. and Herrnstein, R. J. (1985), *Crime and Human Nature*. New York: Simon and Schuster.

INDEX

Written in Blood

A History of Forensic Detection

Colin Wilson

Written in Blood charts the rise and development of forensic detection from poisoners in ancient Rome to modern serial murderers. In fascinating and gruesome detail, it covers many aspects of modern investigation techniques such as forensic toxicology, sexual criminology, blood serology, genetic finger-printing and psychological profiling.

The book presents a gripping catalogue of crimes solved by people with an infinite capacity for taking pains and a growing armoury of scientific discoveries and technical aids. A grisly panorama of case studies shows that it is often the tiniest scraps of evidence that lead to momentous results – for example the murderer of Nancy Titterton was betrayed by a single horsehair.

Colin Wilson examines in depth the surprisingly modern phenomenon of serial sex crime, including the notorious cases of Jack the Ripper, the Moors murderers, Charles Manson and Peter Sutcliffe.

From the mystery of murder to the mystery of crime detection, *Written in Blood* is an authoritative and compelling work that will fascinate the expert criminologist and the general reader alike.

'He has made himself the Philosopher-King of forensic speculation, the Diderot of the path labs'   *Times Literary Supplement*

ISBN 0 586 20842 9

All these books are available from your local bookseller or can be ordered direct from the publishers.

To order direct just tick the titles you want and fill in the form below:

Name: _____

Address: _____

_____

Postcode: _____

Send to: HarperCollins Mail Order, Dept 8, HarperCollins*Publishers*, Westerhill Road, Bishopbriggs, Glasgow G64 2QT.

Please enclose a cheque or postal order or your authority to debit your Visa/Access account –

Credit card no: _____

Expiry date: _____

Signature: _____

– to the value of the cover price plus:

UK & BFPO: Add £1.00 for the first and 25p for each additional book ordered.

Overseas orders including Eire, please add £2.95 service charge.

Books will be sent by surface mail but quotes for airmail despatches will be given on request.

24 HOUR TELEPHONE ORDERING SERVICE FOR ACCESS/VISA CARDHOLDERS –
TEL: GLASGOW 041-772 2281 or LONDON 081-307 4052